Praise for

SACRED SOLDIER: THE DANGERS OF WORSHIPING WARRIORS
By Robert F. Keeler

"A scathing, impassioned, and deeply personal critique of contemporary American militarism. *Sacred Soldier* unpacks in rich detail the contradictions and hypocrisies that beset the relationship between Americans and their armed forces. Robert Keeler has written an important and compelling book."

—**Andrew Bacevich, army veteran, chairman and cofounder, Quincy Institute for Responsible Statecraft**

"The writer writes, the peace warrior nonviolently fights. In the Orwellian tradition, Bob Keeler's words in *Sacred Soldier* come from a writer turned peace fighter who is writing truth to power, both to the policy makers and those on the margins, in hopes of a better humanity going forward. May we heed Bob's clarion call. We are what we do."

—**Jonathan W. Hutto, Sr., navy veteran, author of *Anti-War Soldier: How to Dissent within the Ranks of the Military***

"In *Sacred Soldier*, Bob Keeler wants us to reconsider our veneration for military service on the ground that fighting wars is largely a very bad thing to do. The result is a scathing indictment of American militarism in the post–World War II era. The book's damning bill of particulars calls on all of us to reconsider the role of our armed forces in the life of our country and the larger world."

—**Daniel Akst, author of *War by Other Means: The Pacifists of the Greatest Generation Who Revolutionized Resistance***

"This clear, concise, and highly readable book is a must-read for anyone wanting to understand the true nature of war and of military service. Well written, extensively researched and documented, with Keeler's experience as a journalist, it provides the reader with a broad range of insights and information regarding the mythologization of the warrior, so critical a part of the era of perpetual war in which we live."

—**Camillo "Mac" Bica, Vietnam veteran, author of *Worthy of Gratitude? Why Veterans May Not Want To Be Thanked for Their "Service" in War***

SACRED SOLDIER
THE DANGERS OF WORSHIPING WARRIORS

By Robert F. Keeler

OLIVE
BRANCH
PRESS

An imprint of Interlink Publishing Group, Inc.
Northampton, Massachusetts

First published in 2024 by

Olive Branch Press
An imprint of Interlink Publishing Group, Inc.
46 Crosby Street, Northampton, MA 01060
www.interlinkbooks.com

Copyright © Robert F. Keeler, 2024
Cover design and illustration by Alexandra Zeigler

Library of Congress Cataloging-in-Publication data available
ISBN-13: 978-1-62371-107-8

Printed and bound in the United States of America

For Hailey, Zachary, Annie, Leo, and Dayton,
in the hope that they'll live to see a much more peaceful world.

CONTENTS

Introduction
WAR AND IGNORANCE

My letter from Lyndon B. Johnson came with a subway token.

That 1965 correspondence began formally: "From the President of the United States, greeting." Just one greeting, not even two. Times were tough. Along with the letter, the envelope contained a sheet of directions that helpfully advised me what trains to take from my neighborhood in the New York City borough of Queens to the Armed Forces Induction Station at 39 Whitehall Street in Lower Manhattan. The token was taped to the top of that page. Back then, decades before the introduction of more efficient electronic methods of paying fares, you had to buy tiny brass tokens stamped with the prominent letters "NYC," including a Y-shaped hole in the middle. I imagined that they included the token to make sure I didn't cry poverty as an excuse for not showing up at Whitehall Street. But crying poverty wouldn't have worked. The fare was only 15 cents.

As I held that letter, what I did not know, and did not learn fully until decades later, was the complex and deadly reality of the institution that the president was inviting me to join: the United States military. In the mid-1960s and for years afterward, many sought to avoid being drafted into an increasingly unpopular war that ultimately caused more than 58,000 young Americans to lose their lives in combat—and many more to commit suicide in the years that followed. In sharp contrast, in today's America, it is an institution esteemed above all others—an admiration universally expressed with the five-word blessing that people instinctively bestow on those who have spent time in the military: "Thank you for your service."

Sacred Soldier

How did that happen? How did a military that so many fervently avoided in the Vietnam era evolve into an object of near-worship? In this book, I seek answers to that question, drilling down below that five-word mantra to the reality below, in search of a more nuanced, realistic assessment of our military.

One key reason why we need a more fact-based understanding of our military is that our reflexive admiration of it helps make Congress eager to fund the Department of Defense—and its many civilian weapons makers—at ever-increasing levels. Those appropriations buy weapons systems that don't always work—like the controversial F-35 fighter. But members of Congress keep voting to fund those weapons, because the manufacturers have slyly spread through many congressional districts the jobs involved in producing the weapons. No member of Congress wants to be accused of voting against jobs. What those defense dollars sadly do *not* do is adequately increase the pay of individual members of the military. In fact, far too many of them have to rely on food stamps to feed their families. Nor has Congress given the Department of Veterans Affairs the funding it needs to care properly for our veterans.

As we examine the military, we need to understand the cynical shell game that our political leaders too often play, using the near-universal admiration of the military as a tool to win public support for the wars that they choose to send our armed forces to fight. Another mantra, "Support the Troops," is a not-so-subtle, yellow-ribboned way of saying, in effect: "You love the military. So love the war we have chosen for them, and don't question whether that war makes any sense."

In the past two decades, we should have expended prodigious amounts of energy on keeping young people from marching off to the long wars in Iraq and Afghanistan. The title of a Dexter Filkins book labels that frustrating struggle *The Forever War*. To protect our young people from the ravages of war, we need to give them a realistic idea of what they are signing up for, so that they don't enlist in pursuit of false glory or out of a mistaken sense of obligation to defend "our freedoms," which the Forever War has categorically not done.

For those who do enlist—for whatever reason, from patriotic fervor to the simple need for a regular paycheck or funds for college tuition—we have serious obligations.

To begin with, we must do our best to protect them from multiple deployments—like the four tours in Iraq and Afghanistan for Brent Taylor, the mayor of North Ogden, Utah, and a major in the Utah National Guard. On his final deployment to Afghanistan, in 2018, his mission was to train a commando battalion in the war-torn country's army. His mission—and his life—ended in an "insider attack" by someone he was there to help train. Taylor left behind a wife, seven children, and a grieving city. No matter how many children warriors have, what positions they hold in civilian life, or what factors persuaded them to enlist, no one should have to endure four deployments to combat zones—especially not in a never-ending, unwinnable war. Whether Taylor could have found a way to avoid that fatal fourth deployment or whether he went willingly out of a sense of duty to other soldiers, this much is clear: For Taylor and his family, the correct but imperfectly executed decision by President Joseph R. Biden Jr. to bring home all American troops from Afghanistan came too tragically late.

For survivors of that war and all wars, we must do a far better job of binding up their wounds when they return to "the world," to civilian life. We must find ways to heal the psychic damage of war—post-traumatic stress and moral injury—before they take their own lives. The suicide rate among veterans of the Forever War remains a real problem.

Though I now see all these needs, in 1965 I saw nothing about war clearly. This introduction is my way of recounting what I failed to understand back then, of describing something of what I have learned in the years since that letter from the president arrived, and of using research and writing as a way of doing penance for my ignorance.

All these years later, I still have the page of directions that came with the president's letter—and that subway token—mostly because I hate to throw away any document that might later "come in handy." During most of that time, it had no significance to me. I was 21 years old when it arrived, and I had never given any serious thought to issues of war and peace. I had no sense of its human costs, no concept of the rivers of blood that it spilled, no understanding of what my Christian faith had to say about it, no insight into the essential nonviolence of the Gospel. I lived in a thick fog of unknowing. All I really knew of war was that my father had fought in one and ended up in a Nazi prisoner-of-war camp—after the terror of being in a boxcar in the Berlin rail yards while Allied bombers were attacking those yards.

Then, in late 2001, three months after the 9/11 attacks, and two months after American troops went to war in Afghanistan, I found myself glad that I still had that 1965 document. In that period before the 2003 invasion of Iraq, it did indeed "come in handy," to goad me into examining that disastrous Iraq decision far more critically, in light of my uncritical, ignorant acceptance of the wicked war in Vietnam. In that spirit, I wrote a two-part confessional piece, "War in a Time of Ignorance," for an online publication called *In the Fray*, and I argued fiercely but unsuccessfully on the *Newsday* editorial board against an editorial endorsing the invasion.

In the half-century since I was drafted, events in my own life and my family's life—including my brother's death after his tour in Vietnam—have led me to an increasingly skeptical scrutiny of the nation's foreign policy and its use of the military as a cover for its mistakes. I never say "Thank you for your service," except occasionally to a teacher or a librarian, people whose service does not involve killing anyone. I instinctively focus on the latest story about corruption and incompetence in the military—stories that appear, then disappear, without changing the broad perception that the attitude we owe to the military is adulation. My own changed view of the military has led me to the conclusion that near-idolatrous worship of the warrior is dangerous not only for the nation, but also for the warriors themselves.

In 1965, at the height of the buildup in Vietnam, I was far from skeptical; I was simply ignorant. That brings me back to that communication from President Johnson: Why do I still have it? The reason is probably nothing more mysterious than the nasty strain of compulsive behavior that has plagued me from childhood—not quite obsessive compulsive disorder (OCD), but definitely obsessive compulsive personality. That obsessiveness allowed me to be drafted in the first place. Through my first year at Fordham University, I had received no grade lower than an A—not because any great career goal was driving me, but because imperfection always seemed like such a hideous option. In my sophomore year, terrified that I might have to settle for a B+ in one course, I decided to drop out of school. Smarter, less compulsive people, including the dean of Fordham College, tried to talk me out of it. A Jesuit college in New Jersey offered me a full scholarship. But the threat of that perfection-marring B+ was too much to overcome.

If I had remained on Fordham's Rose Hill campus until graduation in 1967, I like to think that the salutary virus of dissent might have infected me, moving me to protest an immoral war. In that late-sixties period, Students for a Democratic Society opposed the Reserve Officer Training Corps and military recruiters on the Fordham campus. For reasons I can no longer remember—though money for school probably had something to do with it—I had joined the Air Force ROTC and the fraternity-like Arnold Air Society. If I had stayed at Fordham, I now wonder, would I have sided with the ROTC or would I have been enlightened enough to agree with Students for a Democratic Society?

As much as I might now ponder what might have been, the reality remains that I made the breathtakingly neurotic choice to drop out of college. That decision dramatically altered the arc of my life. After leaving school, I took a job as a copy boy and later a desk assistant at the *New York Herald Tribune*. It was my first chance to witness the craft of journalism at a high professional level. Though I loved that job, it had a serious drawback: Unlike the academic world that I had left behind, it offered me no protection from the draft. Worse, in a year when young men of my age were spending much of their time thinking of ways not to get drafted, I was not really thinking about the draft at all.

All these years later, I still marvel at how comprehensively I failed to notice what was happening. On at least one occasion, my job put the fighting right under my nose. The legendary Jimmy Breslin had cabled a column to the *Herald Tribune* from Vietnam. It arrived in one long, unbroken string of words, and my job was to break it into paragraphs. Sadly, I was far more worried that I might paragraph the story in a way that would displease the mighty Breslin than I was about the bloody events that he was describing.

Here's further evidence of my skewed priorities: In April 1965, others of my age had participated in a huge Washington protest against the war, but that August, I focused my own protest on the now-iconic Beatles concert at Shea Stadium, the home of the New York Mets. Beatles fans had been known to shower the band with jellybeans, as a sugary tribute, and 55,000 of these people were coming to our ballpark. To a Mets fan like me, accustomed to bad news, it seemed entirely possible that one of those jellybeans would re-main lurking in the infield grass, where a hard ground ball would later strike it, diverting its course directly into the throat of our shortstop. So, at a time when my brain should have been working overtime on Vietnam, I used it to create a fictitious organization, complete with an acronym: ALBATROSS (Associated Lovers of Baseball Against the Ruination of Shea Stadium). Then my friend Roger and I circled the stadium, protesting the desecration of our sacred home field. The Beatles fans were not amused, but a United Press International reporter was. He interviewed me briefly and quoted me as saying, "The Beatles in Shea Stadium is like a burlesque show in church."

That was the same year when a postal carrier delivered my letter from the president, and I have a vague memory of being surprised. All these decades later, I am still astonished at the murky process inside my head that was masquerading as thought. While so many others of my age were worrying and planning about the draft, I was fretting about the imaginary danger of a stray jellybean in the Shea Stadium infield. If I had been paying attention, the president's frugal salutation and the tiny subway token should have put me on high alert, like the first notes of scary music in a horror movie. I should have concluded by then, as so many had, that the war was a totally immoral enterprise, a conflict that our nation had no business entering. And the arrival of that letter from LBJ should have driven me into a frenzy of belated planning to avoid the draft. Instead, I meekly rode the subway to 39 Whitehall Street. This ugly, fortress-like building near the southern tip of Manhattan eventually became a concrete symbol for the whole war. It stood just blocks away from the site where excavation would begin, a few months later, for the World Trade Center.

Soon after I arrived, I went through the famously humiliating physical exam, brilliantly satirized by folk singer Arlo Guthrie in his song "Alice's Restaurant." The result of my physical would have elated many young Americans, who were known to consume massive amounts of alcohol the night before reporting for examination, so as to seem physically unworthy of military glory. The military classified me 1-Y. That meant I was temporarily ineligible because of some physical defect. Instead of leaping for joy, I was offended: Why would my country reject me?

Whatever the reason for that rejection, the government soon decided that my bodily imperfection was not a threat to national security. Why the change of heart? Without knowing it, I was almost certainly caught up in the government's growing desperation. "As draft quotas shot up in 1965, the military lowered its admission standards," Christian Appy wrote in his magisterial book, *American Reckoning: The Vietnam War and Our National Identity*. What Appy wrote about was a lowering of the standards on the military's intelligence test. Before Vietnam, Appy wrote, the military "routinely rejected men who scored in the bottom two quintiles" on the test. "Beginning in 1965, however, the military admitted hundreds of thousands of draftees and volunteers it once would have deemed unqualified."

Though I don't think I had any trouble on that intelligence test, they had made me 1-Y for some physical reason. But the fast-increasing need for even remotely able bodies had forced the government to lower their physical, as well as their mental, standards. So the imperfection of my body no longer bothered them. They ordered me to report for induction on November 15, 1965—exactly three months after my protest of the Beatles concert and a couple of weeks before the Thanksgiving events in the Berkshires that led Guthrie to write "Alice's Restaurant." I raised my right hand, took one step forward, and solemnly promised to defend the nation. To this day, I look back at the high seriousness of that moment and marvel at the cosmic emptiness of my head. I was not thinking anti-war thoughts. Nor was I swelling with patriotic fervor, eager to kill commies for America. I was just there, a cluelessly compliant recruit.

As I quickly learned, the army did not encourage its troops to think. Whenever a recruit dared to say something like, "I thought," a sergeant would bark, "If you were authorized to think, the government would have issued you a brain." Even so, in that first week in the military, I was still trying to think. I even had a "plan" for my army career. At the *Herald Tribune*, one of my colleagues had attended a military information school at Fort Slocum, on an island just north of the City of New York, and he had become a military journalist. That sounded good to me. So I memorized his MOS—Military Occupational Specialty, the little code that described your job. His MOS was 71Q20, information specialist.

Smugly, I cradled this magic code in my mind as I carried my DA Form 20 through a processing line at Fort Jackson, South Carolina. The DA Form 20 is a soldier's personal military record, printed on stiff yellow paper. Mine was mostly blank as I approached the low-level clerk who was about to assign me to my first job in the army. This was my plan: I would tell him I wanted to be a 71Q20. In his astonishment that I even knew what an MOS was, he would meekly write down the code, and I'd be on my way to training as an army journalist.

As the clerk looked up at me briefly, I spoke confidently: "I'd like to be a 71Q20, information specialist." Ignoring me definitively, he casually penciled in 11A10, armor crewman. It was then that I had my first great epiphany about military absurdity. My destiny was not to write, but to drive tanks. Hell, I was a city boy. I didn't even know how to drive a car.

Before I knew it, I was climbing onto a rickety Saturn Airlines propeller plane, with all my goods in one olive drab duffel bag, bound for Fort Hood, Texas. There, in a tank company recently converted to a basic training unit to help turn out the long lines of men needed to prosecute the war in Vietnam, I learned to be a soldier.

It never occurred to me to question the central premises of our training. The sergeant would demand loudly, "What is the spirit of the bayonet?" We would reply in unison, "To kill!" Instead of seeing in that ritual the cruel reality at the core of all armies, I obsessed about polishing my boots and shining my brass.

At my first permanent assignment, as a personnel clerk in Fort Bragg, North Carolina, I spent my time and energy learning to type officer efficiency reports perfectly. I could have seen the presence at Bragg of the United States Army Special Forces, a remorseless collection of professional killers, as an occasion for reflection on the brutality of warfare. Instead, I just loved the jaunty way they wore their green berets. In fact, I bought one and sent it home as a present to Judy, the young woman I had met at a going-away party just before I left for the army. Now, after being married to Judy since 1969, I cringe at the memory that my first gift to her was a symbol of war.

At Bragg, my brother Richie and I crossed paths for the only time in the army. He was on his way to Vietnam. By then, I had grown tired of being a clerk and soured on life in a barracks that echoed annoyingly with country and western music. So I had decided to apply for officer candidate school, even though acquiring a commission as an officer would extend my obligation from two years to something more than three. As Richie and I said our goodbyes, he reminded me that, even after I had my second lieutenant's gold bars, he would never salute me. We had grown up together, played stickball together, and had always been equals—more or less. He was the better athlete, but I was the better student—the jock and the geek. So, no, I wouldn't have expected a salute from him.

At the Artillery and Missile Officer Candidate School at Fort Sill, Oklahoma, my obsession was learning how to get an artillery round to its target. One day, I led the fire direction center, calculating map coordinates, wind, and other variables, to produce an accurate trajectory. We launched a barrage of timed-fuse rounds, exploding them over a heap of scrap cars on the practice range. Not bothering to ponder what it might have been like to be a person standing below that lethal rain of shrapnel, I rejoiced at this moment of make-believe slaughter, this euphoric exercise in the murderous math of war.

At Fort Sill, as at Fordham, my focus on grades was obscuring the obvious. Instead of thinking seriously about the morality of what American artillery was doing to Vietnamese bodies, I contented myself with conquering trigonometry and finishing first in my class. That distinction had one value: It gave my preference of assignments some weight. So I ended up as an information officer at Fort George G. Meade, Maryland. There, I returned to the fringes of the craft of journalism, as a supervisor of the post's newspaper. I also wrote a patriotic speech or two for the post commander.

After less than a full year at Meade, I received a letter from the Pentagon, with orders reassigning me to the 4th United States Army Missile Command, APO San Francisco 96208. APO meant Army Post Office. I knew that the APO in San Francisco served troops throughout Asia, but I didn't know if this meant Vietnam. With a growing sense of dread, I walked to the post office and asked a clerk where APO SF 96208 might be. Matter-of-factly, he told me: "Korea."

I was relieved, of course, but also curious about the factors that had spared me a trip to the rice paddies. So I called the Pentagon and spoke to the officer who had made the assignment. His reasoning was sound: For a year after graduating from artillery OCS, I had not even come close to a howitzer. If he had sent me to Vietnam as an artillery officer, I would have been a dead man walking. It was odd, but typical of my mindset, that the hazards of being a forward observer had not occurred to me when I chose to leave my clerk's job at Fort Bragg to become an artillery officer. There, too, I lucked out. My artillery battalion at Fort Bragg later went to Vietnam as a unit.

In Korea, the army put me in a deeply contradictory assignment. My primary duty was military intelligence—one of the great oxymorons. Working in the S2, the intelligence section of command headquarters, I found myself the custodian of hundreds of classified documents. As an additional duty, I supervised the production of the command's modest little newspaper and handled public relations. In other words, my job was simultaneously to keep secrets and to deliver the news. Clueless though I was, I did see this as typical army madness.

By then, Judy and I were engaged, and we corresponded often, exchanging letters and taped conversations, because phone calls from Korea were too expensive. Our relationship had unfolded almost entirely by mail, but even at that great distance, we had a deep disagreement. More immersed in the real world than I was, she had already sensed that the war in Vietnam was deeply wrong. But I had swallowed the propaganda of a film that the army showed often during my training, called *Why Vietnam?* I should have listened to her, but I stubbornly refused and moped angrily. Still, I missed her and counted the days until we could be together.

As to all those classified documents, I worried about what would happen to me if I failed to protect them, but I didn't worry about the lives that the targeting documents among them might someday enable my unit to snuff out, many miles away from the launchers. Nor did I have moral qualms about being part of a unit that had the capability of putting tactical nuclear weapons on the tips of its rockets.

But in its own way, the military did teach me something. The army knew from experience that the average young American can cause an astonishing amount of mischief when he leaves an American post and sets foot in any town of the host nation. As a "Cold War instructor," my job was to brief these teenagers about the hard-working people and the ancient culture of Korea before they were allowed off post. I did the best I could, but I had no illusions that my little talks were any match for the hormones and the capacity for mischief of these young Americans.

By the end of my thirteen months at Camp Page, I had grown disillusioned with the army. Even so, my disillusionment was pale and feeble: a sarcastic, jokey reaction to the everyday stupidities of "the army way," rather than an intelligent, principled response to the deeper questions of our presence in Korea. During my time in Korea—all of 1968 and the first month of 1969—I missed an immense amount of turmoil in the United States: the assassinations of the Rev. Martin Luther King Jr. and Senator Robert F. Kennedy of New York, and the turbulent Democratic National Convention in Chicago.

The convention, the chaos surrounding it, and the treatment of the media who covered it were early factors in the declining trust of the American public in journalism. "Even before the Convention began, the *Times*, the *Wall Street Journal*, CBS, and NBC had run stories saying that the war was unwinnable, in contradiction to what the Johnson Administration was telling the public," Louis Menand wrote in *The New Yorker*, in a 2023 article under the headline, "When Americans Lost Faith in the News." In the planning of the convention, Menand wrote, "pains were taken to incommode the news media as much as possible." He listed the obstacles that Mayor Richard Daley placed in front of the journalists covering the convention. Television's coverage of the anti-war protesters outside the convention was limited. Menand quoted media historian Heather Hendershot's account of a letter from an air force colonel: "I noted with delight that the police devoted some richly deserved attention to the prime provocateurs—the press." Hendershot summed up the effect: "The networks generally operated with tremendous fairness in Chicago, and attacks after the fact were unwarranted." But she cited that convention as "a tipping point for widespread distrust of the mainstream media." So, while I was in Korea, counting down the days until I could return to the craft of journalism that I left behind, the start of public distrust of the media was already well underway. Also, while I was in Korea, I somehow decided that Richard Nixon's experience as a vice president would make him a better president than Hubert Humphrey, whose candidacy emerged from that turbulent convention, and I voted for Nixon by absentee ballot. I still regret it.

When my 13 months in Korea ended, I flew back to the states, got discharged from the army, and got on with my life. I resumed pursuing a career in journalism, and Judy and I got married a few months after my discharge. Through the 1970s and '80s, I paid little attention to what was going on overseas. Major events in the war—and the protests against it—somehow flew well below my radar. In recent years, I have often come across reminders of a Vietnam-related event and wrestled with my guilt over failing to notice it or react to it back then. One example was the death of four Kent State University students at the hands of Ohio National Guard troops who were sent to the campus to deal with protests over Nixon's "incursion" into Cambodia.

In James Carroll's 2021 book, *The Truth at the Heart of the Lie: How the Catholic Church Lost Its Soul*, I read his account of a demonstration about Kent State by Boston University students—a sorrowful vigil that he joined, as their campus chaplain. Reading that tale prompted me to wonder what I was thinking and doing then. That was a quarter-century before I started keeping a compulsive diary. So, to see what was occupying my attention at that historical moment in 1970, I had to rely on the yellowing collection of my clips from the *Staten Island Advance*. Among those stories about the quotidian grinding of governmental gears, I found one that appeared the day before the Kent State massacre: a long, sleep-inducing Sunday feature about a new deputy commissioner in the department that oversaw the Staten Island Ferry. That's the kind of nanoscale news that was dominating my attention.

Occupied with the daily demands of deadlines on my beat—the ferry and Staten Island Rapid Transit—I gave little thought to Southeast Asia. I did wake up about the Vietnam War in time to vote for George McGovern, the anti-war candidate, in 1972. But I devoted no real study to what had led to the war, nor to the broad sweep of American foreign policy that had made it almost inevitable. Instead, I focused on my family and my work. Now, many years later, it makes me feel a little less guilty when I realize that someone as smart as Andrew Bacevich, a West Point graduate who saw combat in Vietnam, also took a while to come to full understanding. "With the passage of time, I concluded that classifying Vietnam as either a mistake or a tragedy amounts to little more than subterfuge," Bacevich wrote in *Paths of Dissent: Soldiers Speak Out Against America's Misguided Wars*, which he co-edited. "To use those terms is to evade a much deeper and more troubling truth. In fact, from its very earliest stages until its mortifying conclusion, America's war in Vietnam was a crime."

By the time of the 1972 election, I was a reporter at *Newsday*, still bogged down in daily news of no global importance, still not really focusing on Vietnam. That, of course, is no excuse. There is no reason why I could not have raised my two daughters and my consciousness at the same time. Then in 1983, my brother Richie died, at age thirty-six. One of the hardest things I've ever had to do was to identify his body, horribly decomposed after he had lain, dead, for a day or more in his overheated apartment, where a friend found him. I learned from his friends that he had been suffering from severe headaches for months, and he had odd symptoms, such as a total intolerance for alcohol. But the doctors couldn't give us a definitive cause of death.

As a way of coping with Richie's death and assuaging my guilt over having grown apart from him, I decided to write an article about it for the Sunday magazine at *Newsday*. In the reporting, I contacted some of the men who had served in his combat engineer battalion in Vietnam and discovered that some had displayed the same symptoms that had plagued Richie. I had no positive proof of it, but I suspected—and still suspect—that his combat exposure to the herbicide Agent Orange was what killed him.

Even before I did the reporting that led me to that conclusion, I had a visceral sense that our own government was responsible for his death. It overtook me as I walked into a funeral parlor in Queens for his wake. His coffin was closed, and atop it sat an American flag, folded crisply into a triangle. Without even thinking about it, I removed the flag and threw it roughly on the floor of a closet. From that day to this, I do not take off my hat for the flag, pledge allegiance to it, or find comfort in its colors. The magazine piece closed with the scene at the national cemetery in Calverton, Long Island, where someone handed my father a folded flag and said the rote, ritual words about the country's gratitude. "I wonder whether we'll ever find out why Richie died, before the years had a chance to bring us closer again," I wrote. "I wonder if we'll ever know."

Richie's death should have awakened me completely from my ignorance about our nation's foreign policy. It did not. For the remainder of the 1980s, I should have been studying the way our nation was supporting the murder and the disappearances of the poor in Latin America. But I remained nearsightedly focused on work and family, paying little attention to what was happening in El Salvador and Nicaragua.

The cosmic alarm clock that finally aroused me from my decades-long slumber was Operation Desert Storm. At the time President George H. W. Bush began to utter his bumbling, inarticulate justifications for what became known as the Gulf War, I was working on a long-term project for *Newsday* about the State University of New York. In the all-hands-on-deck situation of Desert Storm, my editors asked me to set aside that project temporarily and help with the war coverage, by writing about the peace movement.

So I found myself flying to Camp Lejeune, North Carolina, with radical attorney Ron Kuby, who represented a group of Marine Corps reservists seeking conscientious objector status. They had joined for a variety of reasons, including the extra money that they could earn as reservists while pursuing other goals in civilian life. Some of them—perhaps influenced by the boastful advertising slogan "The few. The proud. The Marines"—thought it could make them real men.

As dumb as I had been in the army, I never bought into the marine mythology, and I saw marine boot camp as a horrifying prospect. The day I was drafted, a sergeant announced that they needed eight or nine marines. It had not occurred to me that you could be drafted into the marines. But this was the Vietnam War. If they didn't get enough marines from volunteers that day, they'd draft a few of us into the corps against our will. The next few moments were terrifying, but they didn't call my name.

A quarter-century after my own near miss with the marines, I was interviewing a group of young men at Camp Lejeune who had joined the Marine Corps and then had begun to read, think, and have second thoughts about its primary enterprise: mass killing. They had enlisted in the Marine Corps Reserve, later changed their views about the war, and filed conscientious objector applications. Of the 15 objectors, seven were from Fox Company, Second Battalion, 25th Marines, a reserve unit based in the Bronx.

In this proceeding, a marine investigating officer interviewed them. Then so did I. That may have been the first time I encountered what is now known as the economic draft. "I think a lot of people are in it just for the money for school," Doug DeBoer told me, and he joined for exactly that reason. Another objector, Colin Bootman, offered another common explanation for his enlistment: "My father left home when I was pretty young," he said. "I didn't have a male figure to emulate. I thought the military could help shape my character and make me a man."

Another of my Gulf War stories focused on President George H. W. Bush's assertion that the effort to oust Iraq from Kuwait qualified as a "just war." The just war theory goes back to ancient Egypt, China, and India, to Marcus Tullius Cicero in Rome, and to Augustine of Hippo and Thomas Aquinas in the Christian world. That was the first time I had examined the just war theory—as a Christian and as a reporter. In all the years since, I have not run across any case of a war that some nation contemplated but ultimately rejected because it didn't fit the just-war criteria. So, I asked myself, if the just war theory only works to paste a stamp of approval on the killing, but never to stop it, how "just" is the theory, really?

In those early weeks of 1991, before the short and brutal war that quickly destroyed much of Iraq, I spoke with a wide variety of peace groups. For the just-war story, I quoted the Rev. Daniel Berrigan, the Jesuit peacemaker. "I think the whole debate is useless, and that it's a distraction from the main issue and an abandonment of Christ's teaching," Berrigan said. "It's really quite simple: Love your enemies and do good to those who do evil to you, and do not kill."

One of the people I interviewed was Sister Mary Lou Kownacki, the national coordinator of Pax Christi USA, the American section of the international Catholic peace movement. "We do not feel that peaceful negotiations were given all the effort that they deserve," Sister Mary Lou said. "We do not feel that the good achieved by this war will outweigh the possible evils."

From the vantage point of today, Sister Mary Lou was positively prophetic. That war, essentially fought to preserve cheap oil for American consumers and to rescue the despotic regimes in Kuwait and Saudi Arabia that supply much of that oil, was the opening salvo of a conflict that would eventually turn Iraq from an oppressed, autocratic, but mostly functional society under Saddam Hussein into a nightmare of death and rubble. A little more than a decade later, the second President Bush finished the job of destroying that nation.

Something happened to me in my conversation with Sister Mary Lou and my talks with other Christians who objected to the war. The scales fell from my eyes, and I began to see how much my lifelong ignorance had concealed from my view. So I found a local Pax Christi group and joined. My leader was Joop van der Grinten, who grew up in the Netherlands during World War II and was part of the resistance to the Nazis. In the years since, Joop had been fiercely committed to nonviolence. He counseled young men on conscientious objection to the draft during the Vietnam era, and he kept his income low, so the government couldn't tax it and use the proceeds to build bombs. Along the way, he became a white-maned Everyman, as hard at work in the fields of peace and justice as he was in the soil of organic agriculture.

With Joop, and often with Susan Kane, I'd sit in a darkened classroom of a parish school in East Patchogue, a few miles southeast of my home, with a candle flickering and gentle music playing, while we remained silent, Quaker-style, until the Spirit moved us to speak. Joop has died, but Susan (now Susan Perretti) remains a close ally in the peace movement. It was through Pax Christi that I began to think about issues of war and peace—and the military—more critically. Of all the things I learned over the next several years through my involvement with Pax Christi, two lessons stand out: the sad history of Christianity's fall from nonviolence, and the ugly story of American foreign policy in the last half of the twentieth century.

Though I was a "cradle Catholic," I had never really understood how central the principle of nonviolence was in the teachings of Jesus. He entered history at a time when the Jewish people were seething about the occupation by the Romans, and many were seeking violent ways to expel them. Jesus rejected that option. He preached about peace, about loving the enemy, about creative non-violent responses to oppression. The earliest Christians took that nonviolence seriously and declined to serve in the Roman legions. One influential Christian theologian in Rome, Hippolytus, taught that that no one who has embraced professional killing could become a Christian, and no Christian should volunteer for the military. If drafted, he argued, Christians should refuse to kill.

Then, in the year 312, a Roman leader was preparing for a pivotal battle at the Milvian Bridge over the Tiber River in northern Rome, when he thought he saw a vision of a cross in the sky. In the vision, he saw the words "*In hoc signo vinces*," meaning "Under this sign, you will win." Unfortunately, he did win, and soon became Emperor Constantine the Great. The year after that battle, he made Christianity the state religion. From that day to this, Christians have clung to the poisonous embrace of the state. Instead of rejecting the military entirely, Christians now join enthusiastically, providing not only the soldiers to kill in the name of the state, but also the chaplains to bless the bloodshed.

Here's one hideous example of that blessing: Just before Thanksgiving 2001, President George W. Bush appeared at Fort Campbell, Kentucky, before troops of the 101st Airborne Division, whipping them into a frenzied anticipation of battles yet to come. A Christian chaplain closed with a prayer for the commander in chief, and the troops answered the prayer with a resounding: "Air assault! Amen!" That blasphemous blending of prayer and battle lust now makes me ill. In years gone by, I wouldn't even have noticed.

The other pivotal lesson for me was my stunning and much-belated discovery that an idea internalized by all Americans is false: We are the good nation, the only indispensable country, the one that helps people all around the world, the one that stands always for freedom and democracy. To disabuse myself of that simplistic and dangerous view, I needed only to read one 1948 document, written by George F. Kennan, then director of the policy planning staff in the State Department. Though a few have construed Kennan's meaning benignly, his actual words accurately describe an American attitude that has not really changed since those early Cold War days:

"We have about 50 percent of the world's wealth, but only about 6.3 percent of its population. This disparity is particularly great as between ourselves and the peoples of Asia. In this situation, we cannot fail to be the object of envy and resentment. Our real task in the coming period is to devise a pattern of relationships which will permit us to maintain this position of disparity without positive detriment to our national security. To do so we will have to dispense with all sentimentality and day-dreaming; and our attention will have to be concentrated everywhere on our immediate national objectives. We need not deceive ourselves that we can afford the luxury of altruism and world-benefaction.... We should cease to talk about vague and ... unreal objectives such as human rights, the raising of the living standards, and democratization. The day is not far off when we are going to have to deal in straight power concepts. The less we are then hampered by idealistic slogans, the better."

Ever since Kennan wrote this description of American policy, the government of the United States has constantly trumpeted those "idealistic slogans" in public, citing "freedom" and "democracy" and the "threat of communism" to justify a variety of military actions. But the real reason is essentially the maintenance of the "position of disparity" that Kennan described.

For fifty years, American administrations of both parties have done whatever was necessary to keep strong regimes in power in Latin America. That's in keeping with another Kennan dictum. Just a few years after writing the earlier document, he told American diplomatic officials in Latin America that "we should not hesitate before police repression by the local government.... It is better to have a strong regime in power than a liberal government if it is indulgent and relaxed and penetrated by Communists."

Of course, our definition of "communist" has been amazingly broad. It includes any government that seems concerned with economic reform. It also includes bishops. The late Dom Helder Camara, a widely known and respected bishop in Brazil, liked to say: "When I give food to the poor, they call me a saint. When I ask why the poor have no food, they call me a communist."

What I have come to see now, but didn't understand during my army days, is that anti-communism was nearly as destructive a force in the twentieth century as communism. In the name of beating back the red menace, the government of the United States put its money and military might behind some hideously repressive governments. Supported by our taxpayer dollars, these regimes made enemies of priests and nuns who were simply trying to obey the command of Jesus to feed the poor, clothe the naked, and give shelter to the homeless. Instead of seeing these priests and nuns as faithful to the Gospel, these regimes saw them as dangerous subversives. That gave rise to this hateful slogan: "Be a patriot. Kill a priest."

In El Salvador, during the bloody 1980s, the poor endured the assassination of Archbishop Oscar Romero (now Saint Oscar), the rape and murder of three nuns and a lay missionary, and the slaughter of six Jesuits, along with their housekeeper and her daughter. Many of the perpetrators were trained by the United States Army School of the Americas, located at Fort Benning, Georgia. Later, reacting to regular demonstrations against the school, the government cynically renamed it the Western Hemisphere Institute for Security Cooperation. Different name, same shame. Not surprisingly, once people have been victimized by repressive regimes supported by the United States, they tend to view this nation as hypocritical. They think America has a nasty double standard: preaching democracy, but supporting dictatorship, so long as the dictator does what America wants.

In the years since I have finally awakened and seen our nation's many pathologies, I have come to detest the "We're number one, Love it or leave it" brand of patriotism that is so visible right now. My favorite definition of patriotism is the one that the Rev. Jesse Jackson offered years ago: loyalty to the highest ideals of the nation, not to the person who happens to occupy the White House at the moment. True patriotism includes criticizing the government to make sure it is worthy of the nation's highest ideals. Without that willingness to look critically at what the nation is doing, patriotism becomes little more than idolatry—a red-white-and-blue version of the golden calf in the Book of Exodus.

My late awakening to these realities has brought a healthy share of irony into my life. In another century, I thoughtlessly rode the subway to Whitehall Street and became an unquestioning servant of the nation's foreign policy. Now, I am seen as unpatriotic, a card-carrying member of the blame-America-first crowd, even a communist. But all I really want is for America to start spending more of its wealth on making life better for everyday Americans and eliminating the global gap between rich and poor—and a lot less on the military.

In the long list of concrete, life-preserving duties that we owe our military, idolatry should have no place. If people choose to enter the armed forces, they have to be able to do it without succumbing to the myths of glory, without being seduced by the universal worship of our warriors. Other veterans have increasingly been writing books that make arguments similar to what I am saying in this one, and I gratefully cite them throughout. Chipping away at the edifice of warrior worship is a long-term enterprise, and the more veterans who choose to shine the light of reality on our military, the better. This book has been far too many years in the making, but now it's my way of contributing in some small way to that painful process of demythologizing.

Chapter 1
STRIPPING AWAY THE TEFLON

Our society routinely honors the military for "fighting for our freedoms" and for making it possible for the rest of us to go about enjoying our everyday lives. Even in church, the military has a special place: As you sit in the pews before Sunday Mass and read the parish bulletin, you'll find a section asking your prayers for a list of people on active duty in the military, but no other profession merits that routine space in the bulletin. At the airport, members of the armed forces often get to board a flight ahead of others. In shopping center parking lots, some spaces are marked as reserved for veterans.

That admiration and acceptance acts like the Teflon coating on frying pans: It makes sure that nothing nasty, like a negative news story, sticks to the armed forces for long. Oddly, one criticism of the military has gotten some attention, arising from an unlikely source: conservatives with no military experience on their resumes, notably Sen. Ted Cruz, the Texas Republican who ran unsuccessfully for president in 2016, and Tucker Carlson, the Fox News host who got himself fired in 2023. Carlson said the Chinese military is "more masculine" than the "more feminine" American forces. Cruz made a similar comparison of the Russian and American military. "Perhaps a woke, emasculated military is not the best idea," Cruz tweeted in 2021, passing along a propaganda video of Russian soldiers doing shirtless push-ups and looking theatrically manly, plus an American ad featuring a young woman who grew up with two mothers and joined the military.

That "emasculation" analysis was bizarre and off-target on multiple levels. For one, Cruz tweeted the Russian military propaganda video just a few months before Russia invaded Ukraine and lost far more troops in combat than Russian President Vladimir Putin had expected. The resulting near-universal view was that the Russian military was ill-trained and ill-equipped. The shirtless push-ups in the propaganda video appear not to have helped in the fighting. The feminization argument also fails to take into account the toxic masculinity of an institution that has reacted to the increasing numbers of women in its ranks by sexually abusing thousands of them.

Despite that delusional right-wing criticism, the military remains a much-admired institution, as Chapter 3 examines in depth. One measure of that admiration is the proliferation of ads in congressional campaigns that proudly advertise the candidate's military experience. Some veterans have turned their own history in the military into an effective, but not entirely honest, "vote for a vet" campaign slogan—as if time in the military alone is a guarantor of competence in public office. Chapter 4 looks at veterans as candidates and officeholders. And candidates who spent time in the Marine Corps do not hesitate to wrap themselves in all the positive connotations that come with the words "former marine."

Beyond the omnipresence of that phrase, if you drive down any road in America, you're likely to see cars with Marine Corps window decals and bumper stickers that proclaim the Marine Corps motto, "Semper Fi," or a chest-pounding marine addendum to the Book of Genesis: "And on the eighth day God created marines." With all that free advertising, it's no wonder that so many impressionable teenagers, with visions of almost superhuman glory, choose to enlist in the Marine Corps.

Unsurprisingly, marine recruiters don't talk much with prospective recruits about the darker elements at the core of the corps. Most of those who enlist would have at least a rudimentary idea about the brutality of marine boot camp: the screaming drill sergeants, the daily humiliations, the merciless effort to strip new marines of their uniqueness as people and mold them into obedient, buzz-cut war machines. But recruits have no way of knowing the full extent of what happens once they become marines.

Take, for example, some of the words that marines chant as they run, developing their physical endurance and eroding their reluctance to kill. An insight into that phenomenon came from Daniel Hallock, a member of the Bruderhof, a small Christian group firmly committed to nonviolence.

Hallock conducted 40 personal interviews with veterans and drew on nearly 100 written accounts for his book *Hell, Healing and Resistance: Veterans Speak*. In the book, he wrote about what marines used to chant on their five-mile runs: "Rape the town and kill the people! That's the thing we love to do! Rape the town and kill the people! That's the only thing we do! Throw some napalm on the schoolhouse, watch the kiddies scream and shout!" Similarly savage chants show up in other books about Marine Corps culture.

With training like that, it's amazing that more marines don't become war criminals—or sexual predators. Even by the Pentagon's own accounting, sexual predation is a serious problem in today's volunteer military. The Pentagon issues regular estimates of the number of sexual assault incidents in the armed forces, but most of the victims simply don't report these crimes. Why the wide gap between actual assaults and reported assaults? The answer is simple but infuriating: In too many cases, a victim is reluctant to report the abuse to the unit commander, who is also the commander of the abuser, the friend of the abuser, or the abuser himself.

That's why Sen. Kirsten Gillibrand (D-New York) began pushing for a change in the way the military handles sexual abuse. She wanted to take prosecution of those cases out of the hands of unit commanders and put it in the hands of independent professional military prosecutors. That legislation turned out to be a heavy lift, meeting resistance even from Democratic colleagues. Ultimately, Gillibrand's persistence, plus the failure of military commanders to solve the problem, won more than 60 Senate co-sponsors for her bill by mid-2021. Its most important reform—removing commanders entirely from the prosecution of serious crimes—did not make it into the National Defense Authorization Act for Fiscal Year 2022. But the Fiscal Year 2023 NDAA did deal with the rest of Gillibrand's much-needed reforms in the way the armed forces deal with military sexual trauma. Chapter 5 examines this epidemic-level problem.

Like other indicators of imperfection in the military, sexual abuse remains well below the notice of the public, though a story here or there might rise briefly to the level of their attention—stories about military incompetence and boot camp brutality, for example. Once they have appeared, they seem to make no significant change in the collective consciousness of a nation now conditioned to hold the military in awe.

Given the sexual abuse, the brutality, the incompetence, the corruption—not to mention failure to win the 20-year war in Afghanistan—you'd think our attitude toward the military would at least be skeptical. Chapter 6 examines the claim that ours is the "finest" military on the planet. Whatever the truth about the military, we continue to maintain a posture of near-worship, elevating our warriors to almost mythical, superhuman levels. The military is "a distinct social institution that we simultaneously lionize and ignore," wrote Rosa Brooks, a former Pentagon official, in her book *How Everything Became War and the Military Became Everything: Tales from the Pentagon.*

How can we ignore an institution that we lionize? It's easy enough, because only a small fraction of the nation has had any involvement with those who have fought in the two-decade forever war in Afghanistan and Iraq. Vietnam veteran Andrew Bacevich said this in a 2018 column: "The 99% of Americans who were not soldiers learned to tune out those wars, content merely to 'support the troops,' an obligation fulfilled by offering periodic expressions of reverence on public occasions. Thank you for your service!"

How can we lionize an institution as flawed as any other large institution? What kind of attitude toward the military, short of idolatry, is appropriate in our society? That's the aim of this book: to dispel the mythology, strip away the Teflon, and start a conversation that grounds both civilians and warriors in reality, that helps both the troops and the nation.

In that conversation, instead of repeating rote gratitude, we should be asking veterans how their service affected them. What do they need, now that they're back in the world? How can we help?

We should be asking the Veterans Health Administration why people suffering the wounds of war, from lost limbs to post-traumatic stress disorder (PTSD), have to wait so long in some cases to get the care they need. We should be asking Congress why it has consistently underfunded VA. The resulting staff shortages are a pivotal reason why veterans have to wait too long for care in too many instances. We should also be asking conservatives why they want to weaken the VHA by shifting care for veterans to the private sector, where wait times can also be long, and the quality of care is lower than what veterans receive from the VHA. Chapter 8 examines the problems that veterans face, from homelessness to suicide, and the political struggle over the future of their health care.

We should be asking the Department of Defense why we need so many bases around the world—an expenditure that Alexander Hamilton would love, but one that we should examine skeptically, in the spirit of James Madison, who had two nightmares: mob rule (thus, his support for the Electoral College) and a standing army. Chapter 9 examines the conflicting attitudes of the founding generation toward the idea of a standing army, which led to the little-discussed Third Amendment, prohibiting the unwanted quartering of troops in private homes. That issue has long been settled in favor of Hamilton's view, and it's clear that America will always have a standing army. But that doesn't prevent us from asking where that army should be standing, where it should be stationed on our troubled planet.

We should be questioning the practices of recruiters who meet their quotas in part by being less than truthful in promising military jobs that will teach skills useful in civilian life. We should be asking recruiters to issue the military equivalent of the Miranda warning as they speak to potential recruits: a serious lecture about what can come with bearing arms in the nation's wars—or a military version of the admirable honesty of rabbis toward those who wish to convert to Judaism: an account of the suffering that has routinely come to Jews. Chapter 2 examines the ways of recruiters and the work of counter-recruitment activists. Chapter 7 details the way our nation maintains a Selective Service System, requiring men—only men—to register for some possible but unlikely future draft. The existence of this system, even with its spotty record of compliance, gives generals and politicians a theoretical backup source of new troops. It allows them to entertain the idea of a war without having to worry how the public will react to it and how that reaction will reduce the number of young people willing to join an all-volunteer force.

We should ask young Americans to question their own motives for enlisting. Is it an altruistic patriotism or an atavistic yearning for the gory and the glory of combat? In *A Rumor of War*, Vietnam veteran and author Philip Caputo wrote of this phenomenon as "the unholy attraction" of war.

We should be asking our Congress and our president why we keep building aircraft carriers and high-tech fighter planes to combat enemies whose weapons of choice have recently been box-cutters on airplanes and rented trucks or crude suicide bombs in crowded venues.

The message of this book is that we won't get to those vital questions as long as we cling to our current idolatrous attitude toward the military, as long as we lionize it but ignore its inner workings and its flaws. It's time to recognize that our worship of the warriors encourages more young Americans to enlist and discourages us from examining both the wars that we ask them to fight and the shamefully deficient way we treat the wounds they bring home from those wars. It's time to stop allowing idolatry to camouflage reality. It's time to begin looking beyond the camo uniforms at baseball games, the flags, and the jet fighter flyovers, to examine the hard realities of our nation's military: What is it doing right? What is it doing wrong? How big a military do we really need? How big a military can we afford?

Chapter 2
WHY THEY JOIN: GLORY, OLD GLORY, OR JUST A JOB

No quota-driven recruiter had to lure me into the military with slippery promises that wearing combat boots would bring me valuable new skills to use in a triumphant return to civilian life. No recruiter had to make a red-white-and-blue patriotic appeal. No recruiter had to offer me a cash bonus that I could use to pay off college debt or buy a new car. No recruiter wandered the halls of my high school.

All it took to get me into the army, as I said in the introduction, was a letter from the president. My recruiter, in effect, was Lyndon B. Johnson, and he had a powerful recruitment tool that made sweet talk or deceptive promises unnecessary: the draft. Now there is no draft, though there is a troubled and troublesome system for registering young men—yes, still young men only—to fight in some war yet to come. Chapter 7 examines the draft registration system. This chapter focuses on how recruiters operate in the increasingly difficult effort to fill the ranks of the now all-volunteer armed forces and how counter-recruitment activists work to keep young people from signing the enlistment contract. It all starts in school.

NO CHILD LEFT ALONE

My reporting on issues surrounding the draft and recruitment began in 2003 with a column I wrote for *Newsday* about No Child Left Behind, the 2001 reauthorization of the Elementary and Secondary Education Act. The major cause of public uproar against the law was its emphasis on standardized testing. But the part of NCLB that caught my attention was this: If a school district denied military recruiters access to contact information for its students, the district could lose its federal funding. Earlier in 2003, I had argued on the editorial board against an editorial endorsing the Iraq invasion, but the board had gullibly swallowed President George W. Bush's argument that Iraq was producing weapons of mass destruction. Between that and my membership in Pax Christi, the Catholic peace movement, my antennae about recruitment were up.

The law did contain an opt-out provision: If parents did not want their children's contact information falling into the hands of military recruiters, they could sign an opt-out form. But too many parents failed to notice the opt-out information, among the blizzard of forms that children typically bring home from school. So, without parental knowledge, recruiters had a way of reaching out to their children. In one vivid tale from that time, a working mother returned home and found her son entertaining a recruiter who wore a full Marine Corps dress uniform.

The powerful allure of the Marine Corps dress blues is undeniable, at least for those susceptible to uniforms. The white cap, the white belt, the white gloves, the blue trousers with red stripe all act together, with a colorful array of decorations on the chest, to create an image of otherworldly excellence, pride, manliness, and the exclusivity and excellence implied in the phrase "The few. The proud. The marines." The mysterious, dangerous, almost mystical power of that uniform is depicted in a scene in Roxana Robinson's novel *Sparta*, in a conversation between the book's main character, Conrad, and his sister, Jenny. He has just announced he is joining the Marine Corps, which seems wildly out of keeping with his pursuit of classical studies in college. Jenny guesses what has moved Conrad to lose his mind: "The white gloves, right?"

So, imagine a teenager sitting in the family living room with someone wearing that spellbinding uniform. The prospective recruit is still years away from the full development of his prefrontal cortex, which would help him or her weigh wisely the elements of the momentous enlist-or-not decision: the allure of the white gloves versus the possibility of grisly death in a senseless forever war. Too often, the white gloves win.

That image, a Marine Corps recruiter visiting with a boy while his mother was not at home, moved me to write the column about No Child Left Behind. To get a sense of why Congress decided to push schools to give recruiters contact information for their students, I interviewed David Vitter, the Louisiana Republican congressman who had insisted on including Section 9528, what I call the No Child Left Alone provision.

"We had heard through various sources that there were an alarming number of instances where high schools banned military recruiters from contact with their students," said Vitter, complaining that colleges and business recruiters got unfettered access. So, the law reads: "Each local educational agency receiving assistance under this Act shall provide military recruiters the same access to secondary school students as is provided generally to post secondary educational institutions or to prospective employers of those students."

Unlike Vitter, I couldn't believe that the military, with its bottomless budget and an arsenal of scary weapons, would be the underdog in a recruitment competition with a college or a business. As our interview ended, I asked a pivotal question: What could he tell me about his military experience? The answer was that he had none. This one member of Congress, with zero time in combat boots, felt the need to defend the military against the tiny number of school districts that acted to keep recruiters away from their students. His concern became the law of the land.

Trying to understand the forces that led to that provision, I spoke with Rick Jahnkow, who did decades of counter-recruitment work at the Project on Youth & Non-Military Opportunities (Project YANO). The source of Vitter's misinformed view that recruiters were being denied access in schools, Jahnkow said, was recruiters themselves.

"You have to sympathize somewhat with recruiters, because it's really difficult for them when they're not performing according to what they're given in quotas," Jahnkow said. "They went to Congress, and they made some outrageous claims that Vitter echoed. That was manufactured. It was never the case that so many schools were banning recruiters." In the late Nineties, before the passage of NCLB in 2002, the real problem was that the economy was up, and unemployment was down. Jobs were available, and the economic attraction of the military couldn't compete.

But the economy giveth and the economy taketh away. "They passed those provisions, and then the economy tanked," Jahnkow said. "By the time that law actually passed, they were having no trouble meeting their quotas." When jobs are scarce, and young people are hurting, they are more susceptible to "the economic draft," the siren call of recruiters dangling enlistment bonuses and the promise to pay for college education. Still, recruiters have a tough time bringing in enough volunteers. So the Pentagon more than doubled its recruitment budget in the early years of the wars in Afghanistan and Iraq, from 2004 to 2008.

As to the usefulness of the requirement that school districts provide contact information to recruiters, Jahnkow said, "To us, recruiters never favored those contact lists, because they could only be used to make blind or cold calls home." It was much better for recruiters if they had information on a prospect in advance. One paragraph in my column about No Child Left Behind reflected that. The superintendent of schools in Fairport, in upstate New York, sent an opt-out form to the families of 1,200 juniors and seniors, but only 43 chose to let their names go to recruiters. So Superintendent William Cala advised recruiters, You're better off with a list of people who really want your product than with a larger list of "cold calls" to make.

RECRUITER MIND-READING

Even when parents took advantage of the opt-out provision in No Child Left Behind, that didn't totally protect their children. Why? The recruiters now know a lot more than just phone numbers. The person who taught me a lot about that is a counter-recruitment expert named Pat Elder.

In 2015, I read a counter-recruitment piece by Elder in the magazine *U.S. Catholic*, and I interviewed him to learn more about it—my first interview for this book. Elder called himself "a Dorothy Day/Catholic Peace Fellowship/Pax Christi dude" and told me his story. "I ran a real estate title company in a rural jurisdiction in Maryland," he said. "When 9/11 hit, I moved my family to Bethesda. I got immediately into the anti-war movement." He founded the DC Anti-War Network and had police and national security agencies "tracking" him. "There was a period where I didn't work for four years," he said. "It's a rich thing for a guy in his forties to organize and be a revolutionary."

As Elder got further into the movement, he met Rick Jahnkow of Project

YANO in 2005. "He is my guru," Elder said. "He's a great man, and a great pacifist and revolutionary." But Elder might have surpassed his guru in studying military testing. His research led to a book called *Military Recruiting in the United States*, a densely packed must-read for anyone trying to figure out how the military is finding new recruits.

In his book, Elder describes a "quantum leap in the Pentagon's information gathering capabilities" since No Child Left Behind. "From electronic trolling of social websites to purchasing information from yearbook and ring companies, military recruiting services know what's in Johnny's head, if Johnny has a girlfriend, and what *she* thinks of his decision regarding enlistment," Elder wrote. "The information is merged with data from the [Pentagon's] Joint Advertising Market Research and Studies Recruiting Database (JAMRS) and social media sites like Facebook, and the result is staggering."

Recruiters can also use reliable information about a prospect's actual aptitude that they glean from ASVAB, the Armed Services Vocational Aptitude Battery. Note that Armed Services is its first name. The military would like people to believe that it's not so much a recruiting tool as a neutral career-discernment test. But deep into a Marine Corps recruitment manual, Elder found this relatively honest description: "The ASVAB is used by the Armed Forces for recruiting purposes and by school counselors for vocational guidance counseling. The ASVAB's ability for determining civilian job skills has not yet been proven."

In gushing contrast, the website of the United States Military Entrance Processing Command (USMEPCOM) says that the ASVAB career program "helps you identify your skills and interests and encourages you to explore all the pathways you can take to reach your career goals—education, credentialing, licensure and apprenticeship programs, and the Military." Notice how "the Military," reverentially but incorrectly uppercased, is tagged on at the end, almost as an afterthought. In the 2017–2018 school year, 702,000 high school students took the test, the USMEPCOM website says.

Knowing how important ASVAB is to recruiters, the counter-recruiters work to make sure the test is optional, *not* mandatory. Recruiters are not supposed to suggest to schools that ASVAB be made mandatory, but they love it when districts take that step. Beyond the optional/mandatory question, the other ASVAB struggle is about who gets to see the results. The regulations of the processing command set up eight options for reporting of the test results. Options one to six allow recruiters to see the results within varying time frames. Under options seven and eight, the recruiters don't get to see the results at all. Counter-recruiters like Barbara Harris, of the New York Coalition to Protect Student Privacy, keep pushing schools to choose option eight.

Harris has deep roots in peace activism—and a long history with recruiters. On October 17, 2005, she was among 18 women protesting American involvement in Iraq, by showing up at the iconic recruiting station in Manhattan's Times Square and volunteering for enlistment. Though they were not all grandmothers, the idea was to sign up and free up grandchildren from combat in Iraq. "We wanted to speak to the recruiters, and of course, they locked the office," Harris said. One older woman used her cane to knock on the door as the recruiters hid inside, behind their files. Finally, the women sat down on the ramp leading into the office and refused to budge. This earned them a ride in a police vehicle to the police station, where they sat in separate cells. "We had to take the laces out of our sneakers, in case we strangled each other," Harris said.

In a nonjury trial in April 2006, Manhattan Criminal Court Judge Neil Ross acquitted them all of disorderly conduct, because they didn't block pedestrian traffic, and anyone who wanted to enter the recruiting center could do that. Then, outside the court, the women, self-identified as the Granny Peace Brigade, sang "God Help America," to the tune of "God Bless America." In *The New York Times*, Anemona Hartocollis described the outcome: "They came, they shuffled, they conquered."

In addition to her peace activism, Harris had a long career in education. Her latest campaign has been trying to teach educators this lesson: If you allow your students to take the ASVAB, you *must* choose option eight, to keep the results out of the needy hands of recruiters. It's not easy for private citizens to make headway against the most trusted institution in America, the military. But Harris remains stubbornly committed to it. "You can't get tired," Harris said. "You just have to do it."

Harris and Jahnkow serve on the steering committee of the National Network Opposing the Militarization of Youth (NNOMY), which coordinates the counter-recruitment work of peace groups. Elder, whose activism has moved from counter-recruitment to exposing the way the military pollutes the planet, is on the emeritus steering committee. So is Seth Kershner, a pivotal researcher.

In western Massachusetts, Kershner went to a "lily-white" high school with economically advantaged students, not a fertile field for the economic draft. His school was about an hour west of Springfield, which was far more fruitful territory for recruiters. "Springfield is a very segregated city," Kershner said. "The public schools there are majority Black and Latino." Kershner used the Freedom of Information Act to find what high schools army recruiters were visiting—and how often.

"In the early 2010s, there were some years where army recruiters alone would visit a single high school in Springfield more than 90 times—or an average of every other day," Kershner said. "You compare that to lily-white high schools, which have far fewer economically disadvantaged students, where they're visiting two or three times a year."

The roots of Kershner's counter-recruitment go back to the early days of the Iraq occupation, when he was an undergraduate at Massachusetts College of Liberal Arts, a state university campus. Studying philosophy, he found himself surrounded by professors with a strong sense of social justice. His deep opposition to the war moved him to join bus trips to Washington to protest. "It felt like going and doing the symbolic protest, marching through the streets, it just wasn't enough," Kershner recalled. The next step was counter-recruitment in high schools, which offered him a chance to have a more direct impact.

"The people who organized the trips to Washington in my area were this lovely couple who had retired after teaching peace studies for decades," Kershner said. "They were doing counter-recruitment work, and they invited me to come along into the area schools." Those face-to-face meetings with students gave him a sense of making a difference. "In the sixties, there was an understanding that it began with the local draft board, and each generation has its own way of resisting war," Kershner said. "After we got the all-volunteer military, as I've documented in papers and so forth, school militarism became the way that the Pentagon got recruits."

After college, Kershner decided not to pursue his study of philosophy in graduate school, but to study library science at Simmons University in Boston, near Fenway Park. At Simmons, he honed the researching skills that he had used in counter-recruitment. During that time, he met Scott Harding, a professor at the University of Connecticut School of Social Work, who became his coauthor on *Counter-Recruitment and the Campaign to Demilitarize Public Schools.*

"It's based on dozens of interviews that we did with counter-recruiters," Kershner said. Harding got them a grant to help finance their interviews of activists in Texas, Oregon, California, New York City, and Washington, DC. "Many of the most active counter-recruitment organizations are located in conservative parts of the country," they wrote. "Fort Worth, Texas, for example, is arguably one of the most militarized cities in the Southwest."

To combat the incursion of military recruiters into Fort Worth's schools, an organization called Peaceful Vocations sprang up. "Before Peaceful Vocations became active, military recruiters enjoyed carte blanche access at local high schools," Kershner and Harding wrote. They described how army recruiters used customized Humvees, often with $9,000 stereo systems, to get the attention of male students. In sharp contrast to expensive, flashy toys like Humvees and helicopters, counter-recruitment activists have nothing more entertaining to offer than flyers and commonsense talk.

The Kershner-Harding book underlined the importance of counter-recruitment with a quote from Diane Wood, founder of Peaceful Vocations in Fort Worth: "The reason we have the war … is because we have militarism in our schools and because of the military's power to induce kids to go into the military…. I personally believe that counter-military recruitment is the very best anti-war movement that you can ever have."

IS RECRUITING CHILD ABUSE?

The parry-and-thrust battle between military recruiters and counter-recruitment activists is an unequal, still-evolving story. My sense of the evolution of school recruitment efforts sharpened when I read a March 2019 article in *Military Times* by Meghann Myers, which began: "High school seniors have traditionally been Army recruiting's most reliable target audience, but leadership is realizing that as military service becomes more and more rare and fewer American youth actually know a soldier or veteran, they'll need to make up that gap by reaching out to younger prospects."

Myers was reporting from Huntsville, Alabama, the scene of the Global Force Summit of a nonprofit called the Association of the United States Army (AUSA). The heart of her story came from a talk by the army's assistant secretary for manpower and reserve affairs. By the time they reach adolescence, said Dr. E. Casey Wardynski, young people have already begun thinking about what they might want to be when they grow up. The lesson: If recruiters wait to approach them about enlistment until they are nearing high school graduation, recruiters are waiting too long.

"We have to confront this question of, will we wait until they're 17, or will we start talking to them at age 12, 13, 14, 15, when they form the set of things they are thinking about doing with their life?" Wardynski said. "If we wait until they're 17 or 18, we will not be the first impression. Others will have made that for us."

A few months after reading that piece and imagining recruiters chasing younger and younger kids, I heard something that elevated the issue to a higher plane. It was one comment in a long, impressive talk by Danny Sjursen, a retired army major who had led troops in combat in both Afghanistan and Iraq, had become profoundly anti-war, had taught history at West Point, and had only recently left active duty. He was speaking in September 2019 at a major venue for the peace movement on Long Island, the Unitarian Universalist Congregation at Shelter Rock, in Manhasset.

As I arrived, I noticed my friend Marty Melkonian, cofounder with his wife, Margaret, of the Long Island Alliance for Peaceful Alternatives. Marty coordinates speakers, often on peace and war, who visit Hofstra University in Hempstead, where he has taught sociology to thousands of students. In addition to his talk at the UU, Sjursen was appearing at Hofstra that week. Marty introduced me to him, and I listened to his talk. Among the topics he discussed was his research on recruiting practices. The words that really caught my attention were "child abuse." The day after that talk, I bought a copy of his book *Ghost Riders of Baghdad: Soldiers, Civilians, and the Myth of the Surge*, and I began following his writing, his speeches, his podcasts, and later, the book he co-edited with Andrew Bacevich, *Paths of Dissent: Soldiers Speak Out Against America's Misguided Wars*. A little over a month after his Shelter Rock UU speech, I interviewed him and asked him about his use of that "child abuse" phrase.

"It's just biological studies that demonstrate that the human brain, the teenage and the early 20s brain, isn't fully developed," Sjursen said. "Thus, by recruiting 17-to-21-year-olds, which is the core demographic, I think it's in a sense child abuse, because you're taking people who really may not know better, may not be developed intellectually enough or be educated enough…."

In *Paths of Dissent*, anti-war veteran Erik Edstrom echoed the core of what Sjursen was saying: "At the first sniff of adulthood, the military bamboozles children into one of the largest commitments ever conceived: to leave your life, be issued a new identity, and be sent across the world to inflict violence on people you don't know, for political reasons you're not meant to understand. I believe in informed consent, and I'm no longer sure that's what happens when a military commitment is pitched to teenagers too young even to be allowed to drink alcohol or buy a ticket for an R-rated movie depicting gory military combat."

Sjursen's "child abuse" description rings true to Kathy Barker, a microbiologist and professor in the Department of Public Health at the University of Washington, Seattle. In fact, she and a University of Washington public health professor, Amy Hagopian, wrote a paper together that compared the methods recruiters use in high schools to the "grooming" that child sexual abusers use to prepare their victims for the abuse. Unsurprisingly, that paper set off a right-wing explosion of outrage, described below.

Before that 2011 paper, Barker and Hagopian had come to counter-recruitment work at different times and with different personalities: Barker was the more emotional, Hagopian was the more methodical. Over time, Hagopian established her credentials within conservative organizations by performing their quotidian tasks, then used that credibility to bring about serious change within the institution.

Hagopian recalls becoming aware of war and peace issues in 1968, when she was 13, at the height of Vietnam, when students in her school took a stand on war issues. "So I was always aware of this, and I went on to work in the antinuclear movement in the eighties," Hagopian said. "I ended up being elected to the Seattle school board in 1990, and one of the first things I worked on was our policy around military recruiting in schools, to be sure that counter-recruiters had equal time."

In addition to her role on the citywide school board, Hagopian was active for a dozen years on the Parent Teacher Student Association of Garfield High School, which her three children attended. "We started in the fall of 2002 noticing that the US was on the verge of an invasion of Iraq," Hagopian said, and the PTSA took a stand against it. "So, by the time the invasion happened, and the recruiters started swarming our buildings, we were well positioned to have a conversation about military recruiting."

Hagopian and others pushed back against the No Child Left Behind mandate that school districts must give recruiters contact information for their students or lose federal aid. In May of 2005, when Hagopian was co-chair of the PTSA, it voted overwhelmingly for a resolution making clear that "public schools are not a place for military recruiters."

That was not enough to overcome the force of the law. A spokesman for the school district, Peter Daniels, said that the district stood to lose $15 million in federal aid if it disobeyed the law. "The parents have chosen to take a stand, but we still have to comply with No Child Left Behind," Daniels told the *New York Times*, which made the Garfield parents' action national news, as did the *Christian Scientist Monitor*. In a way, simply by taking notice of the Garfield action as something new, those national stories provide evidence of how unusual it is for a high school to push back against No Child Left Behind, and how bogus was David Vitter's concern about widespread rejection of recruiters.

The Garfield story had legs. "It had no legal standing, but it flew around the world," said Barker, whose own counter-recruitment activism began later than Hagopian's, after the invasion of Iraq by a coalition force dominated by the United States and Great Britain, with far fewer troops from Australia and Poland. In addition to the national and international attention, the parent association's action brought some nasty phone calls to the school. The principal, Ted Howard II, a Garfield alumnus and a "gem of a human being," Hagopian said, had to field those calls. All the work that the association had done over the years to support the school had earned his trust and loyalty. "And he stood up for us."

Getting to know each other through their children, Hagopian and Barker had formed an effective counter-recruitment partnership. After the Garfield High School resolution against recruiters, they worked together to get the statewide PTA, which largely represented rural school districts, to take a similar position. "We had a tough sell of it," Hagopian recalled.

IS RECRUITING LIKE SEXUAL ABUSE?

Then, in 2011, Hagopian and Barker became coauthors of a peer-reviewed paper for the *American Journal of Public Health*, under this headline: "Should We End Military Recruiting in High Schools as a Matter of Child Protection and Public Health?" The very first paragraph of the paper's abstract contains this stunning assertion: "Military recruiter behaviors are disturbingly similar to predatory grooming."

In the body of the paper, Barker and Hagopian make their point by quoting first from the army's school recruiting handbook, which advises recruiters how to win the confidence of students: "Be so helpful and so much a part of the school scene that you are in constant demand. Attend athletic events at the HS. Deliver donuts and coffee for the faculty once a month. Offer to be a timekeeper at football games. Martin Luther King, Jr.'s birthday is in January. Wear your dress blues and participate in school events commemorating this holiday." The coauthors called the advice about Dr. King's birthday "a particularly cynical gesture, given Martin Luther King's views on war and militarism."

The paper points out the similarity between that recruiter behavior and what a peer-reviewed article in the *Journal of Sexual Aggression* called "the process by which a child is befriended by a would-be abuser in an attempt to gain the child's confidence and trust, enabling them to get the child to acquiesce to abusive activity."

This comparison led Hagopian to a less-than-hospitable interview by right-wing Fox News personality Bill O'Reilly. He sparred with her and took faux Fox umbrage, as an all-uppercase caption under Hagopian's photo yelled: "OUTRAGEOUS COMPARISON." Hagopian pointed out that the article was not saying that recruiters are actual sexual abusers, but simply that their process looks a lot like predatory grooming. That didn't calm the Fox host.

O'Reilly's outrage in defense of the military is highly ironic. First, there's his knowledge of how the military actually works: During the Vietnam War, he was either in college or teaching. So, no combat boots for him. Then there's his rejection of the idea that recruiters could sexually abuse recruits.

A few years after O'Reilly's exchange with Hagopian, Fox News fired him in 2017 after the *New York Times* reported that he and Fox had settled multiple sexual harassment lawsuits against him. So, he knew a lot about about sexual harassment, but nothing about the military. In contrast, Hagopian is deeply knowledgeable about war and health. Together with another professor, Evan Kanter, she teaches courses on it.

Though the Hagopian-Barker article did not attempt to make a case that recruiters are sexually abusing recruits, it did mention "an Associated Press report of hundreds of rapes of young women by their military recruiters." Soon after my interviews with Barker and Hagopian, I checked out that 2006 investigation. Here are its top two paragraphs:

"More than 100 young women who expressed interest in joining the military in the past year were preyed upon sexually by their recruiters. Women were raped on recruiting office couches, assaulted in government cars and groped en route to entrance exams.

"A six-month Associated Press investigation found that more than 80 military recruiters were disciplined last year for sexual misconduct with potential enlistees. The cases occurred across all branches of the military and in all regions of the country."

As I researched the reporter, Martha Mendoza, I learned that she had also worked on an AP investigation of a war crime committed by American troops during the Korean War. The start of that AP series said: "It was a story no one wanted to hear: Early in the Korean War, villagers said, American soldiers machine-gunned hundreds of helpless civilians, under a railroad bridge in the South Korean countryside."

For that investigation, Mendoza and her AP colleagues—reporters Charles Hanley and Sang-Hun Choe, with researcher Randy Herschaft—won a 2000 Pulitzer Prize for Investigative Reporting. They turned their work into a book called *The Bridge at No Gun Ri: A Hidden Nightmare from the Korean War*. Sadly for them, the book came out right at the time of 9/11. Mendoza and Hanley were on day one of a nine-city book tour, and they had to shelve the book and begin reporting on 9/11. Though it didn't get as wide an audience as it deserved, I had known about the book for years, because I spent 13 months in Korea, because I care about Korea, and because my antennae about war crimes in general were up. Often, driving by a Korean

War monument in front of a Suffolk County office building, I'd think, "What about No Gun Ri?"

In reading about Mendoza, I also learned that she had been part an AP team that won the most prestigious of Pulitzers, the public service prize for 2016. The series dug into abusive labor practices in the seafood supply chain in Asia that brought fish to America. Their reporting freed two thousand people from slavery and led to industry reforms.

So, by the time I spoke with Mendoza, she was a heroine to me. In an era when the president of the United States was daily demonizing journalism as "fake news," I took comfort in great investigative journalism, like high-impact reports in *Newsday* about housing discrimination on Long Island and about how much the fighter-plane manufacturer Grumman knew about the way its toxic chemicals were contaminating the island's groundwater. Combined with my pride in that *Newsday* work, Mendoza's outstanding journalism made me a little emotional during the interview.

The Korea investigation had been her first deep dive into the military. It turned out to be difficult, because some in the Associated Press leadership felt "that we were accusing US soldiers of a war crime, when in fact these things can happen in the fog of war," Mendoza recalled. It took four months of reporting, Mendoza said, but 10 months to get it on the AP wire. In the aftermath, AP disbanded its investigative team.

Mendoza did not bring a cynical attitude about the military into either the No Gun Ri investigation or the story about sexual abuse by recruiters. Her parents were Peace Corps administrators, and she and her siblings had the same experiences as military kids: living in different countries and even shopping in the commissary. "We were definitely not anti-military," Mendoza said. In fact, she had relatives who had been in the military, from Normandy in World War II to the modern Marine Corps, and she spoke with many veterans. "I would say I came out of that with respect for the institution."

But that didn't keep her from pursuing the recruiter story. It began at a National Lawyers Guild conference, where she encountered a lawyer who was representing two women claiming to have been raped by their recruiter. "I didn't necessarily think it was a story, because incidents can happen," Mendoza said. "So, then I filed Freedom of Information requests with all the branches and realized that there was a pattern of abuse." She found that, among the thirteen thousand frontline recruiters in 2005, across all branches, "one out of 200 was disciplined for sexual misconduct. That was high enough to be of concern to me and seemed worthy of a story."

Beyond the Freedom of Information requests and a grasp of the macro dimensions of the problem, Mendoza went right to the heart of it: recruiters and recruits.

"I wrote letters to recruiters who are currently in prison and asked them if they would be willing to sit down and talk to me," Mendoza recalled. "I had one recruiter who was, and so then I went to his prison in New York and talked to him about how it came to be that he did this, what his situation was." He told her about his rape conviction for having sex with a 16-year-old high school student while he was a Marine Corps recruiter. The student caressed his groin while he was driving her to a recruiting event, but he didn't consider that an excuse. "I pulled over and asked her to climb into the back seat," he said. "I should have pushed her away. I was the adult in the situation. I should have put my foot down, called her parents." With help from military public affairs staff, Mendoza spent a couple of days observing recruiters. She also read journals and diaries kept by survivors of sexual assault by recruiters.

Though her investigation showed recruiters sexually assaulting recruits, Mendoza was able to understand the world of recruiters. "It's never going to be okay to sexually assault somebody. But they're under kind of crazy pressure when they're recruiting that I hadn't thought about," Mendoza said. "The whole idea of somebody who maybe is not a good salesperson, has a different skill set, being required to be a recruiter, and having people get in their face and scream at them that they have to get people signed up, to me it just didn't seem like the best way to populate the military."

TOUGH TIMES FOR RECRUITERS

To some extent, the military did address the quotas. Between the time Mendoza did her reporting and the time Major General Allen W. Batschelet became the commanding general of the United States Army Recruiting Command in June 2013, his predecessors had tried to ease the stress on recruiters.

"There were two or three of them that changed the recruiting model from an individual quota system to a unit or team goal system," said Batschelet, who retired from the military and became CEO of Horizon Strategies in North Carolina, whose clients included the military, academia, and corporations. "That took a lot of pressure off the individual recruiters. And it was more reflective of how the army does business. You know, we do things as units, not as individuals. So, that shift addressed that problem, and I would say it was largely successful."

Despite the pressure, being a recruiter has its advantages. Among others, no one shoots at you in a recruiting station. (Well, at least not in this country. Russian President Vladimir Putin's emergency conscription of troops in 2022 to fight in his war on Ukraine brought multiple protests, including a shooting at a recruiting station.) Still, not every recruiter volunteers for the duty. "About one-third are directed to become recruiters for three-year tours," Batschelet said. "The full-time recruiters enjoy being on the frontlines of ensuring the army remains a viable institution and the lifestyle that being a recruiter affords, different than that of a soldier assigned to, say, an infantry unit."

By the time Batschelet's tour of duty at the recruiting command ended in 2015, he had taken part in a further examination of the army's approach. "Before I left, I convinced the secretary of defense—actually, the secretary of the army first and the secretary of defense—that the army's talent acquisition strategy and processes, business systems and so forth, were completely inadequate to the challenges of today and tomorrow," Batschelet said. "So they issued a problem statement, signed by the secretary, that essentially said, 'Fix this.'" What needed fixing? Batschelet called it an "industrial age" system that relied on talking to large numbers of people—something like 50 prospects to produce one enlistment contract. "It was horribly inefficient, and it required a lot of manpower. And so, we were talking to a lot of kids that weren't even eligible."

No matter how the military recalibrates its systems, it still faces significant obstacles in the broader society. "As the army's chief recruiter, I can tell you our mission isn't getting any easier," said Batschelet's successor, Major General Jeffrey Snow, at a 2017 Heritage Foundation event, gloomily titled "A Looming National Security Crisis: Young Americans Unable to Join the Military."

The day before that event, *USA Today* carried a story saying that, reacting to the increasing demand for new soldiers, the army "has reached deeper into the pool of marginally qualified recruits, offered hundreds of millions in bonuses and relaxed the process for granting waivers for marijuana use."

A few years before the Heritage Foundation event, the availability of waivers allowed into the army a troubled young man who went on to commit a horrendous war crime. At the end of January 2005, Steven Dale Green, 19, an unemployed high school dropout, sat in a Texas jail after his third misdemeanor conviction. "Days later, Mr. Green enlisted in a soldier-strapped Army, and was later assigned to a star-crossed unit to serve on an especially murderous patch of earth," a 2006 *New York Times* story reported, noting the army's increase in the use of moral waivers. "The change opened the ranks to more people like Mr. Green, those with minor criminal records and weak educational backgrounds." The year after his waiver-aided enlistment, Green was in Mahmudiya, Iraq, south of Baghdad, with a unit of the 101st Airborne Division. He and four other soldiers drank, changed into black clothes, and raided the home of an Iraqi family. Green shot and killed the husband, wife, and younger daughter, and he and another soldier raped a 14-year-old daughter, shot her, and tried to burn her body. This crime did not become known until after Green had been discharged from the army with a personality disorder. He was convicted and sentenced in 2009. Green was serving multiple life sentences in a federal prison in Arizona when he died in 2014, in an apparent suicide.

Now, at the 2017 Heritage Foundation event about the shortage of young Americans able to enlist, the army's chief recruiter didn't shy away from talking about the *USA Today* story on increased use of waivers. "I'm kind of hoping some of you didn't read it, but if you did, I have to tell you, the army is not lowering standards," Snow said, expressing pride in the work that 9,000 recruiters did. If you add up the total number of recruits who were either in a lower testing category or who needed a waiver for past marijuana use, Snow conceded, the article had that number correct: about 1,800. "That's 2.7 percent of 68,682 individuals we recruited," Snow said. "I have to tell you, that's well within the quality benchmarks."

For the 2018 fiscal year, his recruiters faced an even bigger task—the recruitment of 80,000 new active-duty soldiers—and a big hurdle: Pentagon data showed more than seven out of 10 people age 17 to 24 were ineligible for the military, because of obesity, lack of high school education, or a criminal record. At the Heritage event, Major General Malcolm Frost, then the commanding general of the United States Army Center for Initial Military Training, said that out of 32 million to 34 million people in that age group, only about 10 million are recruitable—and only about 380,000 to 400,000 of them have what Frost called "a propensity to serve."

Frost painted a grim picture of the army's narrow appeal. "Eighty percent of the active-duty army is in five states in our union—five of our fifty," Frost said. "We are rurally based, in the Bible Belt—the smiley face, I like to call it—of America. We are not in urban America. We're not where Americans live, in the cities. We live in military gated communities. We are disconnected from the citizenry we serve, I would argue." In other words, he said, the military is "becoming a warrior class unto ourselves."

Recruiters must also overcome the bloody image of the forever war that young people have. "What they think they know comes from movies and the news," Jeffrey Snow lamented at the Heritage event. "I'm not here to speak ill of either, but you and I know this doesn't paint an honest picture of the work we do every day. Instead of seeing the opportunity to become an engineer, an electrician, a vet tech, a firefighter, an IT specialist, America's youth see only the pain and the hurt. They believe that if they enlist—and I'm troubled by this—it is likely that they will be damaged in some way." The current tally of deaths—both in combat and by suicide—will do nothing to dispel the belief by young people that "they will be damaged in some way" in the military. Many more active-duty military and veterans have committed suicide during the post-9/11 wars than have died in combat. The same was true of the Vietnam era. Chapter 8 examines the grim numbers of the lingering problem of suicide.

In addition to all the other obstacles, the recruiter also has to contend with the "female influencers" in a potential recruit's life, who push back against enlistment. "If there's an adult male in the situation, they are almost always supportive of the young person joining," said Batschelet. "The moms, though, are the hurdles that recruiters have to convince—if not the mom, then whoever that adult influencer is: the grandmother, the aunt, or whoever."

That would account for some of the recruitment ads from Today's Military, an all-branches Pentagon advertising effort. Those ads actually show parents arguing with their children against enlisting. The clever twist in the ads is placing the parents right in the middle of the soldiers' military life, arguing against a choice they have clearly already made. In one, the ad begins with a group of soldiers barging into someone's home, clearly in search of terrorists. "Do you really want to go through with this?" the mother asks her heavily armed, hyper-vigilant son. "Absolutely," he says, without a moment's hesitation. "You've always stood up for what you believed in, but this?" she says. He responds, "What could mean more than this?" A second later, we see him out of uniform, obviously a flashback to the time before he made the enlistment decision. "So, Mom," he says, "what do you think?" She says nothing, but she summons him for a hug, as this admonition appears on the screen: "Their success tomorrow begins with your support today." Obviously, the ad is an attempt to influence the influencers.

Another ad starts with a confident, competent young woman, striding purposefully through her workplace, a military cybersecurity facility. Her mother trails behind her and asks her why she has chosen this career. "This doesn't make sense," the mother says. The young officer answers, "It does to me, Mom." The mother presses the issue: "You're a smart kid. Why do you want to do this?" Calmly, her daughter responds: "I love it. You know that." The mother isn't satisfied: "OK, but why this way?" Her daughter says, "Because I want to take on the world's toughest hackers, and this is where it's done." Then a flashback shows the young woman, in civilian life, asking her mother, "So, what do you think?" The mother sits down next to her and nods her head almost imperceptibly, bowing to her daughter's military dreams. The ad does not mention, of course, the epidemic of sexual harassment, sexual abuse, and rape that women in the military face every day around the world. As in the other ad, the closing words say, "Their success tomorrow begins with your support today," and not, "Their safety tomorrow depends on your refusal today." Chapter 5 tells the story of the dangers women face in the military—not from the "enemy," but from within.

For all the problems they face, recruiters have plenty of advantages, including ads like these two from Today's Military, and even more important, the hyper-adulation of the military. Recruiters also have been able to count on big toys, like the Army's Adventure Van, an 18-wheeler that brought military-themed gaming to hundreds of high schools in the past decade. The army can spend profligately on experimental projects such as the Army Experience

Center, a 14,500-square-foot facility stuffed with video game consoles and a war-games simulator. It opened at a Philadelphia shopping mall in 2008, but closed two years and $22 million later, after multiple anti-war protests. The army denied it had been a recruiting center, but rather, a marketing test. Some 40,000 people participated.

Another example of hugely expensive military toys helping recruiters is the big-event flyover by military fighter jets. One of those is the annual Memorial Day weekend air show at Jones Beach on Long Island, sponsored by Bethpage Federal Credit Union. It has featured both the United States Navy Blue Angels and the United States Air Force Thunderbirds aerial demonstration teams—plus nonmilitary performers. The Blue Angels were the featured performers at the first Jones Beach air show in 2004. The following year, the state's Office of Parks, Recreation and Historic Preservation decided that the first show was such a roaring success that it should be an annual event. An officer of Bethpage Federal Credit Union once told me in an informal conversation that part of the rationale for its sponsorship of this air show is to honor Grumman Aerospace employees. That seems fitting enough, given that Bethpage FCU began as a credit union specifically for employees of that defense contractor, and the Blue Angels have flown Grumman aircraft in the past. But they have never used the F-14 Tomcat, Grumman's signature product, made famous by Tom Cruise in the original *Top Gun*, in 1986. That same year, long before the Jones Beach show began, the Blue Angels started using the McDonnell Douglas F/A-18 Hornet. Still, the credit union sponsors the show.

For years, friends of mine from Pax Christi Long Island, the regional presence of the Catholic peace movement, have gone to Jones Beach during the air show to demonstrate, making a simple point: Memorial Day is supposed to be about remembering those killed in past wars—not about recruiting people for current or future wars. Right there on the beach, undaunted by peace activists, a recruiting station awaits, in the hope that recruiters can interact with anyone who has been inspired by the scary aerial maneuvers and wants to join the military. Once, in a chat with a state parks official, I said that the Pax Christi demonstration might not happen if the recruiters weren't there. He told me what I should have guessed: The Blue Angels are not flying at Jones Beach—or anywhere—unless the hosts of the show make recruiters feel very welcome. Sure enough, the Blue Angels Support Manual for 2019, which laid out in clear language what the hosts need to provide, said this: "Community outreach and recruiting are vital aspects of the mission of the Blue Angels. The Team's air shows and public appearances are Navy and Marine Corps awareness tools. The crowds that the Blue Angels draw provide unique opportunities for officer and enlisted recruiters."

So the philosophy is clear: The air show is about recruiting. But the Blue Angels manual doesn't stop there. It prescribes the size of the recruiting area: "60 feet wide by 80 feet long by 20 feet high," and its location, "in a high traffic area on the crowd line and positioned near center point for recruiting purposes." It also requires that recruiting ads appear in all programs for the event.

Less publicly flashy but more pervasive is America's Army, a video war game hatched in 2002 by the Army Game Studio, in Huntsville, Alabama. People using it have logged billions of rounds of play. But the army doesn't like to acknowledge recruiting as its core goal. They prefer discussing its use in training people who are already soldiers, not its potential for enlisting new soldiers. "We would never expect someone to sign up for the army simply because they played a game," Marsha Berry, a leading official at America's Army, told one interviewer. "Rather, if someone played the game and became interested in the army because of something they learned, he/she could go and talk to a recruiter who would give them the information to make an informed decision."

Many factors go into that decision—from a desire to get away from an oppressive life situation to a feeling of guilt that friends are going away to fight, while you're still safe at home. In that enlistment calculus, economic necessity seems a more frequent motivator than patriotism. I got a cogent summary in a conversation with one veteran, Kayla Williams, a former army linguist and author of two memoirs, *Love My Rifle More Than You: Young and Female in the U.S. Army* and *Plenty of Time When We Get Home: Love and Recovery in the Aftermath of War*.

"I enlisted so that I could get access to the G.I. Bill," said Williams, a former senior fellow at the Center for a New American Security who in 2021 became assistant secretary of the Office of Public and Intergovernmental Affairs at the Department of Veterans Affairs. "I also enlisted to challenge myself and to break out of the rut that I had dug for myself, and to be able to learn a foreign language. Like most people, it's not one single thing that drove me to enlist. It was a combination of factors. In terms of idealism, I would say the component of my decision to enlist that was most idealistic was being acutely aware that our country had invested in me, in that I grew up on food stamps occasionally and knew that I wouldn't have gotten as far as I had without the social safety net, and I felt an obligation to defend the nation and to serve the country that had helped invest in me."

Another author I interviewed, Rory Fanning, drew part of his enlistment motivation from an Oscar-winning film released soon after the 9/11 attacks, *Black Hawk Down,* about an unsuccessful 1993 operation in Somalia. "When you see the two planes hit the Twin Towers, and you're young, and you see all those thousands of people die, and you're full of energy, and you've got a bunch of student loans to pay back, and you don't want to go work in a cubicle, and you've just seen the movie *Black Hawk Down,* and you've grown up in a right-wing Catholic family that believes that the US is a force for freedom and democracy around the world, signing up for the military was an obvious choice," said Fanning. "There isn't really a rite of passage for a lot of young people, and the military becomes the default rite of passage."

Fanning's book, *Worth Fighting For: An Army Ranger's Journey Out of the Military and Across America,* describes both that military rite of passage and two other journeys: his transformation from willing warrior to conscientious objector and his eight-month cross-country walk, in 2008–2009, to raise money for the Pat Tillman Foundation.

Tillman, a former NFL safety for the Arizona Cardinals, joined the army after 9/11 and died in a "friendly fire" incident in the unfriendly mountains of Afghanistan. In an attempt to cover up the embarrassment, the military announced at first that Tillman had been killed by the enemy, but later had to admit that the fatal fire came from his own troops. Fanning had already been deployed once to Afghanistan before he went to the Army Ranger School at Fort Benning, Georgia. It was during that time that he first met Tillman and Tillman's brother, Kevin. By then, he had soured on the forever war.

"It wasn't until I signed up for the military and kind of saw what was happening in Afghanistan, and was feeling more like a bully than anything, that I began to question what the US has been doing around the world,"

Fanning said. "After two weeks of thinking and working up the courage, I walked up to a Ranger School instructor and said, 'I don't believe in what I am doing anymore. I want out,'" he wrote.

That step on the path to conscientious objector status did not go over well—with two exceptions. "The only ones in the battalion who were sympathetic to my case were the Tillman brothers," Fanning wrote. "They weren't scared to talk to me in public. They empathized and said, 'Try not to let it get to you.'"

In his post-army days, Fanning spends his time "fighting to end the unending wars," as his website puts it. That includes pushing back against Junior Reserve Officers' Training Corps in the high schools of Chicago. The United States Army Cadet Command describes its JROTC as "one of the largest character development and citizenship programs for youth in the world." But counter-recruiters see JROTC as another cog in the recruitment machine. In Chicago, where Fanning lives, he does something about it, even though school administrators aren't always receptive to counter-recruiters. "Chicago happens to be the mecca of the JROTC program, because the black and Latinx communities are preyed upon," Fanning said. "So I go into high schools when they allow me. The Chicago Teachers Union actually gave me a grant to get in and meet these kids."

Another enlisted man who joined with college debt as a motivating factor, became thoroughly anti-war, and wrote a book was Jonathan Hutto. Unlike so many recruits, Hutto had already compiled an accomplishment-filled biography before he enlisted, but like so many, it was economic need that propelled him into the arms of the United States Navy.

Hutto was born in Atlanta. Both of his parents were born in the segregated South in the 1940s. His father had started a small business in Atlanta, and his mother had worked to integrate Chattanooga, Tennessee. In 1995, Hutto entered Howard University, a jewel among the historically Black colleges and universities. It wasn't easy financially.

"I come from a background where I was solidly born within the Black middle class, but that crashed when my parents divorced," Hutto said. "So we went from a patriarchal, male-led household—my father had his own business, doing HVAC—to then a child-support household, which had a desperate economic impact on our lives." Until he was almost 10, he had lived in a stable home. "From the time I was 10 years old until the time I left to go to Howard University, I probably moved about 10 times—I mean, constantly. I became a professional at packing a U-Haul truck."

Being accepted to Howard was only the first step. Paying for it was tough. "There was no money saved for me," Hutto said. "There was no college fund. There was none of that. But my dream exceeded that. I mean, Jesse Jackson had a famous quote that he used to say often, ad nauseam, back then that I internalized. He said, 'Use hope and imagination as weapons for survival and progress.' That was what I was doing, when I was 16, 17 years old. My situation did not dictate my aspiration."

Once at Howard, Hutto quickly became politically active. He served as co-coordinator of a student-led voter registration effort and later was elected president of the Howard University Student Association. His brightest memory was hosting Kwame Ture, aka Stokely Carmichael, for his last public address at Howard. After graduation in 1999, he worked for the American Civil Liberties Union of the National Capital Area, doing public education on civilian oversight of law enforcement. Later, he joined Amnesty International's mid-Atlantic office, working with student groups. In 2001, he was a member of Amnesty's American delegation to the World Conference against Racism in Durban, South Africa.

In January 2003, he decided to leave Amnesty. "I had become a full-time single dad and was seeking employment that would grant me the flexibility and time to be a dad and a productive worker," he wrote in his book, *Antiwar Soldier: How to Dissent Within the Ranks of the Military.* He tried a transition-to-teaching program at Howard University, but figured out that teaching was not for him. Enter a navy recruiter, with a promise to help with the $48,000 in student debt that Hutto had amassed at Howard. Hutto signed on the dotted line in December 2003, a few months into the occupation of Iraq, and reported for duty in mid-January of 2004, three months short of his 27th birthday.

In his book, Hutto described the attitude he and his friends had toward the ongoing occupation: "When my buddies spoke of the Iraq War, they talked about the war as being a conflict for profit involving companies such as Halliburton. Most know the situation. However, simply knowing the situation does not end the economic compulsion to join."

That last sentence is a particularly powerful description of the "economic draft." In *Paths of Dissent*, Erik Edstrom wrote: "Only later would I realize that this is a perverse carrot to dangle before you: trade college funding for the formative years of your life. In the richest country on earth, you may literally have to kill, or die, for a decent education." When I asked Hutto about the economic draft, he said simply, "I was already ideologically opposed to the wars of occupation at the time of my enlistment." But his financial situation left him little choice. Later, as he attended the Defense Information School at Fort Meade, Maryland, one of the instructors asked students to describe why they had enlisted, and Hutto offered a positive reason. "I stated the military was the only institution in America that came close to reflecting what the rest of the country looked like (at least in the enlisted ranks)," Hutto wrote.

Assigned to the aircraft carrier USS *Theodore Roosevelt*, Hutto found himself deployed to the Middle East, in September 2005, for Operation Iraqi Freedom. His job was writing articles, taking photos, and anchoring a news program. He also found himself pushing back against racism, including a petty officer who brandished a hangman's noose in front of him and said that another African American sailor needed a lynching. On his return from the Middle East, he became a key organizer of Appeal for Redress, a petition from active-duty troops to Congress to withdraw troops from Iraq.

The arc of his life—from the nomadic youth created by divorce to his college education, employment history, and the accomplished adulthood of antiracism and anti-war activism—makes Hutto atypical. But in one dimension—a sharp economic need that made enlistment seem like a solution—he is similar to the high school students whom recruiters court so assiduously.

"You've got these kids that are helpless, really," said activist Kathy Barker. "We can't fight wars without them. And when you get into these debates with military people around it, they debate this, they debate that, and in the end they say, 'Well, we can't do it unless we get the kids.'"

In the time of the Covid-19 pandemic, getting the kids didn't get any easier for the army. "America's military faces the most challenging recruiting environment since the All-Volunteer Force was established in 1973, driven in part by the post-COVID labor market, intense competition with the private sector, and a declining number of young Americans interested in uniformed service," the army public affairs office said in July 2022, summarizing some of the findings of a joint memorandum by the secretary of the army and the army chief of staff. "Currently, only 23 percent of 17- to 24-year-old Americans are fully qualified to serve. Pandemic-driven constraints like virtual learning have further limited access to the recruiting population in high schools and exacerbated a decline in academic and physical fitness levels."

Another challenge is the attitude of those 18–34 toward the military. In the 2021 General Social Survey from NORC at the University of Chicago, a fifth of the people in that group said they had "hardly any confidence" in the military. At the same time, the military has come under increasing criticism from conservatives for its "woke" efforts at diversity, equity, and inclusion.

So, despite the thank-you-for-your-service and support-the-troops mantras, a recruiter's job is not an easy one.

Chapter 3
STABBING, SPITTING, THANKING

In the quiet emptiness of a dentist's waiting room, a plainly civilian office associated with drilling and filling, not bombing and killing, the omnipresence of the American military showed itself one ordinary day and left me quietly stunned. On a small corner table sat a basket filled with tiny toy soldiers. The accompanying sign, bearing the insignia of the branches of the armed forces and spelled with randomly reverential uppercase letters, urged me, "<u>PLEASE</u> take a toy soldier home and place it somewhere that will remind you to Pray for our Men and Women serving Our Country."

To preserve my sanity, I choose to believe that this display is not typical of all dental offices. But toy soldiers definitely have been part of the American male growing-up experience since the years after World War II. More recently, Hasbro, the company that sells G.I. Joe toys, franchised that iconic miniature soldier to Paramount Pictures. The result was a series of war-themed films, enthusiastically promoted by fast-food giant Burger King, which offered G.I. Joe toys as prizes in its kids meals.

"As in the case of many Hollywood films (from *Top Gun* to *Iron Man*), the Pentagon lent a great deal of equipment and personnel for the making of the *G.I. Joe* films, including Apache helicopters, Humvees, and even members of the Army's 21st Cavalry Brigade," Roberto J. Gonzalez and Hugh Gusterson wrote in the introduction to an essay collection called *Militarization: A Reader*. "The synergy of the Paramount-Pentagon partnership was simple but powerful: free high-tech stage props in exchange for a two-hour recruitment advertisement for the military."

An excellent case in point was the original *Top Gun* movie in 1986. The Navy helped create the film and absolutely *loved* it. *Top Gun* was so successful in attracting future fighter pilots that its star, Tom Cruise, joked in a 1990 *Playboy* interview, "I am totally responsible for World War Three." In that interview, promoting his anti-war movie, *Born on the Fourth of July*, Cruise said it would have been "irresponsible" to make a sequel of *Top Gun*, because the original film provided a "fairy tale" view of military life. But that momentary scruple didn't prevent him from starring in the 2022 sequel, *Top Gun: Maverick*, which attracted rave reviews and quickly sold record-setting hundreds of millions of tickets.

Beyond its value in recruiting new pilots, the first *Top Gun* film performed a valuable service for the military, explained in the terse language of a Pentagon document: "Film completed rehabilitation of the military's image, which had been savaged by the Vietnam War." That line appears within the first two minutes of a documentary called *Theaters of War: How the Pentagon and CIA Took Hollywood*, a deep dive into the way the Department of Defense, the Central Intelligence Agency, and the Federal Bureau of Investigation shape our entertainment. It was just one insight among many that emerged from the documents that the filmmakers were able to acquire through doggedly patient use of the Freedom of Information Act. *Theaters of War* opened on Kanopy, an educational screening service, in May 2022, a week before the second *Top Gun* film premiered on that Memorial Day weekend. *Theaters of War* will never reach as many eyeballs as the *Top Gun* sequel has. But it is a valuable piece of work that many more people need to see, because it makes stunningly clear something that most Americans don't fully realize: that the government is virtually a co-creator of a large segment of our entertainment.

In the documentary, Tricia Jenkins, a professor of film, television, and digital media at Texas Christian University and author of *The CIA in Hollywood*, described the Hollywood-Department of Defense relationship starkly: "The Pentagon is powerful in the film and TV industry because they have expensive toys. They have submarines, they have aircraft carriers, they have extras, they have pilots, they have helicopters." The result is massive influence. "What we've found is that thousands upon thousands upon thousands of products have been affected and are often rewritten at script level by the national security state in the United States," said Matthew Alford in the film. He teaches British politics, American politics, and foreign policy at the University of Bath, in England. Alford's estimate: If you add up theatrical films and episodes of TV series, the Pentagon, CIA, and FBI have influenced roughly 10,000 productions—a staggering number. "Do normal people know about that? No, of course they don't."

Alford is one of the moving forces behind *Theaters of War*, along with another British citizen, Tom Secker, who runs a website called spyculture.com, and Roger Stahl, professor of communications studies at the University of Georgia. It's an unusual team for a film about the Pentagon's influence on the American entertainment industry: two Brits and an American professor from Georgia, an overwhelmingly military state. Wondering what drew them into this field of study and how they became a team, I did brief interviews with each of them.

Alford grew up in the small seaside resort town of Torquay, in the southwest county of Devon. As a young teen from an apolitical family, he thought that the first Gulf War was justified, to remove Iraq from Kuwait. Later in his teens, his view of the world grew darker. When an internet café opened in town in the mid-1990s, he explored the web for the first time. In that initial 45 minutes, he came upon the work of linguist-philosopher Noam Chomsky and printed out about 50 pages. Then he began reading Chomsky's books. As an undergraduate, Alford studied politics and government, but began to feel it was too generic a field. So he earned a master's degree in film, then pursued a doctorate at the University of Bath. His dissertation applied to Hollywood the propaganda theory outlined by Chomsky and Edward Herman in the 1988 book *Manufacturing Consent: The Political Economy of the Mass Media*. Beyond the dissertation, Alford wrote a 2010 book, *Reel Power: Hollywood Cinema and American Supremacy*. Despite right-wing views that Hollywood was a center of communist-influenced anti-American thought, Alford argued that the film capital was a willing servant of the government's preferred narrative: America as a "benevolent force in world affairs."

Growing up in Lancashire and Yorkshire, Secker knew from an early age that he wanted to be a writer, probably a novelist. Then he read *Operation Hollywood: How the Pentagon Shapes and Censors the Movies,* a 2004 book by David Robb. In a library he found Alford's book *Reel Power*, and they communicated and talked about where to go from there. The question was whether they could use the Freedom of Information Act to get the mainstream media to focus on the issue of government influence on entertainment. "If we can find a big pile of documents or something really explosive or attention-grabbing, we can start trying to get more mainstream media attention on this," Secker recalled. The result was a book they coauthored in 2017, *National Security Cinema: The Shocking New Evidence of Government Control in Hollywood.* It got more attention than self-published books usually do. "There was a real public thirst, I think, for that information," Alford said. "So I think we just hit on something."

One of those who noticed was Stahl. His academic focus had been communication studies, starting in his home state, at the University of Nebraska. He earned a master's degree from Northern Illinois University, then worked on his doctorate in communication arts and sciences at Penn State, where he was when the Anglo-American invasion of Iraq happened. "It just blew my mind how that public relations apparatus just kicked right into gear, and how effective it was," Stahl remembered. "So I kind of changed gears." He had been working in a rhetoric department, studying media and persuasion. The Iraq invasion sharpened his focus on the interaction of the military and the entertainment industry. His doctoral dissertation was "War Games: Popular Media and Play in Post-Industrial Militarism." And in 2009, he wrote a book called *Militainment, Inc.: War, Media, and Popular Culture.*

Others had written about the military-entertainment axis before Stahl's book and the Alford-Secker book. The existence of the Pentagon's "entertainment liaison office" in Los Angeles was becoming more widely understood. "We knew about the existence of the office at that point," Stahl said. "We had a little bit of the primary documentation, but not much." *Militainment, Inc.* was written without the benefit of the many thousands of pages of documentation that they later acquired. So the book did not fully explore the day-to-day workings of the entertainment liaison office. "It sort of mentioned it and acknowledged it," Stahl said, "but then kind of set it to the side and talked about what could be accessed from journalistic accounts, mainly, and what officials had said about their inroads into the entertainment industry."

Stahl had begun working on a documentary on the issue when the Alford-Secker book came out in 2017. Before long, they had joined forces to work together on what became the *Theaters of War* film. The key to gaining more granular knowledge of government-edited entertainment was the Freedom of Information Act (FOIA). In the realm of the FOIA, it was Secker who did most of the grinding of governmental gears, both for the Alford-Secker book, *National Security Cinema*, and for the documentary. "He's the brains behind this operation," Stahl said.

One of Secker's first breakthroughs came from his visit to a website called Government Attic, a graphically unappealing but content-rich repository of FOIA information. It provided Secker with the goods on the government's entertainment liaison offices, where the tinkering with scripts happens. What he saw on Government Attic were documents from the early 2000s, "diary-like reports from the army and air force's entertainment liaison offices that just detailed what they were up to, week by week. And I thought, no one's followed up on this." So he did, submitting requests for further, more recent documents. Even though Secker said that the American FOIA process is less opaque than the British version, getting answers to requests is painfully slow work. Some requests have been languishing for years. Alford experienced an egregious eight-year wait when he asked the CIA for material on its interaction with *Argo*, the 2012 film about a CIA operation to rescue six Americans from Iran. "Amusingly, that didn't turn up until 2020, during the pandemic," Alford recalled.

Document by slowly emerging document, they accumulated a deep knowledge of the way the national defense establishment wants productions to portray its activities. Beyond the government's line-by-line comments in the scripts, such as "inject professionalism," they learned that the censors find some elements of productions to be total showstoppers—objectionable enough to earn an outright refusal of government help. In *Theaters of War* a partial list of those showstoppers scrolls on the screen: losing wars, losing control of nukes, failure to prevent terror attacks, military incompetence, oil industry influence, private armies. A film won't get the government's help if it shows the United States engaging in war crimes, illegal arms sales, drug trafficking, chemical and biological weapons, government coups, assassination, or torture. And the Pentagon doesn't want any production to include these behaviors in the military: institutional racism, alcoholism and drug abuse, soldier suicide, sexual assault, and that painfully ironic military oxymoron: "friendly fire."

If the government declines to lend you its toys, you can still go ahead and try to make the film at greater expense, but in many cases government rejection means the film simply doesn't get made. One example: Even major star power was not enough to earn government cooperation with *Countermeasures*, a film set on a navy aircraft carrier. On Secker's spyculture.com website, he offers a postmortem for the movie-that-wasn't: The original plan gave the lead role, a navy psychiatrist, to Sigourney Weaver. Later, it was to have been Geena Davis. In the script, she uncovered a crime ring on the carrier, which is smuggling jet parts to Iran—a sensitive subject in light of the Iran-Contra scandal. That Reagan administration scheme resulted in multiple indictments, convictions, and pardons of high officials. Their crime was selling weapons to Iran, despite a congressional ban, and using the proceeds to support the right-wing Contras in Nicaragua. Reacting to the script, Philip Strub, who ran the Pentagon's entertainment liaison office for three decades, wrote to a Disney vice president and attached a memo griping about depictions of sailors committing sexual harassment or sexual abuse. (The real-world backdrop for that concern was the 1991 Tailhook scandal, involving naval and marine officers sexually harassing women at a Las Vegas symposium. It led to a handful of courts-martial and formal reprimands against more than 30 officers.) But the death knell of the film was not sex or politics. Rather, as a Pentagon document said, "There is no reason to denigrate the White House or remind the public of the Iran-Contra affair." In the end, it was clear: no government-owned aircraft carrier, no movie.

One production that got past the Pentagon's censors was puzzling: *NCIS*. The title of that enduringly popular TV series stands for Naval Criminal Investigative Service. In effect, the basis of the series was people in the navy committing crimes that needed to be investigated. So, why would the navy not try to kill that series? Simple: "They only really care about a situation in which the institution seems to be at fault, or it doesn't solve its problems," Stahl said. "So, the lesson from every *NCIS* episode is that, although things go wrong, we fix our problems."

Despite its record of killing many productions, the defense establishment really does want films getting made—as long as they portray the military the right way. In fact, these films and TV shows are far better than openly government-based propaganda could possibly be: The audience has entered the theater or turned on the streaming devices to be entertained, not suspecting that the government has actually shaped the images on the screen propagandistically. To you, the audience, it's just entertainment. You consume the propaganda while munching on popcorn. Commenting on a 2013 film about fighting the Taliban, *Lone Survivor*, a Pentagon document acknowledged that movies reach much bigger audiences than any news story about the events that they depict: "Audiences going to see the film will voluntarily sit through a two-hour infomercial about the participation of Army Special Forces in one of our many joint missions. It will also show the dedication and professionalism of our soldiers." Yes, that's the Pentagon admitting that a commercial film is an infomercial for the military.

Another major infomercial-in-the-making was a film called *Second to None*. One document in the Alford-Secker-Stahl treasure trove is a long, loving Marine Corps commentary on the project. "USMC input has been crucial to the shaping of the story and its characters," the document boasted. The analyst saw the film's potential to become what the document called a marine "recruiting bonanza," similar to the benefit that *Top Gun* brought to the navy. (In a handwritten change, someone took out "bonanza" and made it "substantial recruiting assist." But you get the idea.) The marine analysis of the film boasted that it would be the "first movie *ever*" about the Harrier jump-jet, a fighter capable of vertical/short takeoff and landing but described by some pilots as "unforgiving" to maneuver. And the document glows in almost hagiographic language about the way the film would portray every marine positively, in such dimensions as "personality, leadership skills/style, technical/tactical proficiency, dedication to duty, sympathetic response to human misery/humanitarianism." The censors did have a spot of trouble with one scene, involving marines dumping human excrement from Harrier jets onto the pirates who are the film's bad guys. The scene in the script was "imaginative, funny, and provides some sort of catharsis," the document conceded, but it cautioned that "it may backfire with the American public and consequently reflect badly on the USMC." Still, the marine analysts loved the project. In the end, this glorious recruiting movie ran into financial trouble and the start of the Gulf War, which made the military hardware unavailable for the film, Secker said. "Then the whole thing just got shelved and never got made."

That document and many others provide clear insights into the behind-the-scenes, script-level control that the government exercises, but the team that made *Theaters of War* continues to push for more. One longed-for treasure trove, Alford said, is a store of more than 200,000 navy documents. And there's so much more to the story than the documentary told. "There's probably like three or four hours of footage that I had to cut," Stahl said. As they continued to push for wider distribution of the film, Stahl—with Alford and Secker—worked on another, more comprehensive book than either his *Militainment, Inc.* or the Alford-Secker *National Security Cinema.* "It's going to be an institutional history," Stahl said. "It's going to be a history of how we came to know what we know, but also the public relations effort to keep it under wraps and to satisfy the public with tiny pieces of information, going back to the 1940s, when people started objecting to it." They also planned a big-data-style quantitative analysis of what the government has been doing with entertainment. "We did a recent study, where we looked at the top ten biggest franchises, the most commercially successful franchises, and the Pentagon had had a large role in four of them—at least four—and a more minor role in another two," Stahl said. "So we're talking about about fifty percent. But it's hard to quantify. It really is."

Before the work that led to *Theaters of War*, others in both academia and the mainstream media had written about the national security state's influence on entertainment, but not nearly as much as the seriousness of the subject demands. "Of course, we cannot expect all subject areas to be explored with alacrity—that's the nature of research—but something as big as the military and security state dominating the entire entertainment industry over such a long time should have generated a lot more discussion, by any measure," Alford said. Now their persistent research has contributed to a widening interest in this field of study. "There's an appetite out there among academics that has not been satisfied," Stahl said. And Secker is not shy about naming their work as a primary cause of that increased interest: "I think it's primarily based on what we've been doing, because I can't see what else has moved the needle."

Whatever the exact size of governmental influence turns out to be, Pentagon-guided movies and TV shows are not the only products that promote a positive, muscular, recruitment-friendly image of the military and a national inclination to genuflect to it. On a sports channel where I watch baseball, for example, it's hard to avoid military-themed commercials for sunglasses and other not-necessarily-military products. One starts with: "Soldiers in battle depend on clear vision to hit their targets. Now you can get that same HD clarity with BattleVision by Atomic Beam." In case you missed the military connection, the words "FMR Fighter Pilot" appear on the screen beneath the BattleVision spokesman, Hunter Ellis, as he sits in a merely civilian aircraft. The array of products in these commercials includes tactical flashlights, tactical lanterns, tactical folding knives, among others. "Tactical" and its shorter little brother, "tac," are the key words to remind you that these non-military products are somehow "military tough."

Toy soldiers and tactical sunglasses live at the lower end of the all-pervasive presence of the military in our society, along with races that honor the memory of soldiers fallen in the forever wars. The upper end of that spectrum includes the Pentagon; the defense contractors who rake in billions of Pentagon dollars to build weapons; the lobbyists—often retired generals—who stalk the halls of Congress to urge appropriations for those weapons, and the members of Congress. Our lawmakers routinely rubber-stamp bloated Pentagon budgets for weapons systems that may or may not work, but they always provide jobs in their home districts because "political engineering" makes sure that bits and pieces of the manufacturing process are spread to as many congressional districts as possible.

"We can call all of this—the massive investments in war and in the public relations of war, and the assorted beliefs that sustain them all—'the military normal,'" wrote Catherine Lutz in *The Counter-Counterinsurgency Manual*, a publication by anthropologists alarmed by the Pentagon's plan to use members of their profession as academic tools in the forever war. "The military-industrial-Congressional-media-entertainment-university complex is a massively entangled system."

Those three words, "the military normal," are an accurate label for the mentality of today's America. The anthropologist behind that phrase has been a formidable force in the long, difficult, almost Sisyphean struggle to educate Americans about war and warriors. A brief summary of her work is a useful way to begin exploring the dimensions of that powerful, persistent military normal.

Lutz is the cofounder and co-director of the Costs of War Project at the Watson Institute of International & Public Affairs at Brown University. She has written, co-written, or edited a series of books on war and peace, such as *Breaking Ranks: Iraq Veterans Speak Out Against the War*, *The Bases of Empire*, and *Homefront: A Military City and the American Twentieth Century*. In *Homefront*, Lutz turns the lens of her scholarship on Fayetteville, the unpleasant military-dominated town near Fort Bragg, North Carolina, the post where I spent some of the unhappy early months of my three-plus years in the army. I was pretty dense in those days, but smart enough to steer clear of Fayetteville.

To the study of war, Lutz brings a distinguished academic background, including a doctorate in social anthropology from Harvard, a past presidency of the American Ethnological Society, and a Guggenheim Fellowship. Long before her higher education, she understood war. As a very young woman, Lutz wrote in *Homefront,* she saw televised "ghostly images of ash and jumbled bones in Nazi ovens and skeletal human forms in the liberated concentration camps," Later, she understood "the ravages of the Vietnam War on bodies and relationships."

In the months before the Anglo-American invasion of Iraq, Lutz joined those who saw that plan as irredeemably wicked. At the time, she was teaching at the University of North Carolina, Chapel Hill. As the war neared, although she had voted for Democratic Sen. John Edwards, she deeply opposed his willingness to go along with the invasion. In October 2002, Edwards voted for the blank-check Authorization for Use of Military Force in Iraq, and he made clear his belief that "Saddam Hussein is a tyrant and a menace; that he has weapons of mass destruction and that he is doing everything in his power to get nuclear weapons …." At the start of 2003, Edwards announced that he was running for president. In February, a few weeks before the "shock and awe" bombing of Baghdad launched the invasion, Lutz joined a protest at Edwards's presidential campaign office in Raleigh. "He was basically supporting the whole invasion narrative, the whole WMD thing," she told me. Along with seven other anti-war protesters, she declined to leave the office, and police hauled them off for a few hours in jail.

That brief claustrophobic episode did not make Lutz any less willing to confront war mentality in all its forms. She soon had a chance to push back against the latest folly, the *Counterinsurgency Field Manual*, a wrongheaded effort by the military to turn around the ongoing disaster that was the occupation of Iraq. In the three years that followed the protest at Edwards's office and the invasion a few weeks later, it had become increasingly clear that the weapons of mass destruction simply weren't there, despite all the pre-invasion assertions in stories by Judith Miller of the *New York Times*, by President George W. Bush, by Vice President Dick Cheney, and—in a memorably wrong speech at the United Nations—by Secretary of State Colin Powell. Instead of the shower of flowers that was supposed to have greeted American forces as liberators, they faced a daily shower of shrapnel from improvised explosive devices. Some of the people behind those devices were former members of the Iraqi army. In one of the greatest blunders of the war, Lewis Paul "Jerry" Bremer III, head of the Coalition Provisional Authority, the top American civilian in Iraq, had fired that country's entire army. Many of those suddenly unemployed soldiers joined the insurgency.

Not to worry, though. In 2006, the United States Army and the Marine Corps published the *Counterinsurgency Field Manual*. The following year, the University of Chicago published a trade version of it, with a foreword by Gen. David Petraeus, the soldier-scholar who in 2007 commanded the Multinational Force—Iraq. A core idea of the manual was that America could turn around the mess in Iraq and Afghanistan by more carefully studying and fully understanding the cultures that its military was currently bombing. Part of the Pentagon's efforts to deal with those cultures was something called Human Terrain Teams, which put anthropologists and other social scientists together with combat brigades. In September 2007, Secretary of Defense Robert Gates announced a major expansion of this initiative, which was widely seen as a Petraeus pet project.

Two years earlier, in 2005, the American Anthropological Association had set up a special commission to look into the ethical implications of anthropologists working with the military and intelligence services. Its report laid out the ethical problems and urged further study. In October 2007, the organization's executive board issued a statement saying that the military's Human Terrain system violated the association's code of ethics. At the association's annual meeting late that year, Lutz recalled sitting down in a Washington hotel restaurant with a small group of anthropologists who agreed that anthropology should not be enlisted for war. So they asked themselves: "What are we going to do? We can't just sit by while they try and recruit us."

One important thing that the Network of Concerned Anthropologists did was to publish the *Counter-Counterinsurgency Manual*. The tone of the book was a blend of righteous indignation and careful explication of the military manual's scholarly failures. In the preface, Marshall Sahlins described how the military wanted to gather a broad array of information about the local culture. "Fact is, it would take many anthropologists with years of training and even more years of fieldwork to do this, by which time pretty much everything would be different," Sahlins wrote. "Another fact is that all the military really wants is some superficial handles on the local culture that will allow them to manipulate the people for better or for worse."

For all its flaws, the military's *Counterinsurgency Field Manual* made a positive impression. One reason for that was the widespread longing for some way out of the morass of the forever war. It also gained acceptance because of its association with Petraeus, the scholar-soldier of the moment—years before his time as director of the Central Intelligence Agency and his resignation in the middle of an extramarital affair with his biographer and allegations that he mishandled classified documents. Whatever the reasons, the military manual drew rave reviews.

Major publications that are usually considered liberal, such as *The New Yorker* and *Harper's*, "climbed on board, running glossy uncritical profiles of the cultural counterinsurgency's pitchmen in glamorous write-ups portraying this new generation of anthropologists as a brilliant new breed of scholars who could culturally co-opt foreign foes and capture the hearts and minds of those we'd occupy," wrote David Price in the *Counter-Counterinsurgency Manual*. Against those stories in large-circulation, high-influence publications, the critique by Lutz and other anthropologists in the *Counter-Counterinsurgency Manual* had a tough time changing public attitudes toward the military, which by then had grown into full-spectrum adulation. But those attitudes weren't always that way.

In her section of the *Counter-Counterinsurgency Manual*, Lutz described a time before "the military normal" arose, from the era of the framers to the twentieth century: "The ascendance of the military came about only relatively recently in US history. While the US, as a state, was born through violence—Indian Wars, the Revolution, and slave repression being the most important forms that violence took—it was founded on a suspicion of standing armies, and with civilian leadership ensured by Constitutional frameworks. Military leaders had relatively limited powers as a result: the public saw the military as a burden in peacetime and at best very occasionally necessary. Government-run armories and shipyards provided limited incentives for politicians and the business sector to argue for increased military spending. Middle class families were reluctant to send their children into a military they saw as a virtual cesspool of vices."

Families deeply skeptical of the military included evangelical Christians. Though they are now a major voice in the worship-the-military choir, it's worth remembering that they were singing a very different tune as recently as World War II. "Even as they supported the war against totalitarianism, many evangelicals nonetheless harbored doubts about the US military," wrote historian Kristin Kobes Du Mez in *Jesus and John Wayne: How White Evangelicals Corrupted a Faith and Fractured a Nation*. "Through the 1940s and into the 1950s, most evangelicals saw the military as a place of moral corruption for young men. Contrary to later myths about 'the good war' and 'the greatest generation,' the military was known as an institution where drunkenness, vulgarity, gambling, and sexual disease abounded."

In the years since World War II, misbehavior in the military has not gone away. As Chapter 5 documents, sexual abuse is a widespread problem that the Pentagon and politicians have so far been unable to solve, and Chapter 6 addresses incompetence and corruption in uniform. So, despite the military's real problems, what accounts for today's almost universal hyper-adulation? One answer is the war in Vietnam and a persistent, pervasive myth that grew out of it: that soldiers returning from Vietnam encountered no parades in their honor, but rather a shower of spit from anti-war protesters. In effect, the myth holds, civilians were stabbing our soldiers in the back and causing them to lose a winnable war. So, believers in the spitting myth argue, we now owe to today's soldiers the honor that the Vietnam-era military did not experience.

How true is the myth? A Vietnam veteran and sociologist, Jerry Lembcke of the College of the Holy Cross, examined that question in his book *The Spitting Image: Myth, Memory, and the Legacy of Vietnam*. His conclusion?

The mass spitting attacks did not happen. In examining the idea that the lack of support by civilians had caused the loss in Vietnam, Lembcke looked back at Germany in the wake of World War I, when Germans demanded to know what had caused their catastrophic loss. Leaders such as Gen. Erich Ludendorff and Field Marshal Paul von Hindenburg laid the defeat at the feet of opponents of the war. "Slackers abounded, and who were they but Jews," said World War I veteran and would-be politician Adolf Hitler.

"To ground the idea that German soldiers had been betrayed on the home front," Lembcke wrote, "the German right popularized the image of war veterans being abused when they returned home," abuse that included spitting on their gray uniforms. This became the legend of the "stab in the back," rendered in German as *dolchstoss*. How important was the stab-in-the-back legend (*dolchstosslegende*)? Lembcke cites a sweeping assessment by William Shirer, author of the magisterial history, *The Rise and Fall of the Third Reich*. This "fanatical belief," Shirer wrote, "more than anything else was to undermine the Weimar Republic and pave the way for Hitler's ultimate triumph."

Decades later, after World War II, the French fought in Vietnam, attempting to restore colonial rule there. The French army lost definitively at Dien Bien Phu in 1954, and its commanding officer there, Gen. Henri Navarre, hurled a *dolchstoss*-like accusation at French political leaders: "They allowed this army to be stabbed in the back," Navarre said.

Not surprisingly, the spirit of *dolchstoss* continued when American troops became ensnared in Vietnam. It erupted in a New York City mayoral race in 1969, when Sen. John Marchi, a conservative Republican from Staten Island, used it in his campaign against Mayor John V. Lindsay, a moderate Republican who opposed the war. Marchi claimed that Lindsay had "planted a dagger in the back of American servicemen in Vietnam," Lembcke wrote.

Though people can cite instances of anti-war college students raucously blaming the warriors and not the politicians for the wickedness of the war, that does not add up to a tsunami-like flow of saliva, with large numbers of demonstrators allegedly spitting on large numbers of returning soldiers. In pushing back against that myth, Lembcke details the anti-war activities of soldiers, before and after their return to civilian life. He writes about anti-war cooperation between those who fought in Vietnam and those who didn't. David Cortright also detailed that cooperation in *Soldiers in Revolt: GI Resistance During the Vietnam War*. But the spitting myth dies hard.

President Richard M. Nixon campaigned in 1968 on a mythical "secret plan" to end the war. But as he ran for a second term in 1972, he hadn't ended it. Still, he eagerly jumped to the "support" of the troops—the same ones whose lives he had endangered by continuing the war. This was the essence of the argument that the administration made: "The thirty thousand GIs who had already died in Vietnam would have been sacrificed for nothing if we were to quit now," Lembcke wrote. "As long as there were U.S. soldiers in Vietnam the war had to be supported; to do otherwise would mean abandonment and betrayal. So it was in the soldiers themselves that Nixon found the perfect reason to continue the war."

That is dangerous thinking. "The will to kill and be killed grows out of sacrifices and acts of destruction already performed," wrote the Trappist monk Thomas Merton in his Vietnam War-era book *Faith and Violence: Christian Teaching and Christian Practice*. "As soon as the war has begun, the first dead are there to demand further sacrifice from their companions since they have demonstrated by their example that the objective of war is such that no price is too high to pay for its attainment. This is the 'sledgehammer argument,' the argument of Minerva in Homer: 'You must fight on, for if you now make peace with the enemy, you will offend the dead.'"

Not even two decades after the Vietnam War had ended, the use of the troops as a reason to support the war cropped up again. President George H. W. Bush was casting clumsily about for the right set of reasons to persuade the public to support his desire to invade Iraq and expel Iraqi troops from Kuwait. It wasn't really working. But the echoes of Vietnam came to Bush's rescue. "It was the myth of the spat-upon Vietnam veteran that galvanized the sentiments of the American people sufficiently to discredit peace activists and give George Bush his war," Lembcke wrote.

Despite Lembcke's efforts at deconstructing that myth, it refuses to go away. I witnessed this for myself in December 2017, at an event sponsored by the Global Institute at LIU Post, a campus of Long Island University. The institute's founder was Steve Israel, a former Democratic member of Congress whose work had brought him in contact with a number of generals, including David Petraeus. The event was to be a conversation between Israel and

Petraeus, and I was curious about what the general might say. Despite his fall in the sex-and-classified-documents scandal, Petraeus is a highly intelligent man with stellar academic credentials. But that background did not prevent him from carelessly blurting out the spitting myth. At the start of the event, Petraeus asked how many in the audience were Vietnam veterans. Quite a few raised their hands. Petraeus thanked them for their kindness to the returning Iraq and Afghanistan veterans, and he made a point of contrasting that loving treatment to what had happened to the Vietnam vets when they returned home. He *told* them that they had endured spitting. He didn't *ask* them. He didn't call for a show of hands on this question: "Did anyone spit on you when you came home?" Though he holds himself out as a history scholar, Petraeus simply repeated the persistent, corrosive, utterly ahistorical myth.

Almost as if reading from the same script as Petraeus, Mayor Domenic Sarno told a gathering of veterans for Vietnam Veterans Day 2022 in Springfield, Massachusetts: "When you came back, instead of being respected you were spat upon. Many were told not to wear their military uniforms when they reentered the country. Yet when it came to showing respect for veterans during Operation Desert Storm and the Mideast conflicts it was the Vietnam veterans who led. They weren't obligated to do that, but they said to themselves we cannot forget. We must always remember how we were welcomed."

This perceived need to make up for the mythical spit storm, by replacing it with worship of warriors, was not the only factor leading to today's military normal. The turnaround of the evangelicals' attitude was also pivotal. During World War II, as we've seen, they thought of the military as a pit of debauchery. But then they took on the mission of converting it. "The military, which had its own reasons to be concerned about the discipline and moral vitality of its forces, welcomed the work of evangelical organizations," Kristin Kobes Du Mez wrote in *Jesus and John Wayne*. By the time of the Vietnam War, after decades of working with the military, conservative evangelicals were wholeheartedly supporting an institution they had once disdained. In the heart of the Vietnam War, an event at the United States Military Academy put a powerfully symbolic seal of approval on the evangelicals: West Point conferred its Sylvanus Thayer Award, for a citizen who exemplifies "Duty, Honor, Country," on evangelist Billy Graham.

Clearly, that evangelical change of heart about soldiering has been a major force in creating the military normal. "They have fostered among the legions of believing Americans a predisposition to see U.S. military power as inherently good, perhaps even a necessary adjunct to the accomplishment of Christ's saving mission," wrote historian-veteran Andrew Bacevich in *The New American Militarism: How Americans Are Seduced by War.* "In doing so, they have nurtured the preconditions that have enabled the American infatuation with military power to flourish. Put another way, were it not for the support offered by several tens of millions of evangelicals, militarism in this deeply and genuinely religious country becomes inconceivable."

Another major factor enhancing the emerging national embrace of the military, of course, was 9/11. Americans were understandably angry and fearful, and they looked to the military for safety—without asking too many questions about how a handful of terrorists armed with boxcutters managed to do so much damage to a nation with the world's largest defense budget. Once President George W. Bush ordered American troops into Afghanistan, then into Iraq, the "support the troops" mantra became universal, even at sporting events. William Astore, who spent 20 years in the air force and has developed a sharp eye for the military normal, took notice of the post-9/11 alliance between two major American institutions. "I was never particularly skilled at any sport, but I did thoroughly enjoy playing, partly because it was such a welcome break from work—a reprieve from wearing a uniform, saluting, following orders, and all the rest," Astore wrote. "Sports were sports. Military service was military service. And never the twain shall meet. Since 9/11, however, sports and the military have become increasingly fused in this country."

Yes, and the Pentagon was happy to amplify that swelling of pride. With its bottomless, congressionally enabled bank account, the Department of Defense had no trouble coming up with millions of dollars to burnish the image of its troops, and no one really complained. Then two unlikely critics, two Arizona Republican senators, the late John McCain and Jeff Flake, decided to throw a penalty flag, to criticize the Pentagon's habit of paying sports teams for not-so-spontaneous tributes to the military.

Looking for material for a weekly report on wasteful spending, someone from Flake's office came upon a National Guard contract with the New York

Jets. The two senators ordered some research and ended up issuing a report in 2015 called *Tackling Paid Patriotism*, with a cover illustration of a football player in a McCain-Flake jersey tackling quarterback Uncle Sam. Among the teams in the National Football League that benefited from Pentagon largesse, they detailed $327,500 in contracts with the Jets for "paid patriotism" items such as recognizing New Jersey National Guard soldiers as "hometown heroes" on the stadium's Jumbotron and displaying "into battle" ceremonies before the kickoff of preseason and regular season games. The report contained details on a long list of contracts with teams in the NFL, Major League Baseball, the National Hockey League, and others. McCain, a Navy pilot and prisoner of war in the Vietnam War, was nobody's idea of a pacifist. Despite his bellicose instincts, McCain found the paid patriotism payments unacceptable. "We appreciate if they honor the men and women in uniform, but not to get paid for it," McCain said, as he and Flake released the report.

My personal introduction to the military's influence on sports was "Military Monday," a New York Mets promotion that included the use of camouflage on the players' caps. That tip of the camo cap to the military didn't work for the team. Even on nights when they played badly enough to wish they could disappear, the camouflage was not enough to hide them. Still, camouflage-themed uniforms have become common throughout Major League Baseball. The Mets also honored a "veteran of the game," presenting each veteran with an American flag and introducing them to the crowd.

Another tip of the cap to the military at sports events—and on local television news—is the sure-to-make-you-misty-eyed surprise reunion of a deployed soldier with his or her family. You have to feel happy for the family. They've obviously been worried about the safety of their soldier in the combat zones of the forever war. Now, suddenly, at a baseball game or in some other setting, their deployed soldier is briefly back home, wearing a camouflage uniform and embracing the family joyfully. It's a powerful feel-good story, which is why local television news desks cannot resist showing footage of every such reunion they can find. But these reunions beg a couple of questions: Won't this happy soldier soon be redeployed to the forever war? For every soldier who gets to play a part in this happy story, how many thousands only come home at the end of their deployment, often physically or mentally wounded, or don't come home at all?

Andrew Bacevich, who did come back from Vietnam, but whose son Andrew did not return alive from combat in Iraq, witnessed one of these emotional reunions at a Fourth of July game at Fenway Park in Boston. He described it in great detail in an opinion piece under the headline "Ballpark Liturgy: America's New Civic Religion," for the TomDispatch website. In keeping with the "liturgy" in the headline, he ended the essay with a theological reflection on the reunion he had witnessed at Fenway.

"Finally, it rewarded participants and witnesses alike with a sense of validation, the reunion of Bridget and her family, even if temporary, serving as a proxy for a much larger, if imaginary, reconciliation of the American military and the American people. That debt? Mark it paid in full," Bacevich wrote. "The late German theologian Dietrich Bonhoeffer had a name for this unearned self-forgiveness and undeserved self-regard. He called it cheap grace. Were he alive today, Bonhoeffer might suggest that a taste for cheap grace, compounded by an appetite for false freedom, is leading Americans down the road to perdition."

Cheap grace is also a fitting category for today's most often repeated five-word sentence: "Thank you for your service." As soon as someone learns that you have spent time in the military, those five words automatically pop out, as if on a recorded message. (If you announce that you're a teacher, though, don't expect to hear that incantation.) Yes, some veterans find it comforting. For years, Alan Reff, a Korean War veteran, "harbored a resentment" of the American public, because in all the praise of the military, nobody mentioned Korea or the veterans who endured that frigid, frustrating, still-lingering conflict. So Reff bought a Korea veteran cap and regularly wears it. "Having the cap on and having people say, 'Thank you for your service,' has totally wiped away my resentment," Reff said.

More typically, veterans I've interviewed about this phenomenon don't really know what to make of it or how to respond. "It's so awkward. Usually, people mean well. So, I typically say, 'Thank you for your support,'" air force veteran Katherine "Kat" Maier said. "I'm never really quite sure what to do."

Some veterans will push back, if the person saying "thank you for your service" seems likely to listen. "I don't feel badly about just saying, 'Thank you,' because that's just something to say," said Ann Wright, a retired army colonel, retired State Department official, and an outspoken critic of the

Iraq misadventure. "But if I find somebody that I think really it will make a difference, I can take the time to talk to them about various ways you serve your country, and it isn't necessarily in the military."

That flexible approach also suits Maggie Martin, an army veteran deployed to Kuwait and Iraq, who later became a leader of Iraq Veterans Against the War. "It depends if I have time to chat with somebody, or if I'm on the move," Martin said, "but I usually like to tell folks, 'Thanks. I've been fighting against the war ever since, and I'm more proud of that work.' Something along those lines."

The adulation makes some veterans uncomfortable because they feel it's out of keeping with their own memories of their time in combat. "People use the term 'hero' or 'warrior,' and I think people feel like anything but a hero or a warrior overseas," said Rory Fanning, whose experience of both joining the army and becoming a counter-recruiter appears in Chapter 2. In Afghanistan, he saw himself as far from heroic. "I felt like a bully," he said. Soon after that, he turned against the war, which gave him further insight into the meaning of the ubiquitous five-word expression of gratitude. "When people say 'Thank you for your service,' I think it's a way of shutting up people who may be questioning the mission of the US military, because heroes don't go steal other countries' natural resources, or heroes don't kill innocent people. So, by using that term, I think it's a way of silencing people and thanking them, because there's an assumption that what they're doing overseas is good. And the second you start speaking out is the second nobody wants to hear from you, and they stop thanking you."

Another anti-war veteran, Camillo (Mac) Bica, approached the thank-you question by writing a book whose title sums it up: *Worthy of Gratitude? Why Veterans May Not Want to Be Thanked for Their "Service" in War*. "I do not want to appear disrespectful or ungrateful, but should we meet on the street one day, do say 'Hello' or 'Fine day' or other such nicety, but please do not thank me for 'my service' as a United States Marine," wrote Bica, now a leader in Veterans for Peace. "I make this request because my service, as you refer to it, was basically, either to train to become a killer or to actually kill people and blow shit up. Now, that is not something for which a person should be proud nor thanked. In fact, it is regrettable, and for me a source of guilt and shame, something I will have to live with for the rest of my life, as the past cannot ever be undone. So, when you thank me for my service, it disturbs me … a lot."

After reading Bica's book, I interviewed him to ask if he had seen any change in the frequency of the thank-you mantra. He had not. "I think they do it more for themselves than they do for anyone else," Bica said. "It's like saying good morning. It doesn't really mean anything. If it meant something, maybe you would ensure that veterans are better treated and ensure that we don't send them to places where we shouldn't be, to take part in adventures and endeavors that are illegal and immoral."

For now, that hyper-adulation shows no signs of slowing down. In fact, the military remains so widely admired that people get into trouble for trying to exaggerate their own connection with it. "Reverence for the military means that there's a real resource that you can grab onto," anthropologist Catherine Lutz said. "'Yeah, give me some of that love. Give me some of that reverence. I'll tell you I did all kinds of things in the war.'" The military is easily the most trusted institution in America, and it's natural enough for people from all walks of life to want to borrow some of that luster, in ways that fall short of honesty.

In fact, out of fear that unworthy people would pretend to be heroic, Congress voted overwhelmingly in late 2006 to adopt the Stolen Valor Act, prescribing prison time for anyone who manufactured, sold, or wore unauthorized military medals. President George W. Bush, a famous non-combatant, signed it into law. Large numbers of people claimed to have received the Medal of Honor from Congress, for example. Many others claimed lesser distinctions, like serving in the Navy SEALs or the Special Forces. In 2012, the Supreme Court ruled the Stolen Valor Act an unconstitutional abridgment of free speech. The following year, Congress passed an amended version of the act. This time, it added the element of criminal intent. If you were fraudulently claiming to have received a medal for valor, not just to brag, but to make money, you could go to prison. President Barack Obama signed it into law.

Reaching for military glory doesn't have to involve medals. One of the most visible examples was Brian Williams, once the much-admired host of *NBC Nightly News*. In 2015, the network took away his anchor seat and exiled him into a less prestigious assignment at MSNBC. Williams had exaggerated an incident that happened in 2003, when he was covering the early months of the Anglo-American invasion and occupation of Iraq. He was in a military helicopter, and he claimed that the chopper "was forced down after being hit with an RPG," a rocket-propelled grenade. Soldiers familiar with that event begged to differ. The RPG-damaged helicopter had actually taken off a half-hour ahead of the group of aircraft containing Williams. Interviewed by the military newspaper *Stars & Stripes*, Williams apologized and said, "I don't know what screwed up in my mind that caused me to conflate one aircraft with another." One possible explanation, of course, is the desire to be associated with military peril and bravery.

Another example is Sen. Richard Blumenthal, a Connecticut Democrat. In 2010, he was the state's attorney general, running for United States Senate. It was during that campaign that he suffered an embarrassing preposition malfunction. He described his time in the military as happening *in* Vietnam, when the correct preposition was *during* Vietnam. Actually, during Vietnam, he was safely stateside, in the Marine Corps Reserve. No rice paddies. No Viet Cong. In 2010, the *New York Times* reported that Attorney General Blumenthal had spoken at a support-the-troops-overseas rally in 2003, telling the crowd, "When we returned, we saw nothing like this." The "we," of course, was a reference to troops returning from Vietnam, where Blumenthal had not actually been, and "this" referred to the support symbolized by the rally. Though it's unclear whether he mentioned the word "spit" in that speech, he clearly was repeating the familiar refrain about Vietnam veterans having been treated shabbily, which is a fundamental element of today's hyper-adulation.

Blumenthal did apologize for his sloppy use of prepositions, but it came back to haunt him in 2018, when he was a member of the Senate Judiciary Committee, sharply opposed to President Donald J. Trump's nomination of Brett Kavanaugh to the Supreme Court. Trump did not spend time in the military, either *in* or *during* Vietnam. He suffered, he claims, from bone spurs. So an actual veteran, Sen. Tammy Duckworth of Illinois, who lost both legs in Iraq, conferred on him the inglorious title of Cadet Bone Spurs. But Trump felt he really had faced danger: the possibility that his widely known promiscuousness would cause him to catch a sexually transmitted disease. "It is my personal Vietnam," he said in one interview. In that perilous battle with STD, Trump said, "I feel like a very great and very brave soldier." Despite his own lack of military experience, Trump did not hesitate during the contentious Kavanaugh confirmation hearings to bludgeon Blumenthal for mischaracterizing his time in the Marine Corps Reserve. Typically, Trump was not content merely to report Blumenthal's preposition problem but felt compelled to exaggerate what Blumenthal had claimed: "He didn't just say, 'Gee, I was in the service.' No, he said, 'I was in the Marines. Da Nang province. Soldiers dying left and right as we battled up the hill.'"

In the current atmosphere of adulation for the military and shameless efforts to bask in its reflected glory, criticism of the institution does not come easy. "People are scared to death to do anything, to say anything bad about the military," said Seattle counter-recruitment activist Kathy Barker. "It's like a religion." It's not that the ranks of people in camouflage uniforms do not contain bad actors, but calling them out is not an acceptable form of discourse in America. "You're not allowed to say that right now," said Kayla Williams, who saw more than her share of military imperfection in Iraq and elsewhere. "I think that that's to our detriment, and it's dangerous. We should not be pretending that all troops are always heroes. We have troops who are in prison. We have to acknowledge that that happens and that not all troops are angels. But right now, civilians, in my opinion—obviously not all of them, but most civilians—at this moment I don't think feel comfortable saying, 'Hey, aren't some of you guys bad?' It's seen as unpatriotic."

So the powerful military normal persists. Pushing back against it can be exhausting. But Catherine Lutz, who has studied and written about the military normal for years and has a deep anthropological understanding of its pernicious growth, does not plan to abandon the struggle. "I've just done it my whole life, because I can't give up," Lutz said. "And I do have some optimism—or had some optimism at various points." She quotes Antonio Gramsci, an Italian Marxist philosopher, who talked about pessimism of the intellect and optimism of the will. "I understand intellectually that this is a system that is so entrenched, so much at the service of powerful interests, that a group of citizens, even millions of citizens, are still relatively powerless in a country that's not truly a democracy, where those lobbyists and campaign funders who want more government contracts through the Pentagon, a few of them are going to win out over the many of us. That's the pessimism. But then the optimism of the will is just the sense that the struggle is necessary, and that there's a beautiful community of people who just have to do it, have to say no, have to do whatever they can do. It's never enough."

Chapter 4
VOTE FOR A VET?

The vocabulary of political ads these days is filled with words designed to take advantage of the hero worship of veterans. Voters should "Vote for a vet" or "Send in a marine." The images aim for the same effect as the words, showing a younger version of the candidate in a marine dress blue uniform or the ready-to-fight army camouflage. The implied message is simple: You can thank me for my service by voting for me.

But it doesn't always work. Nor should it. In primary elections in the pivotal midterm-election year of 2022, for example, these magic words and images failed to deliver victory.

In rural Vermont, Gerald Malloy ran in the Republican primary for United States Senate to replace influential Democrat Patrick Leahy, who chose not to run for a ninth term. Malloy's website and his lawn signs proclaimed, "Deploy Malloy," using a verb that has come to be associated with military combat. Malloy's bio emphasized his West Point education and his more than two decades in the army. His Republican opponents were an investment banker and a former federal prosecutor. He narrowly won the primary. In the general election, he ran against Democrat Peter Welch, who had held Vermont's only seat in the House of Representatives since 2007. Welch won the seat in a landslide and carried every county in Vermont. The slogan "Deploy Malloy" did not work. Malloy failed to be deployed to Congress.

In the Pennsylvania Republican primary for United States Senate, ads for hedge fund millionaire and West Point graduate David McCormick called him "battle-tested" and "Pennsylvania true." And those words were correct. He had deep roots in Pennsylvania, finished at the top of his class in the United States Army Ranger School, and experienced combat in Iraq in the Gulf War in 1991. Somehow, despite those credentials, he lost to Dr. Mehmet Oz, an import from New Jersey whose military experience was in the Turkish army, but who boasted endlessly of the enthusiastic endorsement of a former president with zero military experience, Donald J. Trump. In the general election, Oz lost to the Democratic candidate, Lieutenant Governor John Fetterman.

In the GOP primary for Pennsylvania governor, Bill McSwain, a Trump-appointed federal prosecutor, asked voters to "send in a marine." (If McSwain had done more research, he might have discovered that the "send in a marine" mantra hadn't worked in the 2018 election cycle, when Bob Hugin, a Republican candidate for the United States Senate in New Jersey, ran against Democratic incumbent Bob Menendez, whose 2017 corruption trial had ended in a hung jury. Hugin's "send in a marine" plea didn't help. The people of New Jersey chose an ethically challenged incumbent over a marine.) McSwain played the marine card, but he finished a distant third to Doug Mastriano, who had a long army career, retiring as a colonel in 2017. Mastriano wore an Operation Desert Storm cap at his victory party, and as his campaign went on, his social media featured multiple images of him in uniform, with the headline "Doug Mastriano Fighting for Freedom." It got to the point that the army reminded him about government policy on the use of military images in campaigns, and he removed photos of himself in uniform. On his Twitter account, he added a disclaimer that his use of his military rank, job titles, and photos in uniform did "not imply endorsement" by the Department of the Army or the Pentagon.

His reminders of his time in combat boots were not the only over-the-top aspects of Mastriano's campaign. He focused heavily on his deep belief in Trump's claim that Democrats stole the 2020 election. "I saw better elections in Afghanistan than in Pennsylvania," he said during the campaign. Mastriano, who regularly spouted QAnon conspiracy theories, was present for the insurrection at the Capitol on January 6, 2021, though he insisted that he left when the crowd became unruly. Mastriano was not the only veteran present that day. An analysis by National Public Radio found that almost 20 percent of the people who were charged for their role in the insurrection had some sort of military background. In the general election, Mastriano, the veteran who had defeated another veteran in the Republican primary, lost to the Democrat, Attorney General Josh Shapiro, a veteran politician, but not a military veteran.

When veterans use their time in the military as a résumé item in a campaign for public office, some of them have been known to embellish the extent of their actual military experience. That became an issue, for example, in the campaign in the 9th Congressional District in Ohio. The long-time incumbent, Democrat Marcy Kaptur, faced Republican J.R. Majewski, who advertised his time in the air force. But the way he described that time became a controversy that resulted in a *New York Times* story under this headline: "House Candidate's Claims About His Military Record Unravel Further." The subhead went on to say: "J.R. Majewski promotes himself to Ohio voters as a combat veteran, but the Air Force has no record of it. Now, there is evidence he was demoted for drunken driving." Whatever the truth of Majewski's air force days, that time in the military did not help in the election. Kaptur easily retained her seat.

The Pennsylvania gubernatorial primary featuring McSwain and Mastriano was hardly the only political contest that had a veteran running against a veteran. In New York's 18th Congressional District, for example, both Democrat Pat Ryan and Republican Colin Schmitt were not shy about mentioning their military service. Ryan graduated from West Point and was twice deployed to Iraq. Schmitt's time in the National Guard included neither deployment overseas nor the 180 days of continuous active duty that the National Guard considers necessary for a person to be called a veteran. In addition to the differences in their military histories, Ryan and Schmitt differed sharply on issues. Ryan narrowly prevailed. In the 2020 general election for House and Senate seats, a veteran faced a veteran in 17 of those races, said With Honor Action, an organization that promotes veterans for elective office. That vet-versus-vet scenario makes perfect sense in the current environment of near-worship of all things military. If one party nominates a vet, the other party feels the need to look around for one, too. Whether it's a veteran running against another veteran, or a veteran running against someone with no military experience, one thing is clear: Though veterans got to be veterans by wearing a uniform, they are not uniform in their beliefs or their behavior. Nor are they all exemplary.

"We need military veterans who aren't just there because they happen to have served in the uniform," said Danny Sjursen, the anti-war retired army major and former history professor at West Point. "You know, there's good vets and there's bad vets."

Looking back at American history, it isn't difficult to spot the "bad vets" who had a distinctly negative impact on the world, going all the way to the earliest days of the nation: Benedict Arnold rose to the rank of major general in the Continental Army during the Revolutionary War, but he defected to the British side and later commanded British troops against Americans. His name has become a universal synonym for treachery. In the modern era, Lee Harvey Oswald, a former marine, assassinated President John Fitzgerald Kennedy before Kennedy had a chance to act on his plan to get America out of Vietnam. Arguably, that assassination of a veteran by a veteran led to the deaths of 58,000 Americans in combat and the suicides of another 50,000 to 100,000 Americans, scarred by their time in Vietnam. Timothy McVeigh, a Gulf War army veteran, bombed the Alfred P. Murrah Federal Building in Oklahoma City, killing 168 people. Jeffrey Dahmer drank far too much in the army but got an honorable discharge anyway, then became a serial killer who mixed murder with necrophilia and cannibalism. In recent history, Duncan Hunter, a former marine, won a California seat in Congress as a Republican, but later pled guilty to federal charges of misusing campaign funds. Prosecutors alleged that some of that campaign money subsidized his extramarital affairs with five women. Hunter was sentenced to prison but pardoned by Trump. And Elmer Stewart Rhodes III, a Yale Law School graduate and former army paratrooper who founded the right-wing Oath Keepers, played a key role in the January 6 attack. In 2022 a federal jury found him guilty of seditious conspiracy.

The veterans in Congress in the early 2020s come in many ideological shapes. Some are hyper-conservative. Some are progressive. Some support the repeal of the Authorizations for Use of Military Force (AUMF) that have given successive presidents the power to continue the forever wars in Afghanistan and Iraq. Some oppose repeal. Some, like Sen. Tom Cotton, the Arkansas Republican, have a distinctly militaristic, interventionist bent. And some veterans organizations feel that not enough congressional veterans support trims in defense spending. "We want to see much more aggressive cuts in military spending, much more accountability, as far as the military goes, and larger reductions, base closures, things like that, that we don't see from a lot of the veteran politicians," said Garett Reppenhagen, executive director of Veterans for Peace, who spent 13 months in combat boots in Iraq, didn't like the war he was seeing, and wrote about it in his blog. "We as an organization reject a lot of the nationalism that I think drives our war culture. To get into office these days, many candidates have to appeal to that patriotic side, to be able to win votes."

All that diversity of veterans' views in Congress poses a problem for voters: Instead of automatically voting for someone who puts out "vote for a vet" lawn signs or wears marine dress blues in a TV ad, voters have to ask themselves what else the candidates have to offer and what positions they take on important issues, military and otherwise.

"I think that saying you should vote for somebody simply because they're a vet is actually kind of dangerous," said Dan Caldwell, senior advisor at the conservative-leaning Concerned Veterans for America. "Some of the most partisan members of Congress are veterans, and that's on the Right and Left. So, I don't think that military service guarantees that somebody is going to be a good member of Congress."

Though Caldwell's organization takes positions on the future shape of the Veterans Health Administration that are different from what other veterans groups advocate, he has worked with more progressive groups on repeal of the AUMFs, to return to Congress the war powers that it has meekly ceded to the presidency. "I would just say that, overall, military service hasn't been indicative one way or another of support for war powers reform," Caldwell said.

It's also true that veterans don't always derive from their military experience a strong urge to trim defense spending and keep America out of future fruitless wars. "They come to office on their military credentials, but then don't have a lot of thoughtful, bold ideas about anything besides the militarization of American foreign policy," said Gregory Daddis, a retired army colonel and director of the Center for War and Society at San Diego State University. "For these folks that are putting their military service front and center, they're appealing to the crowd that sees American strength stemming almost exclusively from military power." Veterans have the experience that should equip them for a debate about the costs of our defense budget. "It should be the Tom Cottons that are leading the charge, saying, 'We're spending too much. I know. I've been there,'" Daddis said.

Cotton's name pops up because he has been so visible, from his earliest days in the Senate, and his obvious hawkishness has not endeared him to anti-war veterans. "I tell you, he is my least favorite congressional veteran, maybe in history," Sjursen said. "I mean, he's that bad." Cotton, a not-an-nounced-but-obvious aspirant to the presidency, has a proven knack for making headlines, and that prominence makes him the most important—some would say the most dangerous—veteran in Congress. So he is worthy of an extended examination in this chapter.

Cotton's intense demeanor and Shakespearean appearance—"Yon Cassius has a lean and hungry look"—was fully on display from the very start of his Senate career. His maiden speech on the Senate floor, on March 15, 2015, was a grim piece of our-enemies-are-coming-for-us oratory. It painted a dark picture of America's "retreat" and declining status in the world, raising concern about rising threats from Russia and China and a list of other nations. To react to those threats, Cotton set out national goals of "global military dominance" and "hegemonic strength," and he made absolutely clear where he stood on defense spending: America needs more—a lot more. As he explained, even a one-year $200 billion increase in defense spending wouldn't entirely satisfy him. "Our military, suffering from years of neglect, has seen its relative strength decline to historic levels," Cotton said.

The speech offered a pessimistic counterpoint to what Cotton described as then-President Barack Obama's unwarranted optimism about the progress of the fight against terrorists: "During his last campaign, the president was fond of saying Al Qaeda was on the run. In a fashion, I suppose this was true. Al Qaeda was and is running wild around the world, now in control of more territory than ever before." His criticism of Obama continued with the president's decision to withdraw troops from Iraq. Cotton did not mention that it was President George W. Bush who had agreed with the Iraqi government to withdraw all troops from Iraq by the end of 2011. Obama's administration worked to alter that commitment and keep some American troops in Iraq, but those negotiations failed to produce an agreement. That withdrawal, Cotton argued, gave Al Qaeda a chance to regroup, and it "morphed" into the Islamic State, whose murderous ways he went on to list. "The Islamic State aspires and actively plots to attack us here at home, whether by foreign plot or by recruiting a lone wolf in our midst. The president's suggestions, in other words, that the war on terror is over or ending are far from true. Indeed, the director of national intelligence recently testified that, when the final accounting is done, 2014 will have been the most lethal year for global terrorism in the 45 years such data has been compiled. Yet the president won't even speak our enemy's name."

From the Islamic State, Cotton moved on to Iran, describing its role in international terrorism. "My objections to the ongoing nuclear negotiations are well known and need not be rehearsed at length here. I'll simply note the deal foreshadowed by the president, allowing Iran to have uranium enrichment capabilities and accepting an expiration date on any agreement, to quote Prime Minister Benjamin Netanyahu, doesn't block Iran's path to the bomb. It paves Iran's path to the bomb."

Cotton was not kidding when he said, in a triumph of understatement, that his views on the pending nuclear deal were "well known." In fact, just days before he stood up to give that speech, the youngest member of the Senate had already ignited a firestorm by leading 46 other Republican senators to sign a March 9 letter to the Iranian leadership about the pending deal. The letter warned that any future president could revoke any agreement not approved by Congress, and any future Congress could alter it. The message was clear, even though the letter didn't use these exact words: Mullahs, you should think twice about signing this deal that our president is offering you.

The day after the letter, Cotton's image appeared on the front page of the conservative *New York Daily News*, next to photos of senators Mitch McConnell, Ted Cruz, and Rand Paul, a page anchored by the stark main headline: "TRAITORS." Another headline on that page proclaimed: "GOPers try to sabotage Bam nuke deal." Inside, on page four, an image of the letter itself appeared, with the headline "Backstabbers." And the editorial page weighed in, under the headline "Un-patriot games," with a strong editorial criticizing the letter and its signers.

"Regardless of President Obama's fecklessness in negotiating a nuclear deal with Iran, 47 Republican U.S. senators engaged in treachery by sending a letter to the mullahs aimed at cutting the legs out from under America's commander-in-chief," the *Daily News* editorial said. The members of the editorial board made clear that they, too, worried about the ultimate shape of the nuclear deal, but they didn't like the way Cotton and the others had chosen to express that same concern. "Rather than offer objections domestically in robust debate, as is their obligation, ringleader Sen. Tom Cotton of Arkansas and his band trespassed on presidential turf by patronizing Iran's leaders with the suggestion 'that you may not fully understand our constitutional system.'"

Notice the editorial's designation of Cotton as the "ringleader" of the letter to the mullahs. In the Senate, an institution where seniority is everything, how did the youngest senator, at age 37 and with only two months of seniority, manage to persuade 46 other senators, with a total of 4,775 months of seniority (390 years), to join him in this bold venture? Was it the power of his intellect? There's no question that Cotton is smart and well-educated: Harvard College and Harvard Law School. Was it his status as a veteran who had been in combat in Iraq and Afghanistan? Or was it the incipient aura of a future presidential candidacy?

The day after the letter to the mullahs was released, a Republican Arkansas state senator, Bart Hester, apparently already convinced that Cotton was presidential material, introduced a bill that would allow House and Senate candidates to appear at the same time on the ballot for president or vice president. That was obviously aimed at helping Cotton, who would run for re-election to the Senate in 2020, which was also going to be a presidential election year. Before the month was out, Gov. Asa Hutchinson had signed it into law. As it happened, Cotton did not run for president in either 2016, when Trump emerged from a large field to win the GOP nomination and the presidency, or in 2020, when Trump was running for re-election. Nor has Cotton made it clear that he wants to be president. But his biography, his veteran credentials, and his muscular hawkishness have led many to view him as a future White House contender. A news analysis from McClatchy News Service, published soon after the Iran letter controversy, cited Cotton's down-on-the-farm upbringing and his Harvard and combat pedigrees, calling him a "conservative dream from central casting." The analysis quoted Janine Parry, a University of Arkansas political science professor, who paired Cotton's name with that of a powerful right-wing funding family: "If the Koch brothers tried to grow a politician in a laboratory, it would have grown Tom Cotton."

The Iran letter was not the only time Cotton made headlines. In 2020, after a Minneapolis police officer murdered George Floyd by kneeling on his neck until he died, protests broke out around the nation and the world. To Cotton and others, the sporadic violence arising from those protests was serious business. Cotton had long ago made clear his views on the issue of race relations. During his Harvard days, he had written conservative and controversial columns for the *Harvard Crimson* on a variety of subjects, such as feminism and affirmative action. He also wrote a review of a book about race for the *Harvard Salient*, a conservative journal. Cotton claimed to have seen real progress on the issue of race, and all America really needed to do was to just quit talking about it so much. "If race relations are better now than at any time in our history and would almost certainly improve if we stopped emphasizing race in our public life, what would the self-appointed 'civil rights leaders' have to do with themselves? For this reason, they continue to make hysterical and wholly unsubstantiated claims that inflame public opinion and create a gnawing cynicism in the American people."

Suddenly, in 2020, that progress seemed to have ground to a halt with the murder of George Floyd and the ensuing protests. So Cotton weighed in loudly with an immediately controversial op-ed in the *New York Times* about the looting and violence that had broken out at a limited number of the protests. "A majority who seek to protest peacefully shouldn't be confused with bands of miscreants," Cotton wrote. "But the rioting has nothing to do with George Floyd, whose bereaved relatives have condemned violence. On the contrary, nihilist criminals are simply out for loot and the thrill of destruction, with cadres of left-wing radicals like antifa infiltrating protest marches to exploit Floyd's death for their own anarchic purposes." His solution: Invoke the Insurrection Act and call in the military.

Cotton's op-ed, under the headline that the *Times* chose, "Send in the Troops," caused an immediate uproar inside the *Times*. Dozens of staffers complained, many of them tweeting this line: "Running this puts Black @NYTimes staff in danger." It didn't take long for the paper's leadership to issue an unusually earnest apology for not vetting the piece more carefully. "After publication, this essay met strong criticism from many readers (and many *Times* colleagues), prompting editors to review the piece and the editing process. Based on that review, we have concluded that the essay fell short of our standards and should not have been published."

The "editors' note" went on to say that some of Cotton's assertions about the protests were inaccurate, and the paper of record should have done a better job of fact-checking. "Beyond those factual questions, the tone of the essay in places is needlessly harsh and falls short of the thoughtful approach that advances useful debate." In the uproar, the paper's opinion editor, James Bennet, acknowledged that he had not even read Cotton's op-ed during the editing process and admitted that it was the *Times* that had invited the senator to write the piece. Just a few days after the op-ed ran, Bennet resigned from his senior position at perhaps the most powerful newspaper in the country. Cotton clearly has the power to shake things up.

Years earlier, in 2006, when he was still an officer in the combat zone in Iraq, Cotton had also tried to get the *Times* to publish his opinion. The *Times* and other papers had carried a story about a government effort called the Terrorist Finance Tracking Program. Like some who were then in Congress, Cotton felt that the *Times* journalists involved—two reporters and a senior editor—should be tried for espionage. Their work on the story, he argued, "gravely endangered the lives of my soldiers and all other soldiers and innocent Iraqis." On that occasion, when Cotton was still a soldier and not a senator, the *Times* did not publish what he wrote, but his letter did get published on a conservative blog and went viral. The journalists did not get prosecuted for espionage. But Cotton's hostility to investigative reporting about government secrecy did not fade once he became a senator. One illustrative example was his vigorous opposition in 2022 to a bill called the PRESS (Protect Reporters from Exploitative State Spying) Act. "This bill would prohibit the government from compelling any individual who calls himself a 'journalist' from disclosing the source or substance of such damaging leaks," Cotton said, in an article by the investigative journalism site *The Intercept* about his influence in blocking the bill. "This effectively would grant journalists special legal privileges to disclose sensitive information that no other citizen enjoys. It would treat the press as a special caste of 'crusaders for truth' who are somehow set apart from their fellow citizens."

National security is not Cotton's only issue. Like most Republicans, he reflexively accuses Democrats of being soft on crime. Statistics show that the United States is zealous about prison as the answer to criminality. The Vera Institute of Justice says that the United States, with 4 percent of the world's population, has 14 percent of the world's prison inmates. "The United States is the epicenter of mass incarceration," the institute says. "It's time to end that." In her book, *The New Jim Crow: Mass Incarceration in the Age of Colorblindness*, Michelle Alexander argues that our criminal justice system imprisons racial minorities out of all proportion to their presence in the population, and this harsh reality constitutes a new form of the oppressive Jim Crow laws that replaced slavery. Despite the statistics and the widespread calls for criminal justice reform, Cotton's view is exactly the opposite: America, he says, suffers from under-incarceration.

For a still-very-junior senator, Cotton has demonstrated an ability to wield influence all the way up to the presidential level. One example revolves around Trump and his favorite president, the slave-owning, Native American-removing Andrew Jackson. When Trump became president, he made sure that a painting of Jackson adorned the Oval Office. As a candidate in 2016, Trump had criticized as "pure political correctness" a Barack Obama-administration plan to remove Jackson's image from the $20 bill and replace it with the face of Harriet Tubman, who led slaves to freedom and fought for women's rights. Trump suggested an alternative: Put Tubman's face on the $2 bill (which is no longer printed). Once Trump became president, the Tubman $20 bill simply didn't happen. Then, in 2020, protesters were agitating for the removal of a statue of Jackson in Lafayette Square, just beyond the White House grounds. Cotton noticed—and made sure that Trump did, too.

In his book *In Trump's Shadow: The Battle for 2024 and the Future of the GOP*, David Drucker reports that Cotton called Trump and said, "Have you looked out your window to see what they're doing across the street?" More than that, Cotton put his staff to work searching for a remedy. "The senator told Trump about the Veterans Memorial Preservation Act, a law that makes it a crime (with penalties of up to ten years in prison) to deface, desecrate, destroy, or otherwise harm a monument or statue of someone serving in the US military; ditto regarding any memorial that depicted a veteran's military service," Drucker wrote. "As a former president, Jackson was a political figure. But he was also a celebrated military general." With that nudge from Cotton, Trump wasted no time in invoking the Veterans Memorial Preservation Act and authorizing the arrest of anyone who "vandalizes or destroys" monuments covered by the act.

Cotton also vibrated on the same frequency as Trump on the issue of education about the nation's shameful history of slavery. Not long after his op-ed in the *New York Times* suggested sending in the troops to control those protesting the police murder of George Floyd, Cotton introduced legislation grandly named the "Saving American History Act." It would have prohibited the use of federal funds to support an elementary- and secondary-school curriculum based on the 1619 Project, a *Times* study of the legacy of slavery. "Cotton's bill did not move forward, but it inspired many similar efforts, perhaps most prominently the 1776 Commission, an advisory committee formed by President Donald Trump to respond to the 1619 Project and other attempts to advance a more complicated narrative of the American past," Jake Silverstein wrote in the *Times*. That commission did issue a report, soon after the attack on the Capitol on January 6, 2021, but President Joseph R. Biden Jr. wasted no time in disbanding the commission.

Despite his obvious influence on Trump, Cotton declined several times in a televised interview after the 2022 Russian invasion of Ukraine to comment on Trump's repeated praise for Russia's president, Vladimir Putin. "If you want to know what Donald Trump thinks about Vladimir Putin or any other topic, I'd encourage you to invite him on your show," Cotton told George Stephanopoulos on ABC's *This Week*. "I don't speak on behalf of other politicians. They can speak for themselves."

In response to that non-stance, Reed Galen of the anti-Trump Lincoln Project tweeted a comparison of Cotton to an exotic critter endowed with very large ears for dissipating the African heat and scoping out prey: "Tom Cotton is wily, like a Fennec fox. He'll come up, look around, listen, then skitter back into his hole until the time is right." Cotton's display of slipperiness about Trump and Putin, plus his intelligence, hawkishness, thirst for ever more military spending, and willingness to "protect" America's children from learning about the nation's original sin, all make him a congressional veteran who needs to be watched.

Cotton may be the one to keep an eye on, but there are other veterans with sharply differing views. Perhaps the most visible in the period after the 2020 election—and the "Stop the Steal" madness that Donald Trump created when he lost to Joseph R. Biden Jr.—was Rep. Adam Kinzinger of Illinois. The conservative Republican and air force veteran reliably voted with Trump on legislation, and he voted against the 2019 House resolution to impeach Trump for the first time. Then, in response to Trump's often-repeated, evidence-free claims that the 2020 election had somehow been stolen, Kinzinger spoke out against him. After Trump's rhetoric helped to cause the attack on the Capitol on January 6, 2021, Kinzinger called on Vice President Mike Pence and the cabinet to invoke the Twenty-Fifth Amendment to remove the soon-to-be-former president from office. When the House of Representatives offered a resolution to impeach Trump a second time, Kinzinger voted yea. Predictably, an army of Republican primary challengers lined up against him. Faced with that flow of venom from Trump loyalists, Kinzinger ultimately decided not to seek re-election in 2022.

Despite that decision not to run again, Kinzinger turned out to be anything but a lame duck—more like an avenging eagle. In the closing months of his final term in Congress, he played a pivotal role in the investigation of Trump's criminality in the January 6 insurrection and the ongoing attempt to undo the results of the election. He supported House legislation to create an independent national commission, similar to the nonpartisan 9/11 commission. That effort fell short of the 60 votes needed to overcome a filibuster in the Senate. But House Speaker Nancy Pelosi came up with another plan: Instead of a national commission, she proposed a select committee of House members. She rejected the inflammatory, grandstanding members proposed by House Minority Leader Kevin McCarthy of California, and she extended an invitation to Kinzinger and Rep. Liz Cheney of Wyoming to serve as the Republican members of the committee. Both accepted, and both played significant roles in the committee's carefully choreographed televised hearings in the summer of 2022. At the committee's climactic prime-time hearing on July 21, focusing on Trump's actions and inactions on January 6, Cheney chaired the hearing and Kinzinger led the exposition of the facts and the questioning of witnesses, along with another veteran, Rep. Elaine Luria, a Democrat from Virginia. Near the end of the evening, Kinzinger summed up its significance.

"Whatever your politics, whatever you think about the outcome of the election, we as Americans must all agree on this: Donald Trump's conduct on January 6th was a supreme violation of his oath of office and a complete dereliction of his duty to our nation," Kinzinger said. "It is a stain on our history. It is a dishonor to all those who have sacrificed and died in service of our democracy. When we present our full findings, we will recommend changes to laws and policies to guard against another January 6th. The reason that's imperative is that the forces Donald Trump ignited that day have not gone away. The militant intolerant ideologies, the militias, the alienation and the disaffection, the weird fantasies and disinformation, they're all still out there ready to go. That's the elephant in the room."

As valuable as he was on the select committee, and as much as he ultimately differed from Cotton on the loyalty-to-Trump scale, Kinzinger shares with Cotton something of the same approach to national defense—and, possibly, a desire to run for president. "He's been generally supportive of a more interventionist foreign policy abroad," said Dan Caldwell of Concerned Veterans for America, the conservative group that supports repeal of the existing Authorizations for Use of Military Force (AUMF). Kinzinger routinely opposed repealing the AUMFs that have ceded so much war-and-peace power to the presidency. His argument: The nation needs only one commander in chief, not 535. Kinzinger is not the only veteran in Congress who opposes AUMF repeal. "Dan Crenshaw is another one," Caldwell said. "And then Lindsey Graham, of course."

Graham, the Republican senator from South Carolina, was a Judge Advocate General's Corps attorney in the air force, though his name does not leap immediately to mind in listings of veterans in Congress. Crenshaw, a Texas Republican, is the former Navy SEAL who lost his right eye to an improvised explosive device in Afghanistan. His public visibility rose exponentially when *Saturday Night Live* comic Pete Davidson poked fun at him for wearing an eye patch. The following week on *SNL*, Davidson apologized to Crenshaw. On most issues, Crenshaw is stoutly conservative, such as his resistance to gun control legislation, his support for repealing the Affordable Care Act, and his resistance to mask mandates during the Covid pandemic.

In late 2021, Crenshaw hosted a Houston youth summit, where many of the two thousand conservatives expressed enthusiasm for him as a possible future face of the post-Trump party. In a *Washington Post* analysis of the event and the congressman, Ben Terris wrote that Crenshaw is "both Trumpy and not. He criticized Trump before he was elected but voted against both impeachments. He spoke at the 2020 convention but made waves by not mentioning Trump's name once. In December, after Trump lost, Crenshaw was one of 126 Republicans who signed an amicus brief supporting a lawsuit that aimed to delay certification of presidential election results in certain, strategically important states that President Biden won—tantamount to co-signing Trump's false narrative that Democrats had cheated. (The U.S. Supreme Court snuffed out that legal challenge.) However, when 147 Republican members of Congress later voted against certifying Biden's win, Crenshaw was not one of them."

All factors considered, Crenshaw will not have the support of VoteVets, a progressive veterans group that endorses and supports veteran candidates, from the presidency (Pete Buttigieg in 2020) down to the local level. "I think he's a Trump Republican," said Jon Soltz, cofounder and chairman of VoteVets. "I think that's a legacy he'll have to live with." But VoteVets won't be trying to return Crenshaw to private life. "If we thought he was beatable, we would spend money to defeat him, but his district is just too Republican," Soltz said.

VoteVets is sharply focused on its choices of where to spend money on veteran candidates. "We've got to mass assets in places where we can win," Soltz said. "Sometimes that's going to be in a safe Democratic seat, where we can build seniority, rather than a seat that's going to go back and forth." In the 2022 cycle, though, VoteVets did choose to back a veteran running in a very Republican district, held by perhaps the most consistently visible and outrageous Trump-and-conspiracy-theory-loving member of Congress, Marjorie Taylor Greene. Marcus Flowers, an army vet, took her on, but lost. VoteVets regularly supports progressive veterans in the House of Representatives, such as Ruben Gallego of Arizona, Ted Lieu and Salud Carbajal of California, Jason Crow of Colorado, Mikie Sherrill of New Jersey, and Seth Moulton of Massachusetts, who ran briefly for president in 2019. In the Senate, it has endorsed Democrats Mark Kelly of Arizona, Tammy Duckworth of Illinois, Gary Peters of Michigan, Tom Carper of Delaware, and Jack Reed of Rhode Island.

"Part of what we focus on is defeating Republican veterans," Soltz said. In the 2022 cycle, the first congressional election since the madness of January 6 and Stop the Steal, the top Republican target of VoteVets was Mike Garcia, who represents the 27th Congressional District in Los Angeles. His campaign website featured a logo labeling him "Fighter Pilot Mike Garcia." VoteVets was unimpressed. "Mike Garcia is a traitor to America. He's in a district in Los Angeles where Joe Biden won his district by 10 points," Soltz said. "And he voted to decertify the election. He hides behind his Naval Academy service and his service in the United States Navy." Unseating Garcia was never going to be easy. Soltz griped that "most people aren't even tracking there's somebody in a Biden district that voted to decertify the election." In the end, Garcia prevailed over Democratic candidate Christy Smith, helped by the endorsement of another veterans group, With Honor—yet another reminder that it's impossible to file all veterans in Congress, or all veterans groups, under one convenient label. Congressional veterans disagree on policy issues, and so do the activist veterans organizations. Sometimes, they work together, despite their disagreements. Concerned Veterans for America, for example, works well with the more progressive VoteVets for AUMF repeal, though the two organizations have very different approaches on other matters.

The list of veterans organizations includes the younger, smaller, more activist groups, such as VoteVets, Concerned Veterans for America, With Honor, and Common Defense. It also includes the older and larger traditional veterans service organizations (VSOs), known as the Big Six: the American Legion, Veterans of Foreign Wars, Disabled American Veterans, AMVETS, Paralyzed Veterans of America, and Vietnam Veterans of America. Sometimes, a given issue can galvanize broad agreement among the veterans groups. One example was the Honoring Our Promise to Address Comprehensive Toxics Act of 2022 (Honoring Our PACT). It required the Veterans Administration to grant a presumptive disability rating to veterans affected by toxins from burn pits and other sources in combat zones.

"I think a grand total of 65 veterans groups ended up signing on to support this, and that included all of the major ones and many smaller ones, including us," said Naveed Shah, the political director of Common Defense. When it came time to vote on the bill, in the summer of 2022, veterans in Congress, including Tom Cotton, were not totally consistent. Initially, Cotton joined other Republicans in voting for it in June. But the House amended the bill. In July, Cotton was one of 25 Republicans who voted against cloture, ending debate and proceeding to a vote—including veterans Dan Sullivan of Alaska and Joni Ernst of Iowa. Veteran Lindsey Graham voted yea. The naysaying Republicans argued that the House had amended the bill in a fiscally irresponsible way. But supporters of the legislation suspected that the Republican votes against it were nothing more than a concerted fit of pique, because Democrats had agreed on a sweeping bill to fight climate change and reduce inflation. Whatever the reason for that cloture vote, Republicans became the target of widespread anger, led by entertainer Jon Stewart, who had been advocating for the bill. Less than a week after that no vote, Cotton and the other Republican nay votes on the bill became yea votes.

On a variety of issues facing Congress, Shah described the older VSOs as walking a fine line, avoiding the appearance of partisanship, and focusing entirely on veterans' concerns. But Common Defense takes a broader view. "We really believe that there are many structural and systemic issues in society, and veterans have a unique opportunity to change the narrative around many of the problems that our country faces," Shah said. "One example that I like to use is that, when you talk about entitlements or welfare, the argument from the conservative side is that, well, people don't need welfare. Welfare is only for people who are lazy and don't want to work. But the fact of the matter is that 25 percent of military families are on food stamps. So, are they lazy and don't want to work? Or is it that the cost of goods is greater than the income of our working-class people, and we need to make their lives better and easier? As a country with the most number of billionaires in the world, I think we can afford to do that."

The lesson to be learned from the diversity of beliefs and approaches among veterans groups and congressional veterans is this: Simplistic "Send in a marine" or "Vote for a vet" appeals during political campaigns need to be seen for what they are: empty gimmicks. Yes, the military can give a person some skills. "It demonstrates that you can work in diverse and large organizations, and that, if deployed overseas, it shows that you can handle difficult challenges," said George E. Reed, a professor at the University of Colorado and the author of *Tarnished: Toxic Leadership in the U.S. Military.* "But it should not be the sole determining factor in whether or not somebody votes for you, or whether or not you should vote for somebody."

Despite his book-length examination of bad leadership traits in the ranks, Reed is still stoutly pro-military. But he rejects the "unfortunate belief" that people in combat boots are better than those in the civilian world. "I was a military policeman," Reed said. "All I did for most of my career was deal with people in the military who were engaged in various levels of misconduct. So I knew very darn well that, morally speaking, just because you were in the military, it doesn't mean you were more moral, or a better person, or more ethical than anybody else."

For any voter who walks into a polling place to decide for or against a veteran on the ballot, the task is to look at where that veteran stands on all the issues and what kind of person the veteran is. Voting for someone simply because the candidate is a veteran is a losing proposition.

Chapter 5
DON'T MAKE EYE CONTACT

The calculus that took Rebekah Havrilla from South Carolina to combat in Afghanistan was simple: she needed money for her education.

"For me, it wasn't about the politics," she recalled. "I did a cost-benefit analysis of what I would get out of the military ... I can't afford to pay for college. So, getting a college degree and knowing the G.I. Bill would pay for it, three hots and a cot, and health care. For me, it wasn't about being a patriot."

But enlistment wasn't going to be easy, despite the military's increasing need for recruits for the wars in Iraq and Afghanistan, and despite her high scores on the Armed Services Vocational Aptitude Battery (ASVAB). "I had open heart surgery when I was a kid," she said. So she had to go through a long process to get a medical waiver to enlist. During that delay, she had a chance to ponder what Military Occupational Specialty (MOS) might fit her. One dangerous job that appealed to her—and to other women she met—was explosive ordnance disposal (EOD). "Had I been a boy and had a penis, I would have definitely wanted to try to be a Ranger or Special Forces or something like that," she said. "I wanted to be a badass." But first she had to face rejection. "The marines were like, 'Hell, no.' The air force, too. They were just like, 'We don't care. We're not dealing with all the paperwork involved to try and get one person.'"

But the army gave her a chance. In 2004, she signed her enlistment contract on the final day of the army's fiscal year, at 11:15 PM. "Literally, they were down to their final recruiting push for the year," she said. "It was also the height of the Iraq surge, and they were pretty much taking anything that walked." She had to choose an MOS, and her five choices were cook, parachute rigger, signals intelligence, petroleum supply, and EOD. She chose EOD, partly because of the badass factor and partly because it would get her moving through the system faster than the other jobs. "I'd been waiting a year and a half to get my medical waiver, and I was ready to go."

As she had known before signing the enlistment contract, EOD was almost certain to get her deployed to Iraq or Afghanistan, where dangerous unexploded ordnance awaited. And for 13 months, from September 2006 to September 2007, in the war-torn eastern provinces of Afghanistan, that was her job. "I blew shit up." She clearly was good at it, rising relatively quickly to sergeant.

The first time I met Bekah Havrilla was in November 2013, at Molloy College, in Rockville Centre, Long Island. The occasion was a performance of *In Our Own Voice: Women Veterans Tell Their Story*. That play-in-monologues featured Equity actresses voicing the words of women veterans. After the actresses had completed the performance, actual veterans got up on stage to answer questions from the audience. Havrilla was a frank and fearless voice in that civilian-veteran dialogue.

As a volunteer for the play, I had helped to persuade Molloy to host a performance. The previous year, my last at *Newsday*, I had written a column about an earlier Long Island performance of *In Our Own Voice*, at the Unitarian Universalist Congregation at Shelter Rock, in Manhasset. For the column, I did telephone interviews with two women who had become friends through a women's liturgy group and had brought the play to life: Beverly Coyle, a novelist and playwright who taught literature at Vassar College, and Mary Ragan, a therapist at the Psychotherapy & Spirituality Institute in Manhattan, an interdisciplinary, nonprofit pastoral counseling center. I also interviewed the director, Steven Ditmyer. At the end of that Shelter Rock performance, I watched Ragan skillfully lead the veteran-audience dialogue. When I retired at the end of the year, I volunteered to help them arrange future venues and interview more veterans.

The idea for *In Our Own Voice* flowed from Ragan's desire to have the Psychotherapy & Spirituality Institute help returning veterans. "It was a few years after the start of the Iraq war, and because we're a mental health group, we wanted to do something proactive regarding this entire disastrous situation," she recalled. "What we decided was that we would try to provide mental health services for returning veterans. What we discovered was that veterans were able to get free, confidential, licensed mental health support, not only at the VA, but there's another veterans group that they can get it from."

Once it was clear that veterans could get mental health services elsewhere, Ragan and Coyle talked about what the institute could do instead. "Suddenly," Coyle said to Ragan during a 2021 joint interview, "you were saying, 'What about women?' And suddenly, 'What about interviewing women?'" That made sense to both of them, because women in the military were vastly underrepresented in the media.

Finding women to interview turned out not to be easy. But they both began attending a civilian-veteran dialogue hosted by a New York nonprofit group, Intersections International. At one of those sessions, they made a pivotal connection. "There was one young woman veteran there," Coyle recalled. "We just made a beeline for her." That veteran, Erica Cano, became the first woman they interviewed. They had decided to keep the questions simple: Why did you enlist? What was your experience in training and in deployment? What happened when you returned home?

Before long, they met with a woman whose story went beyond those initial questions to the plague of sexual assault in the military. That wasn't the only time that disturbing subject came up, but they didn't make it a central focus of their interviews or the resulting play. For one thing, another play, *The Lonely Soldier Monologues (Women at War in Iraq)*, by Columbia University journalism professor Helen Benedict, had debuted in 2009. And as the review in the *New York Times* put it, "Sexual harassment and assault by fellow soldiers is a constant theme." In addition, they felt the need to be delicate in approaching this subject. "You had to be very careful not to re-traumatize people," Ragan said. "We were extremely concerned about the ethical requirements of what we were doing. Even though we wanted the women's stories, we didn't want to exploit the women's stories. And so, whatever they wanted to tell us is what we wanted to hear."

As a result of that obedient listening, *In Our Own Voice* did offer a few brief insights into the sexual harassment problem. "You learn to put up with just about everything sounding sexual," said Actor A in Coyle's script, describing the way male soldiers could put an erotic spin on anything. "Really. They can't even say 'Pass the salt and pepper' without making it sexual," added Actor D. A moment later, Actor B responded, "As a female you have one of three choices from them: You're going to be labeled a 'slut,' a 'bitch,' or 'one of the guys.'" Actor D added this bit of advice: "With guys you don't work with, you can't make eye contact. Walking from point A to point B on the base, you don't make eye contact. In the mess hall, same thing." The clear implication: If you make eye contact with someone not in your unit, you're inviting an unwanted sexual advance. Sadly, women are not really safe from men in their own unit, either.

Describing a post-deployment, back-in-the-world chat with an army friend from Iraq, Actor B recalled her frustration with the friend's inability to grasp what women went through: "Can I just ask you, didn't it ever occur to you that female soldiers have to be on guard at all times? He's like 'No.' And that's when I had to explode: 'Chad, I had to watch my back with men every minute of every single *day*!'"

Those words and others in the script, crafted by Coyle from women's own testimony, were my introduction to the issue of military sexual abuse. Not long after that, I heard a sickening statistic: The Pentagon estimated 26,000 cases of sexual abuse in the military in fiscal year 2012. Then Ragan and I interviewed a victim of military sexual abuse who gave us a stark story of the ugliness of abuse. Our interviewee was Bekah Havrilla. Since the 2013 event at Molloy College, where she impressed us with her intelligence and fearlessness, Havrilla had been moving on with her life. Ultimately, she agreed to an interview, and in April 2015, Ragan and I spoke with her at length by phone.

"My commander hated women," Havrilla told us. "He didn't want me there. I spoke to the man three times the entire time I was in that unit, and that was all business-related. He didn't give a shit about me. And then, my first sergeant: I was warned off my first sergeant before I even got there. When I was at EOD school and people found out—I was stationed at Fort Riley—I literally had like three people tell me, 'Watch out for your first sergeant. He's a dirty old man.'"

As it happened, the first sergeant was not a good leader, and "he did make some inappropriate comments from time to time, but he was not really terrible, compared to some of the people that I experienced," Havrilla recalled. "My second team leader that I worked with was very kind of abusive, sexually harassive, made it very clear that he just wanted to fuck me. He would do things like try and pull me into bed with him or come up behind me and put his hands up my shirt and try and like tickle me or kiss the back of my neck. And one time he just blatantly just told me he wanted to fuck me."

But Havrilla did not endure her worst single incident of sexual abuse until days before she was scheduled to leave Afghanistan and return to the United States. It involved a dog handler from a military police unit. They had worked together. "Basically, I had to return some things to him, and he decided that he wanted to have sex," Havrilla said. "And I'm like, 'I'm getting on a chopper, and I'm leaving, and I don't want to have sex with you right now—or ever, because I'm leaving.' So he pretty much just made sure that I knew that I wasn't leaving until he got what *he* wanted…. I said no, and I tried to leave. And, you know, he wouldn't let me, and put his hands on me, and then proceeded to take advantage of me."

Havrilla was unambiguous about what had happened to her. "There was no alcohol involved," she said. "There were no drugs involved. There was no party scene. It was literally, a 'No, I'm leaving,' and it was a 'No you're not, until I get what I want.'" Her verdict on the incident: "That was straight-up rape."

But the horror didn't end there. Months later, Havrilla was working as a civilian contractor at Fort Leonard Wood, Missouri, and also doing some training as a reservist, when she ran totally at random into the man who had raped her in Afghanistan. Casually, he said, "Hi," as if nothing ugly and life-changing had happened between them. "I was like, 'Hi? What are you doing here?'" The man who had raped her then explained that he was now stationed at Fort Leonard Wood. He added, nonchalantly, "Well, maybe we should hang out some time." And he left.

Understandably, that bizarre encounter, that out-of-nowhere reminder of the rape, drove Havrilla into what she called a mini-meltdown. "The irony of it is, this is the first time I had been in full uniform in training in a military environment in a very long time, like a year and a half, and then I run into this guy in a freakin' shoppette," she said. "So, I was like, 'Done, not doing this anymore. I'm removing myself from training.'"

She needed to talk about what had just happened. So her boyfriend arranged for her to visit a chaplain on post. They entered his office together, but the chaplain asked her boyfriend to leave, so he could speak with her privately. She gave her permission, and her boyfriend left the room. "That's when he basically starts quizzing me about my relationship with God, and all of this kind of stuff," Havrilla said. "And he's like, 'Well, you know, things happen for a reason, and this was just God's way of trying to get your attention, because you're not right with him and you need to go back to church.'"

That bizarre, even blasphemous bit of vengeful-God theology was not what she needed to hear at that moment. "I pretty much told that chaplain to shove it," she said. "I'm in the middle of a major crisis right now, and you don't say that to victims."

By that point in her life, Havrilla had already decided that organized religion was toxic. "I grew up as a fundamentalist, independent, Bible-believing Baptist, where Southern Baptists were liberals going to hell, because they listened to Christian rock and wore jeans," she said. When she was in high school, the boys' basketball coach was accused of molesting boys on his team. "When he was actually confronted and caught, he ended up killing himself," Havrilla said. "They basically ostracized the boys that he molested and booted them from the school and gave him like a huge funeral service and touted him as just this individual that was in a dark place." That foreshadowed what she would learn in the military: The people in charge tend to make excuses for the perpetrator and treat the abused persons badly. "So, when that experience with the chaplain happened, I was already kind of angry and turned off by religion anyway."

A little more than a half year after that horrific 2009 day at Fort Leonard Wood, Havrilla endured another searing reminder of the rape in Afghanistan: A close friend stumbled upon some photos of Havrilla that the rapist had taken of her during the act and had posted online. Her face was clearly identifiable in the photos. The shock of that realization pushed her to a new step, filing a formal, unrestricted report about the rape. When the rape first occurred, she had filed a restricted report. That essentially means that she became a statistic, a part of the far too large number of people reporting sexual abuse by military colleagues, but it did not entail formal charges against the rapist or a full investigation. When she encountered the rapist in the shoppette at Fort Leonard Wood, she filed another restricted report. Only after learning about the photos did she finally file an unrestricted report.

"That made it very public," Havrilla said. "It changed everything for me. I'm like, I'm not going to sit here anymore. Then again, I had just run into him like six months earlier. So I was like, Fuck you. You're going to lose some sleep now, too. Whether nothing comes of this, I'm going to make you sweat."

This dual system of reporting sexual assault arose to serve the needs of survivors who don't want all the pressure of a full investigation and trial but do need some health or mental health services. Before the system was installed, in the early years of the century, survivors of assault took a real risk in seeking medical help.

"If they went to the hospital, unless they went off base and were willing to pay for themselves, out of pocket, to get any kind of treatment, that was going to be reported to the chain of command as well, and it would start an investigation," said retired Air Force Col. Don Christensen, president of Protect Our Defenders, a nonprofit human rights organization that advocates for victims of sexual violence, sexual prejudice, misogyny, and racism in the military. "So, a lot of women were complaining, 'I just want to get a pregnancy test or to be treated or to get checked for STDs or talk to a provider. I didn't want to go through this process, and now I'm being forced to go through this trial.' With the restricted/nonrestricted process, survivors of assault get to choose. "So you can go to special victims counsel, victim advocate, mental health, doctor, chaplain, and you can just say, 'I don't want this to go any further.' About 20, 25 percent of allegations are restricted."

In Havrilla's case, the unrestricted report that she filed brought no real results. "The commander didn't want to press charges. They did a full investigation. They contacted my best friend and his [the rapist's] wife. They contacted people in Afghanistan that I worked with in Afghanistan," Havrilla said. "That's when they found out he was married. He admitted to having sex with me while married, which is technically a crime under the UCMJ."

But the Uniform Code of Military Justice did not adequately protect sexual assault victims, because it left the choice of how to handle the assault allegation up to unit commanders. That led to far too many built-in conflicts. The unit commander who got to decide how to handle the case was too often the commander of both the survivor and the perpetrator. Sometimes, the commander actually *was* the perpetrator.

"He was never punished for anything," Havrilla said. "I have no idea if he's still in the military."

Sadly, the consequences for survivors of abuse are more severe than what the perpetrators usually endure. Iraq and Afghanistan Veterans of America has surveyed its members, and 73 percent of those who have suffered military sexual assault report that they have been retaliated against in the aftermath, said Tom Porter, IAVA's executive vice president for government affairs. And the RAND Corporation, a regular supplier of military studies, found a correlation between a person's experience of sexual abuse and an increased likelihood of leaving the military.

The absence of justice in Havrilla's own case did not deter her from seeking a better system for abuse survivors. She worked at Service Women's Action Network (SWAN), a national voice for military women. Among other jobs, she managed SWAN's national help line for legal and social services, working with over six hundred service members, veterans, and their families on issues related to military rape, sexual assault, and sexual harassment. On March 13, 2013, she testified before the Senate Armed Services Subcommittee on Personnel, chaired by Sen. Kirsten Gillibrand, a New York Democrat, about her own bitter experience and about the need to fix the way the military decides on prosecuting sexual predators in its ranks.

"The military criminal justice system is broken," Havrilla told the committee. "Unfortunately, my case is not much different from the many other cases that have been reported. I feared retaliation before and after I reported. The investigative process severely retraumatized me. Many of the institutional systems set up to help failed me miserably. My perpetrator went unpunished, despite admitting to a crime against the UCMJ, and commanders were never held accountable for making the choice to do nothing. What we need is a military with a fair and impartial criminal justice system, one that is run by professional legal experts, not unit commanders. We also need an additional system that allows military victims to access civil courts if the military system fails them. Without both military criminal justice reform and access to civil courts, military sexual violence will continue to be widespread and a stain on the character of our armed forces."

Months before that powerful congressional testimony, Havrilla had joined a civil lawsuit by 25 women and three men who had suffered rape or other sexual assault while they were on active duty. The complaint in *Cioca v. Rumsfeld* alleged that two former defense secretaries, Donald Rumsfeld and Robert Gates, "knowingly and intentionally violated the laws passed by Congress to reduce sexual predation in the military, and by these violations deprived the rape survivors of their Constitutional rights."

The legal theory underlying the suit was rooted in a 1971 Supreme Court decision, *Bivens v. Six Unknown Named Agents of the Federal Bureau of Narcotics*. In *Bivens*, the court basically said that people could sue federal officers for violating their constitutional rights under the Fourth Amendment's prohibition of "unreasonable searches and seizures." Soon after, the court expanded the reach of *Bivens* to violations of constitutional rights guaranteed by the First, Fifth, and Eighth amendments, including protections against suppression of free speech, self-incrimination, violations of due process, and imposition of excessive bail. After the turn of the century, the Supreme Court took a more cautious approach toward allowing *Bivens* claims.

The suit alleged not only that Rumsfeld and Gates had deprived them of their rights by failing to implement congressional protections against sexual predation, but also that the survivors had been labeled "troublemakers" and "drummed out of the military" in various ways. The suit also listed the lenient treatment that the perpetrators had experienced. But the facts ended up playing a subordinate role to judicial interpretation of how far the *Bivens* case permitted them to go in allowing lawsuits.

Havrilla attended arguments before Judge Liam O'Grady in the United States District Court for the Eastern District of Virginia. And she was there in December 2011 when O'Grady dismissed the case. He described the abuse allegations as "troubling" and "egregious," but in the end, he went along with judicial deference to the military, holding that military discipline should be left to elected officials, not to the courts. Sitting in his courtroom, Havrilla had the impression that O'Grady was feeling something like regret that he had to rule that way.

In July 2013, the United States Court of Appeals for the Fourth Circuit upheld O'Grady's dismissal of *Cioca v. Rumsfeld*. In sharp contrast to the simple words of the plaintiffs' appeal, about the stunning lack of consequences for the perpetrators and the ignominy and rejection that befell the survivors, the Fourth Circuit spoke in language that bordered on the Orwellian.

"In concluding that Plaintiffs lack a *Bivens* cause of action in this case, we do not downplay the severity of Plaintiffs' allegations or otherwise imply that the conduct alleged in Plaintiffs' Complaint is permissible or acceptable," the appeals court wrote. "Rather, our decision reflects the judicial deference to Congress and the Executive Branch in matters of military oversight required by the Constitution and our fidelity to the Supreme Court's consistent refusal to create new implied causes of action in this context. Those principles, as clearly expressed in *Chappell, Stanley*, and *Feres*, counsel that judicial abstention is the proper course in this case."

Judicial abstention, of course, is the dry phrase that the judges chose to express a legal approach that resembled the rude rejection that Dorothy and her friends encountered at the gates of the Emerald City of Oz: "The Wizard says, 'Go away!'" In making that point, the judges cited the *Feres* case, a key underpinning of "judicial abstention" and deference to Congress and the executive branch. *Feres* is all about what the court thought Congress meant in enacting the Federal Tort Claims Act in 1946, which gave American citizens the right to sue the federal government. Just four years later, in *Feres v. United States*, the Supreme Court interpreted the claims act narrowly. In its decision, the court issued what plaintiffs' attorneys have called "a judicially created exception" that goes against the clear congressional language in the text of the federal tort legislation. In *Feres*, the court decided that members of the military could *not* sue for damages when the injury they sustained was "incident to military service."

In a similar lawsuit by sexual assault survivors, the defendant was Defense Secretary Leon Panetta. But *Klay v. Panetta* suffered the same outcome as *Cioca v. Rumsfeld*: the trial court dismissed the suit, and the appeals court in *Klay*, the United States Court of Appeals for the District of Columbia, upheld that dismissal.

The attorney for the plaintiffs in both cases, Susan L. Burke, knew the military well, long before filing those lawsuits. "My dad was career military. So I grew up on army bases," she said. "For me, the military is not a mythology. It was part of my life growing up. I didn't glorify it … I always knew some things were good and some things were really messed up."

One of the "really messed up" things Burke encountered as an attorney was a woman who told her that a friend of her soldier husband had raped her. "She'd gone to the military police," Burke recalled. "They court-martialed the guy, but then they lost the physical evidence that she had given them, her underwear." That case prompted her to research deeply the issue of rape in the military. "I just put the word out that I was willing to take on cases," Burke said. "Basically, through veterans' community gatherings, people just spread the word, and so then I just started getting tons of calls from all sorts of people."

Her strategy was to move on multiple fronts, Burke said. "I filed separate suits, trying different angles, different victims, kind of on the theory of, All right, we've got a brick wall here. Let's try to hit it at a few different places, see if we can find any weak spots." Stubbornly, the brick wall remained standing.

After circuit courts upheld the district courts' dismissal of both *Cioca* and *Klay*, Burke did not seek Supreme Court review of either. She and other attorneys focusing on sexual abuse chose a long-term strategy. "We basically wanted to kind of do a second wave," Burke said. "There's a movement to try to get rid of the *Feres* doctrine."

Erasing that doctrine, established in the mid-twentieth century, has proven to be a Herculean task for attorneys representing sexual assault victims. Another case that ran up against the deference that the courts give the military was *Doe v. Hagenbeck*. This involved the rape of a West Point cadet, Jane Doe, by an older male cadet. Doe filed suit against two officials of the United States Military Academy: Lt. Gen. Franklin Lee Hagenbeck, the superintendent, and Brig. Gen. William E. Rapp, the commandant of cadets. She alleged that Hagenbeck and Rapp had failed to protect female cadets from sexual predation. The district court rejected all but one of the four causes of action in *Doe*. The United States Court of Appeals for the Second Circuit decided that the trial court should not have allowed even that one claim to proceed. So it sent the case back down, with instructions to the trial court to dismiss the remaining claim. In its decision, the Second Circuit cited a reluctance in other cases to "require military leaders to defend their professional management choices."

Dissenting from the Second Circuit's decision in *Doe*, Circuit Judge Denny Chin cited evidence of the "misogynistic culture" at West Point, quoting some of the sexually hostile verses from chants used during team-building exercises, like this one: "I wish that all the ladies/were statues of Venus/and I was a sculptor/I'd break 'em with my penis." Chin argued that Doe's injuries were not "incident to military service," adding: "When she was subjected to a pattern of discrimination, and when she was raped, she was not in military combat or acting as a soldier or performing military service. Rather, she was simply a student, and her injuries were incident only to her status as a student."

So, survivors face a legal system that is stacked against them, thanks to the Supreme Court's unwillingness to undo the *Feres* doctrine. A few Supreme Court justices, conservatives such as Clarence Thomas and the late Antonin Scalia, have questioned *Feres*. So did the late Ruth Bader Ginsburg. So far, though, no case challenging *Feres* frontally has managed to get the required four justices to agree to a full Supreme Court hearing. In another approach to the sexual abuse epidemic, Protect Our Defenders and Connecticut Veterans Legal Center filed a lawsuit in federal court in 2022 against the Department of Defense and the Department of Justice. The plaintiffs wanted records of prosecution agreements between the military and civilian authorities over the previous 15 years and information on prosecution of sexual assault and other serious crimes at military bases in California, New York, Texas, and Virginia. "The records are likely to show that the military justice system fails victims of servicemember crimes—who have less judicial recourse than victims of nearly identical crimes perpetrated by a civilian—by under-prosecuting sexual assault in particular," the complaint in the suit argued. Clearly, though the courts have not been a friendly venue for those trying to curb sexual abuse, the legal battles will continue.

Just as deference to military commanders has led the courts to reject lawsuits by sexual assault survivors, the same deference also makes meaningful legislative change difficult. Over the years, as *Cioca v. Rumsfeld* pointed out, Congress had taken a variety of actions to curb military sexual abuse. But one crucial step that the Congress had not taken was to remove the prosecution decision from military commanders and put it in the hands of professional prosecutors, outside the chain of command of both accuser and accused.

In May 2013, two months after Bekah Havrilla told her story to Sen. Kirsten Gillibrand's Senate Armed Services Subcommittee on Personnel,

Gillibrand and a bipartisan group of senators introduced the Military Justice Improvement Act of 2013. Its primary goal was to remove decisions over prosecutions of serious crimes, including sexual assault, from the chain of command and to put those decisions in the hands of experienced military prosecutors. The only crimes not affected by this change would be those considered uniquely military, such as Absent Without Leave and disobeying orders.

The introduction of the bill came just a week after a Pentagon survey had estimated 26,000 cases of sexual assault in the military, sharply up from 19,000 in the previous survey. Even more disturbing to some in Congress was the number of actual reports of assaults, a bit north of 3,000, and the number of prosecutions, only about 300—shockingly low numbers compared to the estimated 26,000 military sexual assaults.

In the days before the introduction of the Military Justice Improvement Act of 2013, other bits of military sexual abuse news helped raise congressional awareness. One was the allegation of sexual abuse by a senior army sergeant responsible for handling sexual abuse cases at Fort Hood, Texas. Less than two weeks earlier, an Air Force lieutenant colonel in charge of sexual-assault prevention programs was arrested for groping and battering a woman in a parking lot. Some indications of sexual problems in the military had cropped up a little more than two decades earlier, as the military adjusted clumsily to the rising number of women in uniform. The most famous incident took place in September 1991 at the Tailhook Symposium, a gathering of retired navy and marine aviators, where women complained of having to run a gauntlet and endure groping and verbal abuse. Ultimately, an investigation by the inspector general and the Naval Criminal Investigation Service (before it became a TV series) turned up 80 to 90 victims. The scandal damaged or ended the careers of 14 admirals and nearly 300 aviators.

In 1996, five years after Tailhook, 12 drill instructors at the army's Aberdeen Proving Ground in Maryland were accused of sex crimes. Four drew prison sentences, and eight either received nonjudicial punishment or were discharged. In 2003, at the Air Force Academy in Colorado, 70 percent of the 579 women enrolled as cadets said they had been victims of sexual harassment. And 12 percent of the women who graduated that year said they had been the victims of rape or attempted rape at the academy.

So, by the time Gillibrand introduced the Military Justice Improvement Act, the headlines had made members of Congress increasingly aware of the endemic problem of sexual abuse in the nation's military. But members of Congress, like judges, reflexively defer to military commanders. As a result, despite the scale of the problem, lawmakers wanted to wait and see how the military performed in controlling it, based on earlier, smaller-scale congressional action, before they would take the more fundamental step of removing prosecution decisions from the commanders.

Gillibrand worked diligently to nudge reluctant colleagues toward passing the Military Justice Improvement Act. She kept a whiteboard in her office where she kept track of the senators who had joined her cause and those who still needed persuasion. But it took eight long years before she achieved a real breakthrough—with a significant boost from a book, a play, and a documentary film.

The creator of the book and the play was British-born author and Columbia University journalism professor Helen Benedict. Her journey into the issue of military sexual trauma began in March 2004, when she joined a small crowd in the City of New York, gathered to honor those killed in the first year of the Anglo-American invasion and occupation of Iraq.

"When they invaded Iraq in 2003, I was horrified, because I knew, being a relatively well informed citizen, that Iraq and Saddam Hussein had nothing whatsoever to do with 9/11," Benedict told me. "And the idea of bombing civilians and sending our soldiers to get killed for no reason was absolutely unbearable to me. What can I do about it, other than march and go on protests and vigils? I'm a writer. So I have to write about it. Then the next question was, what to write about that everybody wasn't already saying."

At that New York event, Benedict heard for the first time Iraq veterans talking about the realities that they faced in that unlawful, unnecessary, unwise, wrapped-in-lies military action. She heard about soldiers having to fight without sufficient armor, without adequate food, and without sufficient clean drinking water. As Benedict saw it, no one at the time was really writing about those adverse conditions facing young Americans in Iraq. "So first I thought, well, I've got to follow whoever I can, to try and find out more about this," Benedict said.

Benedict began looking for events where she could find soldiers. On one of those occasions, in a classroom at the City University of New York's Graduate Center in midtown Manhattan, some male anti-war Iraq veterans were speaking to members of the public. "The audience was tiny, which showed how uninterested the public still was," Benedict recalled. "And that's where I saw these two young women standing in the back of the room. Everyone was in civilian clothes, but I could tell from their postures that they were military, because they stand up very straight."

Walking up to the two women, Benedict asked if they were veterans, too. They were. One of them, Mickiela Montoya, added, "I was in Iraq getting bombed and shot at, but people won't even listen when I say I was at war, because I'm a female." Benedict didn't hesitate, and her answer set her on a course to write extensively and influentially about women at war. "I'll listen," Benedict said. And she did. Benedict interviewed about 40 soldiers—most of them women. "As I was doing research, that's when I discovered that more women were being deployed to this war than ever before in American history," she said. "That's what got me onto the subject of women."

The result was the 2009 book *The Lonely Soldier: The Private War of Women Serving in Iraq*. A companion play, *The Lonely Soldier Monologues: Women at War in Iraq*, debuted in 2009 at Theater for the New City, an off-off-Broadway venue on First Avenue in Manhattan. Benedict's own concept of the book was more expansive than simply a focus on military sexual trauma.

"The book is about women's experience in the Iraq war," she said. "It's about why they joined up, what happened to them in the war, and how they were changed by war. That's what the book is about. Sexual assault is part of it, because it's part of women's lives in the military. The book is not a book about women being assaulted in the military. That's the way it's been portrayed, because that's the most shocking part of it all…. All along, my larger idea was to show what war does to the human heart."

Still, as she continued her interviews and found more and more women talking about sexual abuse, Benedict wrote an article that appeared in *Salon* in March 2007, all about that issue. "I have talked to more than 20 female veterans of the Iraq war in the past few months, interviewing them for up to 10 hours each for a book I am writing on the topic, and every one of them said the danger of rape by other soldiers is so widely recognized in Iraq that their officers routinely told them not to go to the latrines or showers without another woman for protection," Benedict wrote.

A few paragraphs down, she cited an outrageous evidence of latrine fear. It involved Col. Janis Karpinski, who had commanded the infamous Abu Ghraib prison and was reduced in rank from brigadier general after the scandal over the torture of Iraqi prisoners there. She was the only officer punished for those abuses. She claimed that she was scapegoated, and she has become a sharp critic of the military's treatment of women. In 2006, at a mock trial called the Bush Crimes Commission, she testified that three women soldiers in Iraq had died of dehydration in 2003 because they declined to drink water late in the day. Why? If they drank the water that they needed, in order to stay hydrated in the searing Iraqi heat, they might have to walk in the dark to an unlit outdoor latrine, where they feared being raped by male soldiers.

In the article, Benedict also quoted the young veteran she had met at the start of her research: "Spc. Mickiela Montoya, 21, who was in Iraq with the National Guard in 2005, took to carrying a knife with her at all times. 'The knife wasn't for the Iraqis,' she told me. 'It was for the guys on my own side.'" And she wrote about an ugly phenomenon called "command rape," which describes what happens when commanders not only ignore the problem of sexual abuse but engage in it themselves.

One appalling story of "command rape" that Benedict cited involved Spc. Suzanne Swift, deployed to Iraq in 2004. One commander coerced her into sex, and two others harassed her. When she finally told her story, other soldiers shunned her as a traitor. She went AWOL while on leave, got arrested, and refused the army's deal: If she'd sign a statement that she had never been raped, they'd drop the charges. She declined. They court-martialed her, and she spent time in prison. In contrast, the men who had abused her received letters of reprimand. That's the stark, too-common reality. "If you tell, you are going to get punished," Benedict wrote in *Salon*. "The assailant, meanwhile, will go free."

That *Salon* article played a pivotal role in elevating awareness of military sexual trauma because it came to the attention of a documentary filmmaker named Amy Ziering. She read Benedict's article and found it deeply affecting and disturbing. After reading it, she felt the need to share it with Kirby Dick, her co-owner and partner in Los Angeles-based Chain Camera Pictures.

"I walked into Kirby's office and said, 'Did you know anything about this? How is it possible that these women have no recourse to an impartial system of justice?'" Ziering recalled asking her partner. Dick encouraged her to contact the author. So she got in touch with Benedict and asked her whether the *Salon* article had caused the media stir that it obviously merited. "She said, 'No, nothing. It didn't go wide,'" Ziering said.

Soon after Ziering spoke with Benedict, Chain Camera Pictures got the green light from HBO for another project and went to work on that. A couple of years later, Ziering and Kirby took another look at the sexual abuse issue that Benedict had raised. They found that other publications still had not picked up Benedict's *Salon* article and run with it. "So, we just circled back into this issue and started doing our own research and found out that everything that she had uncovered was not only true, but that it was really an epidemic," Ziering said. "It was just the tip of the iceberg."

Though the magazine piece did not initially get the attention it should have, Benedict's reporting did lead to an important new contact for herself, and then for Dick and Ziering, as they tried to figure out the shape of a documentary on military sexual trauma. "I had received this really exciting telephone call that any journalist would love to hear, which is, I got a call from a lawyer called Susan Burke, and she said, 'I've read your book, and I've seen your play, and I figured out how to sue the Pentagon,'" Benedict recalled. "I told Amy about that ongoing case, and I put her in touch with Susan Burke, and that's what gave them the plot for the movie."

But Dick and Ziering did not limit themselves to interviews with the plaintiffs in Burke's lawsuits. In all, they interviewed something like 100 women—and men—who were survivors of sexual abuse in the military. As painful as it was for those survivors to tell their harrowing stories, Ziering went through some of her own trauma during the interview process. "That was my first introduction into secondary PTSD," Ziering said. "I was clueless."

One of the other producers on the film, Tanner Barklow, had scheduled Ziering and Dick to do three or four interviews a day. "We were driving across country, just me and Kirby," Ziering recalled. Several days into that demanding cross-country series of interviews, they interviewed an abuse survivor in upstate New York. As they left the woman's house, Ziering recalled, "Kirby said to me, 'How do you think that went?' And I know that sounds so innocent, but we have our own language. I knew that was an implicit criticism as a partner. I knew he thought it didn't go well."

That night, at their motel, what Ziering had been hearing in the interviews began to make her hyper aware of her surroundings. "I was like, 'Oh, I'm in a room by myself. Oh, I'm looking out at the parking lot. Wait! I need to check if my door is locked.' This is *so* not me." The next morning at breakfast, she acknowledged to Dick that she hadn't been herself during the interview. "I looked at him, and I said, 'I think I know what happened yesterday, in the interview,'" Ziering said. " 'I showed up, but I wasn't there. It's why you asked me, how did I think it went. I didn't want to hear it. I couldn't do it anymore.'"

From that breakfast conversation emerged a sense of what the interviews could do to the interviewers, and it prompted changes in their procedures. "That's when we learned about secondary PTSD, and we decided we would scale back," Ziering said. "We wouldn't do as many interviews a day, and we booked places more expensive, so I could have a treadmill in the morning and exercise." Still, Ziering had to begin using sleeping pills after the film, and Chain Camera Pictures put in place mental health protocols for everyone who works on their films, to protect them from the caustic effects of their work on traumatic subjects. As to the lingering impact of this film on her own health, Ziering put it this way: "When I'm asked, I use it as a teachable moment. I say: 'Look, if someone like me, with no first-degree relationship to this issue, can have this, just imagine how horrible it is for people who go through this and for their loved ones and for all of that. So, that's why we really need to take action.'"

Beyond the problems of the interviews, the film faced the obstacle that most documentary films encounter: raising the money to finance it. In this case, the subject matter—an ugly, ongoing, widespread moral flaw in the consistently most admired institution in America—made fundraising an even more mountainous task than usual. "It was horribly difficult," Ziering said. She and Kirby Dick together put up $75,000 of their own money. They also saved on costs. "A lot of the scenes he shot himself," Ziering said. "We went around ourselves, just the two of us, no crew." Given their résumé, it should have been easier. By the time they started raising funds for the sexual abuse film, their documentaries had already appeared on the BBC and on HBO.

"So, we were a known entity, and we could not get anyone to fund this, left or right or center—any funders. So we did it ourselves, and then, very, very late in the game, PBS came in, thank God."

They also got a break when they pitched the film at a San Francisco gathering of independent filmmakers called Good Pitch. At that event, someone in the audience told them about a woman they needed to meet, who happened also to be in San Francisco. This was just before the renowned Sundance Film Festival, where they wanted to show the film, but they had very little money to fund it. So Ziering did not hesitate to seek out the woman they'd been told to meet. She found the woman, Regina Scully, at a fundraiser. Scully listened to her pitch and said: "Oh, my God, it was meant for us to meet. Sexual trauma is exactly my issue." Scully's family had experienced that trauma, and it had changed the trajectory of their lives. Scully said she'd be in Los Angeles soon and asked if they had any part of the film to show her. So they put together a brief trailer and met her in Beverly Hills. "She looked at the trailer, and she said, 'You're going to Sundance.' And she wrote us a check," Ziering said. "She's actually been a major funder ever since of all our projects. It's been an unbelievable, crazy happenstance, a fairy tale story."

The Invisible War made its debut at the Sundance Film Festival in January 2012. Those interviewed made clear the scope of the problem. Amy Herdy, author of *Betrayal in the Ranks,* a series in *The Denver Post* about sexual abuse, cites an old figure that 200,000 women have been sexually assaulted in the military. "If you take into account that women don't report because of the extreme retaliation, and that was more than a decade ago, I would say you could easily double that number, and it's probably somewhere near about half a million women have now been sexually assaulted in the US military."

Beyond merely talking about the macro situation, the film tells powerful micro stories that were difficult to ignore. The two women whose names became part of the title of two lawsuits that Susan Burke had filed against the government, *Cioca v. Rumsfeld* and *Klay v. Panetta*, played key roles in the film.

Kori Cioca, a young woman from Ohio, had wanted to join the navy, but she ran up against a one-year waiting list. The coast guard offered almost immediate enlistment. So she joined, expecting to help people, but got something else: the unwanted scorn and sexual attention of one of her supervisors at her station in Saginaw River, Michigan, where she was the only woman in her section.

At 4 feet 11 inches tall, Cioca was no match for the 6-feet-3-inch, 240-pound man looming above her in the chain of command, who began by disliking her intensely and publicly. Once, when she made a mistake in a knot-tying quiz, in front of others he called her a "stupid fucking female" and said she didn't belong in the military. When his harassment continued, including grabbing her buttocks, she complained to his higher-ups in the chain of command. But she said some of them were his drinking buddies. That complaint brought no results, and the harassment continued and increased.

Her supervisor would leave voice mails threatening her life. He'd break into her room at night and masturbate in front of her. She began keeping a knife under her pillow. Once, as she bent down to pick up trash, he jammed his groin into her rear. She and a witness went to her commander, and she requested a transfer. The only result: further threats. Toward the end of 2005, he broke into her room, tried to get her to touch his erect penis, and when she screamed, he hit her hard in the face, propelling her across the room and into a wall. Again, she reported the incident to her chain of command, with witnesses. That did not help. Two weeks after the supervisor had hit her in the jaw, he raped her. The documentary shows Cioca's long, frustrating efforts to get the Veterans Administration to deal with the lasting damage to her jaw.

Another horrifying story in the film involved Lt. Ariana Klay. She recalled being impressed with the marines as a young girl and seeing a marine lieutenant colonel running laps around the high school track. "He said, 'You'd be perfect for the Marine Corps, because you're really fit and smart, and that's what the Marine Corps needs,'" Klay recalled. "The professionalism, the camaraderie, everything about it, inspired me."

So she entered and excelled at the United States Naval Academy. As a young marine officer, she was deployed to Iraq from 2008 to 2009. She was so impressive that her commanding officer recommended her for an assignment at Marine Barracks, Washington, DC. This was an elite post: guarding the White House, marching with the silent drill team, protecting dignitaries. "I was excited," Klay said. "It was the tip of the spear, as far as the Marine Corps was concerned."

But she quickly learned that this dream assignment had frightening nightmare elements. As Klay recalled it, in her first conversation with one senior officer at the barracks, he told her, "Female marines here are nothing but objects for the marines to fuck." She discovered that the barracks had a mandatory partying and drinking culture. Women marines had no choice but to down shots of liquor on command. In August 2010, the senior officer's warning about the purpose of female marines became vividly real for Klay. A senior officer and his friend raped her.

"The actions of my seniors, both in the assault and in the ensuing investigations, have really destroyed me," she said, tearfully. "I think the thing that makes me the most angry is not even the rape in itself. It's the commanders that were complicit in covering up everything that happened." The betrayal is even worse, one psychiatrist said in *The Invisible War*, because a military unit is supposed to be a band of brothers—and sisters—but for the canny abuser, the military is "a target-rich environment for predators." Sexual abuse in that band-of-brothers-and-sisters context is very much like incest.

Suffering deeply from her experience, Ariana Klay remembered seeing a high school-age girl running along the road wearing a Marine Corps T-shirt. "I thought that, if she joins, then she's going to have to accept rape and destruction of her life," Klay said, fighting back tears. "In good faith, I cannot recommend anybody to join, with the way the organization is set up now. I would not wish that on anyone."

The film powerfully shows the post-rape struggles of Cioca, Klay, and others. Cioca speaks about contemplating suicide. Klay's husband, Ben, also a former marine officer, weeps as he tells of using one hand to call the police and the other to keep his wife from committing suicide. They obviously both believed in the Marine Corps as a valid expression of loyalty to country, and they both suffered immensely when that institution did nothing to help Ariana. But neither Cioca nor Klay quit. They joined and became the very public faces of Burke's lawsuits on behalf of sexual abuse survivors.

In the months after its appearance at the Sundance Film Festival at the start of 2012, the film had more than 100 private screenings. "But perhaps the most important was for an audience of one," Rebecca Keegan wrote in the *Los Angeles Times* in June 2012, just before the film was to open in theaters. "In April, U.S. Secretary of Defense Leon E. Panetta watched a DVD of the film on a plane. Two days later, he held a news conference to announce new rules on how the Pentagon would handle sex crimes. Most dramatically, he said that the military would move responsibility for handling sexual assault complaints higher in the chain of command so that victims are not in a position of reporting crimes to a direct commander (who may be a friend of the perpetrator, or may even be the perpetrator)."

But moving the prosecution decision higher in the chain of command fell far short of the more sweeping reform of moving that decision out of the chain of command entirely. Putting the prosecution of sexual abuse in the hands of trained military attorneys and taking it away from unit commanders—whose training has focused predominantly on killing large numbers of "enemy" people—is a heavy legislative lift. In the yearslong effort to enact that legislation, *The Invisible War* played an important early role, helping to energize Sen. Kirsten Gillibrand's dogged pursuit of the needed reform, despite the obstacles. Kirby Dick, Amy Ziering's co-owner at Chain Camera Pictures, described her role as pivotal.

"Amy was really brilliant at handling the interacting with the Defense Department, interacting with Congress," Dick said. "Kirsten Gillibrand: Without her, this would not have happened. But I think without Amy, it's possible Kirsten Gillibrand wouldn't have happened."

Ziering in turn credited Nicole Boxer, one of the executive producers on the film, for bringing *The Invisible War* to the attention of a powerful voice in Congress: her mother, Barbara Boxer, who served as a Democratic senator from California until Kamala Harris succeeded her 2017. Gillibrand also viewed the film and began to take action. "Her chief of staff reached out to us, Jess Fassler, and said, 'When are you next in DC? She wants to meet with you,'" Ziering recalled.

Though she was happy to meet with Gillibrand, Ziering brought to that meeting a less-than-glowing image of politicians. Her only real contact with that tribe had been at glitzy Los Angeles fundraisers, which had shaped her view of public officials: not deep, sophisticated, and intelligent, but reliably shallow. Looking back now, Ziering recalls heading into that meeting with "stupid prejudices" and stereotypes, not knowing exactly what to expect. But Gillibrand quickly exceeded her expectations.

"I was blown away," Ziering said. Gillibrand suggested that they have dinner, and the senator chose a plain, serve-yourself venue—not one of Washington's high-end restaurants. Like everyone else in the restaurant, Gillibrand fetched her own food, seeming far less interested in cuisine than in learning more about the sexual abuse issue. She got right down to business, without a trace of introductory small talk.

"It was like, 'We've got an hour. Download everything I need to know about this issue,'" Ziering recalled. "She had the right questions. We answered everything. 'What do I do? Who do we need to leverage? What's the issue? What did you find the answers are?' It was incredible, and very to the point…. There was no quid pro quo, either. It was not like, 'I'm coming out to LA, can you host a fundraiser?' which, from all my stupid prejudices, I had expected. So, no, she was completely honest, completely no-nonsense."

Beyond meeting with Gillibrand, Ziering did some of her own lobbying with members of Congress but did not find a reception nearly as laser-focused and accepting as the New Yorker's. To Ziering, the Pentagon liaison staff in the Capitol had far too much influence on the thinking of lawmakers. "So, with those whispers in these senators' ears, it was hard sometimes to get traction," Ziering said. "They had a lot of their pushback talking points. 'Don't worry. We got this. Don't worry. You can't mess with the chain of command. This isn't as big a problem.'"

But Gillibrand kept at it, undeterred by the skepticism of her colleagues and their willingness to take the word of the military. "She's the real deal," Ziering said. "I was super impressed. Without her, this would have languished." Gillibrand's attitude, Ziering recalled, was simple and unrelenting: " 'I am in. This is outrageous. Let's do this.'"

Don Christensen found himself similarly impressed. "When I made the decision to leave the air force and come to Protect Our Defenders, that is when I had the opportunity to actually meet her and talk with her, and have talked with her a lot since then," he said. "I can say that this is something she is a hundred percent committed to. I know that she has other issues that she's concerned about, but I would say this is her signature issue, to try to reform this. She has worked tirelessly to get other senators."

Along the way, obstacles arose not only from Republicans, but even from her own party. Sen. Claire McCaskill, a Democrat from Missouri, had her own approach, one that Christensen described as "around the edges" reform.

It nibbled delicately at the problem but left the prosecution decision in the hands of commanders.

"I think part of it was—I'm just guessing—she knew she had an upcoming Senate race in a more conservative state, and I think she thought she was walking a tightrope between wanting reform and also wanting to appear like she didn't go against the military," Christensen said. McCaskill ran for re-election in 2018, lost to Republican Josh Hawley, and became a political commentator on progressive-leaning MSNBC. "She did a lot of good stuff, but this is very frustrating because she gave top cover to those in 2013 who were opposing reform, because they could say, 'Well, Claire is a former prosecutor, and so we're going to follow her.' I think if she had followed Gillibrand and aligned with that, this would have passed seven years ago."

Christensen rendered that judgment in late 2020. A few months later, in March 2021, he appeared before Gillibrand's subcommittee of the Senate Armed Services Committee. "There are about 14,500 commanders in the Department of Defense, but the ability to send (or refer) a case to a court-martial is vested in only a tiny fraction of commanders known as convening authorities," Christensen said, following with a statistical analysis of how many commanders have jurisdiction over different levels of courts-martial. "Thus, of the 14,500 commanders, only a little over 3 percent actually send cases to either a special or general court each year. The vast majority of commanders do their jobs with absolutely no authority to court-martial their troops."

In other words, what we have is a clear mismatch between the ongoing scourge of sexual abuse and the inability—and, too often, unwillingness—of commanders to use the Uniform Code of Military Justice to solve the problem.

One horrendous case brought intense attention to the failure of commanders to halt the abuse, and it helped persuade lawmakers that waiting for commanders to solve the problem was just not going to work. It was the murder of army Specialist Vanessa Guillén by another soldier at Fort Hood, Texas. Guillén had told family and friends that she had been sexually harassed. An independent civilian review commission found that the command climate at Ford Hood allowed a "permissive environment for sexual assault and sexual harassment." In the aftermath, the army either suspended or relieved of their positions 14 leaders. Rep. Jackie Speier (D-California), who has been advocating reform as persistently as Gillibrand, called her bill the I Am Vanessa Guillén Act.

Over the years, unit commanders and the stars-on-their-shoulders generals above them have routinely opposed any serious steps to remove that prosecution decision on sexual abuse from the chain of command and put it in the hands of trained military attorneys outside the chain of command. But their obstruction was a poor opponent for Gillibrand's persistence—and the growing impatience of senators with the military's pallid response, especially after the Guillén case.

Just a month after Christensen's testimony before Gillibrand's subcommittee, he stood with her and a startlingly bipartisan group of senators at a Capitol press conference to announce landmarks in the drive for reform. One was a change in the bill. Iowa Republican Sen. Joni Ernst, both an Iraq and Afghanistan combat veteran and a victim of sexual assault in college, had suggested greater emphasis on training and prevention, and Gillibrand had agreed. The amended legislation was dubbed the Military Justice Improvement and Increasing Prevention Act. It honored Gillibrand's primary goal: taking prosecution decisions for major felonies, including sexual assault and others, out of the chain of command. It also added measures such as making training in sexual abuse issues a condition for promotion and strengthening physical security at military installations.

"From 2004 to 2019, Congress enacted 249 statutory requirements related to sexual assault response and prevention," Ernst said at the press conference. "But only nine percent of those were focused on prevention. The new bill increases prevention-focused training and education from the very highest levels to the lowest cadets in our academies and ROTC programs, officers and enlisted."

In joining as a cosponsor of Gillibrand's bill, Ernst became part of a filibuster-proof list of more than 60 cosponsors—a truly amazing display of bipartisanship in a time of bitter political warfare and multiple presidential impeachments. Even Ted Cruz, the fiercely partisan, widely loathed Texas Republican, spoke firmly in support. "This is a bill whose time has come," Cruz said. "None of our daughters and sons should face the risk of assault from their fellow service men and women. It is horrific. It is unacceptable that sexual assault is as prevalent as it is today in the military."

The senators who spoke at the event talked repeatedly about Gillibrand's tirelessness and relentlessness. She justifiably reaped widespread praise for building such across-the-board support for the bill. But even the impressive list of cosponsors didn't entirely bulletproof the reform. It ran into static in the Senate Armed Services Committee from both the Democratic chair, Jack Reed of Rhode Island, and the Republican ranking minority member, James Inhofe of Oklahoma, who shared a bipartisan deference to the military and resisted Gillibrand's efforts to get a quick floor vote on the bill.

Perhaps Inhofe's greatest moment of fame had occurred in 2015, when he brought to the Senate floor a snowball fashioned from snow just outside the Capitol, his idea of proof that global warming is not really happening. During the struggle over the Gillibrand bill, Inhofe again became something of a comedic figure. Reporting on that issue in the *New York Times*, Jennifer Steinhauer quoted him: "Those of us in the military have very strong feelings about the role of the commander." In a deft swipe at his warrior credentials, Steinhauer added, "he said, referring to his past life as a private first class."

The committee chairman, Reed, another supporter of the prerogatives of commanders, also liked to talk about his military experience. "He always harkens back to his days as a captain in the army," Christensen said. "It has nothing really to do with prosecuting cases, but he always talks about when he was a captain in the army, and has a huge deference to generals and admirals."

In the summer of 2021, the Pentagon announced a four-tier system for removing prosecution decisions from the chain of command. But Gillibrand and others continued to push to enact that reform into statute as the process of adopting the annual National Defense Authorization Act (NDAA) continued.

It came to a head on the floor of Senate on December 8, 2021, when Gillibrand rose to ask for an up-or-down vote on her reform bill, as she had done more than 20 times since May 24. That request requires unanimous consent. So it only takes one senator's objection to block a vote on the stand-alone bill, and some senator was always willing to object. So she had to hope that the NDAA would include the language of her bill.

"The Military Justice Improvement and Increasing Prevention Act was included in the Senate Armed Services NDAA bill and passed out of committee 23 to 3," she said on the floor. "That is a pretty decisive vote. But, despite all of the claims that we follow regular procedure and everyone's voices would be heard, when the doors closed for conference, the story changed. Our votes were not respected. Our voices were silenced. Those promises were broken. The House and Senate Armed Services leadership gutted our bipartisan military justice reforms, stripped them from the NDAA and did a disservice to our service members and our democracy. Committee leadership has ignored the will of a filibuster-proof majority in the Senate and a majority of the House in order to do the bidding of the Pentagon.... Despite claims otherwise, the NDAA does *not* remove sex crimes from the chain of command, because the commander remains the convening authority, a central role to the military justice system. Every single court-martial will still begin with the words 'This court-martial was convened by order of the commander.' Commanders can still pick the jury, select the witnesses, and allow service members accused of crimes the option of separation from service instead of facing a court-martial—a total denial of justice."

A week later, on December 15, the Senate voted overwhelmingly to pass the NDAA, but Gillibrand voted nay. The senior senator from New York, Senate Majority Leader Charles Schumer, voted yea. So did 87 other senators. Though Gillibrand did put out a statement about some of the "victories" and "several positive steps" in the huge bill, she clearly was not happy with the outcome. "I will never stop fighting until our service members have a system they can trust and is worthy of their sacrifice."

Similarly, Don Christensen's statement on the final bill pointed out both the gains and the shortcomings of the NDAA's reforms on sexual abuse, compared with the Gillibrand bill that he supported. "Empowering independent military prosecutors is key to tackling the military's sexual assault crisis, and it's also key to boosting military readiness and retention," Christensen's statement said. "If you care about the health and well-being of those who serve our nation and the military as a whole, then today's reforms—which also include significant sentencing reform, enhanced victim's rights, and the criminalization of sexual harassment—are a big win. But there is much more work to be done. Because commanders retain convening authority, they will still wield influence over the process by selecting court-members, approving or denying immunity requests, and the hiring of expert witnesses and consultants." And, as Gillibrand had said a week earlier on the Senate floor, commanders can simply let the accused sexual abuser leave the military, rather than face a court-martial.

Gillibrand's bill had envisioned trained military prosecutors taking over the process completely for all serious crimes, but the NDAA reforms did not include all felonies. The law did remove military commanders from prosecution decisions for 11 crimes, including rape, sexual assault, murder, manslaughter and kidnapping—"special victims" crimes—but left commanders with authority to prosecute or not prosecute for other felonies.

Early in his term, Defense Secretary Lloyd Austin had made addressing sexual abuse a high priority, and in February 2021 he appointed an independent review commission to make recommendations. Asked about Austin's commitment to the issue, Christensen said: "We did get major reforms. So, when it came to sex offenses, he was consistent with his word." Though the scope of Austin's review commission was limited to the special victims crimes, Christensen's conversations with commission members left him convinced that "if they would have been allowed to look at other crimes, they would have been broader in their recommendations, more akin to Gillibrand's legislation." Still, he remained hopeful that Congress may do more than this NDAA had done. "This covers 60 to 70 percent of the felony cases now," Christensen said. "Why not just include the rest of them?"

As to empowering trained military prosecutors, the NDAA for fiscal year 2022 did that to some extent. All of the military branches have attorneys, generally called JAGs, an acronym for Judge Advocate General's Corps. The NDAA bill changed their structure. "It's a hybrid," Christensen said. It creates a special trial counsel office in each branch of the military, reporting directly to the secretary of each branch—not to unit commanders or to the Judge Advocate General. On the 11 crimes included in the NDAA, the special trial counsels would decide whether or not to prosecute. "All the JAGs will come from current JAGs," Christensen explained. "But rather than having the thousands of JAGs that are now involved in this, you'll have a smaller cadre of JAGs that hopefully are specializing in it and have the experience to be making the right decisions." Christensen said that Protect Our Defenders would be monitoring the appointments to these high-level special trial counsel offices. "So much of it's going to depend on who they select."

No matter how good those appointments may be, a giant question faced the trained prosecutors: What happens if they decide to prosecute a sexual abuse perpetrator, but the convening authority, the commander, decides simply not to convene a court-martial to try the case? The answer to that question remained unknown after passage of the NDAA for fiscal year 2022, Christensen said. Even with prosecution decisions in the hands of trained military lawyers, even if commanders go along, there is no guarantee that the plague of sexual abuse will disappear. The prosecution may be highly professional, but the mere existence of prosecution confirms that the problem is still there. As Joni Ernst said at the press conference with Gillibrand on the revised bill, "By the time we have a survivor and a perpetrator, we have failed."

A few months after Congress passed the National Defense Authorization Act for Fiscal Year 2022, with the watered-down Gillibrand reforms, the military itself offered evidence that the scourge wasn't going away. In the summer of 2022, the Pentagon issued the Fiscal Year 2021 Annual Report on Sexual Assault in the Military. Far from showing progress, that report documented the highest-ever level of the problem: 36,000 members of the military reported some form of unwanted sexual contact.

Given that staggering number, military brass have to face the reality that something about the military itself makes sexual abuse possible—even inevitable. Call it toxic masculinity. If you don't think that phenomenon exists, just listen to the chorus of right-wing, never-wore-combat-boots elected officials and cable television pundits, like Tucker Carlson, expressing existential angst about the feminization of the military. That phrase produces millions of Google hits, a seat-of-the-pants hint that people are worried about it. And there's ample evidence that masculinity lies at the heart of the military—not just in America, but even in Canada, our neighbor to the north, often stereotyped as being reliably, even excessively polite.

An insight into the universality of this bad-boy behavior comes from the work of folklorist Carol Burke. In the late 1980s and early 1990s, while a civilian professor at the United States Naval Academy, she was working on a book about women in prison, an institution, like the military, where those in charge have absolute power over those below them. Seeing that similarity, she began to research the military culture. The result was *Camp All-American, Hanoi Jane, and the High-and-Tight: Gender, Folklore, and Changing Military*

Culture. At the start of a chapter called "Sex, GIs, and Videotape," she describes how Canadian paratroopers engage in a disgusting boys-will-be-boys ritual. Keep in mind that when paratroopers jump out of perfectly good airplanes, defying the laws of gravity and common sense, a key force impelling many of them is not intelligence but the need to prove masculinity by doing something that looks brave.

"Twenty-three Canadian Airborne soldiers were lined up in a row, made to drink beer until they were drunk and to chew soft bread rolled up with chewing tobacco," Burke wrote. "The first to vomit was required to urinate on the masticated wad and put it back in his mouth before he passed it on to the next soldier. One soldier struggled to perform pushups in excrement while another urinated on him. A couple of soldiers smeared feces on the face of the one black soldier in the unit, a practice known within the Canadian military as 'bearding.' He was also led around by a leash while he crawled on all fours. On his back in camouflage paint was inscribed 'I love the KKK.' An onlooker shouted, 'We're not racist—we just don't want niggers in the Airborne.' Soldiers urinated and defecated on one another, simulated sodomy and masturbation, all in broad daylight, all under the watchful eyes of officers and in front of the lens of a video recorder."

Even without women among them, male members of the military are capable of vile sexual behavior toward one another. A professor at the United States Naval Academy told political scientist Aaron Belkin, whose work focuses on sexuality in the military, that male midshipmen rape each other regularly. Belkin assumed that the professor was speaking metaphorically, but she insisted that she meant it literally. His years of studying the academy and the military in general eventually led Belkin to this conclusion: The Naval Academy professor hadn't been kidding. Males in the military indeed "penetrated each other's bodies" with metronomic regularity—and some have suggested that this penetration constitutes a particularly revolting form of male bonding.

"They forced broom handles, fingers and penises into each other's anuses," Belkin wrote in his 2012 book, *Bring Me Men: Military Masculinity and the Benign Façade of American Empire*. "They stuck pins into flesh and bones. They vomited into one another's mouths and forced rotten food down each other's throats. They inserted tubes into each other's anal cavities and then pumped grease through the tubes."

In the minds of many male soldiers, the arrival of larger numbers of women in the military in recent years challenged their own sense of masculinity. If women could perform some of their jobs—eventually, even join them in combat—men could perceive women as feminizing the military and threatening their masculinity. As British psychologist Norman F. Dixon described in his book *On the Psychology of Military Incompetence*, proving masculinity is for many men the whole point of joining the military in the first place.

"The argument is simply that a proportion of those youths who opt for a career in the armed services do so out of an underlying fear of being unmanly," Dixon wrote. "Such individuals will be attracted to organizations which set upon them the seal of masculinity. By being admitted to a society of men bent upon the most primitive manifestations of maleness—violence and aggression—the individual achieves the reassurance he requires."

Even in studying America's hundreds of overseas bases, David Vine, an anthropologist at American University in Washington, DC, could not avoid the question of sex. Around those bases, prostitution flourishes—as it does around military bases inside the United States. "Throughout history, women's sex work has been used to help make male troops happy—or at least happy enough to keep working for the military," Vine wrote in his book *Base Nation: How U.S. Military Bases Abroad Harm America and the World.*

In his analysis, Vine paraphrased the work of political scientist Cynthia Enloe, who wrote about the ways that this pervasive, institutionalized prostitution shapes the behavior of male soldiers. "It trains men to believe that using the sexual services of women is part of what it means to be a soldier and part of what it means to be a man," Vine wrote. "It helps shape what Enloe and others have called a 'militarized masculinity,' involving feelings of power and superiority over women. And a willingness to inflict violence on anyone deemed inferior."

Add to that training the growing presence of women in the military, working right next to them and all around them, and men have acted out, not merely out of lust, but out of anger at the feminization of the military and the presence of soldiers they consider inferior because they are women. That toxic formula contributes to the ongoing problem of sexual abuse and sexual harassment that surrounds women in uniform.

"When they run obstacle courses, men line up to ogle their bodies," Helen Benedict wrote in *The Lonely Soldier*. "When they walk into the food hall, hundreds of eyes undress them. When they reach or bend to pick up something, men whistle, groan, and stare. This can go on every hour of every day and creates an excruciating sense of oppression that few men ever experience."

Benedict's book also focused on the debased, dismissive, misogynistic language that women in the military must hear daily: "Even with a force that now includes women, gays, and lesbians, and rules that now prohibit drill instructors from using racial epithets and curses, instructors still denigrate recruits with words like pussy, girl, bitch, lady, dyke, faggot, and fairy; the everyday speech of ordinary soldiers is still riddled with sexist and homophobic insults; and soldiers still openly peruse pornography that humiliates women and sing the misogynist songs that have been around for decades: 'This is my rifle, this is my gun [penis]; this is for killing, this is for fun.'"

This is true through throughout the military, but there are different levels from branch to branch. "The Marine Corps is the worst, when it comes to rape, sex assault, and sexual harassment," Don Christensen said. Carol Burke, who studied the military deeply, concurred, citing the macho marine culture. "There are great marines, and a lot of them are friends of mine," Carol Burke said. "But I think that, with young recruits who are attracted to the Marine Corps, enlisted guys, some of them are attracted because it's the most hyper-masculine branch of the service."

The military has taken some bureaucratic steps to address the issue, at least optically. In February 2004, then-Secretary of Defense Donald Rumsfeld directed a task force to review the sexual abuse problem. That April, the task force issued its report, calling for the establishment of a "single point of accountability" in the Pentagon for sexual abuse. In 2005, the Department of Defense established the Sexual Assault Prevention and Response Office (SAPRO). Below the department level, the Sexual Assault Response Coordinator (SARC) is the person designated to deal with the issue. But the abuse continued, and the failure of commanders to solve the problem brought about the congressional miracle of more than 60 Senate cosponsors on Gillibrand's bill.

No matter how many offices and acronyms they create, the military doesn't much like talking about this scourge in its midst. One example: When

Carol Burke taught as a civilian at the Naval Academy, she did what folklorists do: collecting examples of the prevailing culture. That included the words of marching chants. She vividly recalls one day in her first semester at Annapolis hearing a group of wannabe marines running and chanting repeatedly, "Rape, maim, kill babies, hooah!" When she told her students of her shock, one said, "Oh, ma'am, after a couple of weeks, you don't really hear the words that they're saying anymore." But she began collecting those words anyway.

Once the midshipmen learned what Burke was up to, they volunteered to give her some of those words. The faculty members also contributed. "So, even my military colleagues, when they found out I was working on this, they would bring me things—even these guys in uniform," Burke said. "They thought it was so cute that folklorists have the term *latrinalia* to describe graffiti in johns."

Anyone who has been in the military after World War II can attest to the hyper sexuality and violence built into those lyrics. "Such chants celebrate the need to repudiate pleasures associated with a recruit's civilian past and to embrace a martial future (or, more literally, to leave your girl and love your rifle)," Burke wrote.

After she had left the Naval Academy and was working at Johns Hopkins University, Burke published an article in *The New Republic* about the marching chants, before her book came out. The navy made it pretty clear that it didn't like the public knowing the exact words of those chants. The magazine sent the piece to Patricia Schroeder, then an immensely quotable Democratic member of Congress from Colorado, who coined the phrase "Teflon president" to describe Ronald Reagan. "She called up the secretary of the navy, just left a message and said, 'If what Burke says in this is true, then we know where Tailhook came from,'" Burke recalled.

Something upset the navy, whether it was Schroeder's reference to the infamous 1991 navy sex scandal, or simply the article's honest depiction of the sexually explicit and gruesomely violent words of the chants. "They started a whole investigation of me, interviewing my friends at the academy," Burke said. "This was coming from the secretary of the navy. He called. He wanted to talk to the president of Hopkins. He was away, and so he talked to the provost. This guy called me up, and he was really upset, and he said, 'Carol, we've just gotten this call.' He said to me, 'Do you realize how many millions of dollars in indirect costs we get from the navy?' One of the research centers of Hopkins is the applied physics laboratory, and that's where the Tomahawk [cruise missile] was developed, things like that, for the navy. I only learned afterwards that a lot of their indirect costs came and funded our library on the main campus."

The book came out in 2004, the same year as the scandal of sexualized torture of prisoners at Abu Ghraib prison in Iraq at the hands of American soldiers, male and female. Burke found herself being interviewed about Abu Ghraib and expressing no surprise, given what she had learned and written about sexualized initiation rites in the military. On radio shows, for her honesty, she found herself called a "member of the feminarchy" and part of a "cabal seeking to destroy the military." Both accusations are crude, fevered echoes of right-wing fears about feminization of the military.

In her book, Burke even finds a scriptural antecedent of the hostility that women face every day in the military. "Even when women demonstrate their strength, their stamina, and their battlefield expertise, as they do in field training exercises, detractors, pressed to the point where they confess their religious dread, have recourse to an argument drawn from Leviticus: women are unfit to serve in combat because they menstruate," Burke wrote. "If soldiers can only attest to their manhood in battle, according to the myth propagated by the Marine Corps and its admirers, then mixing masculine blood spent in proving one's manhood with feminine blood has the force of a taboo."

With this deep, abiding fear and loathing of women, plus lust, it is fair to wonder whether even Gillibrand's reform would be enough to control this epidemic of sexual abuse. Too many women have suffered already, and hundreds of thousands who have survived the abuse are still living with its imprint on their lives. That includes such women as Kori Cioca, Ariana Klay, and others who appear in *The Invisible War*. It also includes Bekah Havrilla. Her name appears in the end credits of the film as one of the veterans who helped, but she did not appear in the film itself. What happened to her in Afghanistan and at Fort Leonard Wood is not something she dwells on daily. She is too busy with the hard, day-in-day-out work of healing—herself and others.

She left the army with PTSD, which accounts in large part for the finding by the Department of Veterans Affairs that she is 80 percent disabled. Havrilla believes her PTSD arose both from her experience in combat and from the rape. "The way that I've always viewed that is that combat trauma, while there were some incidents that were very traumatic, those are part of the job," Havrilla said. "I chose to do that job." But she did not choose to be sexually assaulted by another soldier or to experience the betrayal that left her feeling "completely unsupported, not having anywhere to turn," not getting any help from the people above her in the chain of command who were supposed to have her back. "I think those two things compounded themselves."

With the formal diagnosis of PTSD, she has gone through a variety of treatment approaches, including medication and talk therapy. "I've jumped through all of the hoops." Those hoops have included interaction with multiple VA hospitals, where she encountered and learned to disdain what she sees as the VA's overreliance on pharmacological solutions. "That's one of my frustrations with our society and culture: 'Here, take a pill, and it will fix everything for you.' I'm like, 'No, healing is a process, it takes time. It's really hard. And you have to be committed to it, or you won't do it.'"

Havrilla's approach to healing is far from pharmacological. She has read widely on PTSD, including two books by Laurence Gonzales, *Deep Survival: Who Lives, Who Dies, and Why* and the sequel, *Surviving Survival: The Art and Science of Resilience*. "His was the first book that I read about PTSD and traumatic incidents that actually made sense to me on a scientific, neurological level," she said. "He talks about it from a very neurological perspective in a lot of ways, of how the brain is actually physically rewired when you go through these experiences." So she focuses on healing that is "somatically informed, neurobiological," she works on "how to recreate and dismantle neurological systems that are formed in the process of trauma," and she depends on "breath work, meditation." This former army sergeant, who "blew shit up" in combat, can poke a little fun at herself for so easily falling into what could sound to some like New Age terminology. "I've definitely gone down the woo-woo hole a little bit," she said. "But I still approach things from a very logical, scientific perspective."

She completed her higher education, earning a bachelor's degree from Drury University in Missouri. Her senior thesis at Drury focused on sexual violence, with an emphasis on the military. Then she earned a master's degree in international affairs from The New School in New York City. Despite the trauma of combat and sexual assault, her original plan when she enlisted, to get her education paid for, has worked. Two VA education programs, the Montgomery G.I. Bill and the Post-9/11 G.I. Bill, covered her undergraduate costs. And the VA's Yellow Ribbon Program paid for her graduate school. Now she is a licensed massage therapist in eastern Tennessee.

"It is definitely a journey in progress," Havrilla said. "But it feels like the one I'm supposed to be on. There's a lot of people out there that want what I have to offer, and there's a lot of people that relate to me, because of what I've been through." What she went through in the army and soon after her discharge made her feisty, even angry, back then. She is still direct and assertive, even aggressive, when the situation calls for it. Situations do come up that can trigger her post-traumatic stress. But she is doing the healing work that she needs to do, having survived what she survived.

"I don't even like the term 'survivor' anymore," she said. "Yes, I was a victim of something, but I'm not any longer, and I'm going to start surviving. There's also a point where surviving isn't what we need to be doing either. We need to start trying to thrive."

As we talked, I commented that it's difficult to believe that the man who raped her is thriving as well as she is. But she has read so much about toxic masculinity in the military that she has come to understand the forces that shaped him and led him to feel he could do what he did. "When I look at him, I harbor a lot less ill will toward him than I do my commander and my team leaders," Havrilla said. "I don't know that he thought he was doing anything that horrible. He just wanted something at the time, and what does the military, hyper-masculine mentality teach boys? 'Just take what you want.' I have more of a peace, I guess, about that situation than I do about a commander that told me, the day I walked in the unit, that he didn't give a fuck about me and what happened to me, because I was a woman—and the team leaders that constantly harassed me and abused me and assaulted me, because they could. That's the stuff I still struggle with."

And that chain of command, so unsupportive of those who suffer military sexual assault, has been the persistent roadblock to reform for much too long. The power of the Pentagon became clear with the December 2021 passage of the National Defense Authorization Act, which contained some elements of reform but still left commanders with significant control over the process. But

Gillibrand continued to push for full reform. A year later, Congress passed the NDAA for fiscal year 2023, which included this key element: removing from military commanders prosecutorial authority over a list of offenses that include sexual abuse. "This completes the major reform initially encompassed in Senator Gillibrand's Military Justice Improvement Act," said Christensen, who had joined Protect Our Defenders to enact that reform and left the organization soon after he had been part of finally accomplishing that historic mission. "The next stage is to ensure the military faithfully follows the congressional mandates."

It had been a long struggle for Gillibrand and Speier in Congress, and Christensen and others outside Congress, to bring meaningful reform to the way the military handles sexual abuse in its ranks. For all the years before that reform finally made its way through Congress, far too many of those who volunteered for the military had suffered sexual harassment, sexual abuse, and retaliation—but had seen little real justice. That was comprehensively, irredeemably wrong. Now that the statutory framework for fairer treatment of victims is in place, it remains to be seen whether that will be enough, or whether the toxic masculinity deeply rooted in the military will continue to add to the already-too-large list of victims. As Sen. Joni Ernst said in her 2021 press conference with Gillibrand, "By the time we have a survivor and a perpetrator, we have failed."

Chapter 6
FINEST FIGHTING FORCE?

Unquestionably, the United States military is the best funded and best trained on the planet. It has routinely enjoyed the confidence of a higher percentage of Americans than major institutions such as the church, the Supreme Court, Congress, and newspapers. All politicians feel a bipartisan need to sing its praises, using superlatives like the one that former President Barack Obama employed in his final State of the Union address: "the finest fighting force in the history of the world." Vice President Kamala Harris used nearly identical phrasing in her commencement address at West Point in 2023. The sentiment even appeared on the olive drab-colored New Era cap that major-league ballplayers wore on Armed Forces Day 2023: "Our Nation's Finest."

Still, this nagging reality persists: The American military has not won a major war since 1945.

That assertion sounds almost heretical, as I learned when I mentioned it in a speech to a group of senior citizens, including veterans. One of them came up to me afterward and said, "What about Grenada?" That 1983 show of overwhelming force, unleashed for dubious reasons on a tiny Caribbean island, hardly counts as a major war. Nor does the 1989 invasion of Panama, to depose its dictator, Gen. Manuel Noriega. Longer, far more consequential post-World War II conflicts—Korea, Vietnam, Afghanistan, and Iraq—have not ended in anything remotely resembling unambiguous, parade-worthy victory. In a column about an imaginary commencement speech at the United States Air Force Academy, one of its former professors, retired Air Force Lt. Col. William Astore, wrote: "Since World War II began, the air forces of the

United States have killed millions of people around the world. And yet here's the strange thing: we can't even say that we've clearly won a war since the 'Greatest Generation' earned its wings in the 1930s and 1940s."

But why? For starters, you can blame a given failure to win on generals, as Daniel Bolger did in his book *Why We Lost: A General's Inside Account of the Iraq and Afghanistan Wars*. "I am a United States Army general, and I lost the Global War on Terrorism," Bolger wrote. "Time after time, despite the fact that I and my fellow generals saw it wasn't working, we failed to reconsider our basic assumptions. We failed to question our flawed understanding of our foe or ourselves. We simply asked for more time. Given enough months, then years, then decades—always just a few more, please—we trusted that our great men and women would pull it out. In the end, all the courage and skill in the world could not overcome ignorance and arrogance. As a general, I got it wrong. And I did so in the company of my peers."

Generally, questioning generals and their civilian leaders in the Department of Defense makes sense, as our recent history amply demonstrates. The Pentagon Papers, published by the *New York Times* in 1971, showed how much the defense establishment had lied about progress in Vietnam. More recently, Craig Whitlock of the *Washington Post* used the Freedom of Information Act and an aggressive legal struggle to acquire documents from the special inspector general for Afghanistan reconstruction. Those documents, which became known collectively as the Afghanistan Papers, included interviews and other items that showed the failures, mistakes, and misrepresentations by military and civilian leaders of the Afghanistan effort.

The military's inability to accomplish the mission in these wars is far less attributable to individual soldiers or units than to the mission itself, too often an elusive goal poorly conceived by politicians, with some help from generals who are anxious to please their civilian bosses. "We're trying to solve problems with military force that can't be solved with military force," said Lindsay Koshgarian, program director of the National Priorities Project at the Institute for Policy Studies. Katherine "Kat" Maier, an air force veteran from Kansas, summarized the forever-war situation in a memoir. "This isn't winning, no matter how many pretty bows we tie around it," Maier wrote. Later, she told me: "We're in unwinnable wars at this point. There's no metric for winning in these situations. I mean we're destabilizing an area, no matter what we do. We're trying to westernize places that might not necessarily need our influence."

Veterans of these wars often question whether the conflicts were really worth all the blood and tears that they cost. In a 2019 Pew Research report, 64 percent of Iraq veterans and 58 percent of Afghanistan veterans said that the war they had fought in was not worth it. A 2021 survey by Associated Press and NORC at the University of Chicago showed similar attitudes among the public at large, with 62 percent saying Afghanistan wasn't worth it, and 63 percent expressing the same view about Iraq. At the end of her 2006 book, *Love My Rifle More Than You: Young and Female in the U.S. Army,* Kayla Williams wrote: "What was it all about? Not having an answer for that makes it hard. Makes it feel dirty." When I asked her about that sentiment years later, her view was still bleak. "You know, the US going into Iraq did not increase stability," Williams said. "It did not reduce terrorism. I can no longer remember what the stated goals of our intervention were, but I don't know that we met them in any way that would make sense. And that's hard. The US does not have a great record of the aftermath of our intervention in other countries' affairs."

So the nation has a clear duty to steer clear of unwinnable wars, to prevent members of the military from dying on those futile missions or returning home from them mentally or physically scarred for life. America needs to do a wiser, more realistic job of picking its fights and rejecting the marginal and the impossible. Looking back on the current forever wars, the Quincy Institute for Responsible Statecraft issued *19 Years Later: How to Wind Down the War on Terror,* a 2020 report written by Steven Simon. At the core of its findings was this sober warning: "If the U.S. wants to avoid the tremendous toll of civilian death and injury and the expenditure of blood and treasure in response to a future terrorist attack on U.S. soil, it will first avoid large-scale expeditionary operations in failed or failing states with the professed aim of establishing a durable civil order."

Yes, the failure of the American military to win any real war after 1945 is primarily the fault of civilian leaders who ordered the armed forces to accomplish impossible missions. But the military itself is a flawed institution, marred by multiple problems. Chapter 2 examined one of those problems: the difficulty that recruiters have encountered in finding enough suitable recruits. Chapter 5 explored the scourge of sexual abuse in the ranks. This chapter looks at military incompetence. And it raises questions such as: Are we spending too much money on the military? Have we configured the armed forces the right way? Does the United States really need to station troops in about 750 overseas bases?

BOUNDLESS BILLIONS AND TRILLIONS

First, the spending. One striking figure, provided by the Costs of War Project at Brown University's Watson Institute for International and Public Affairs, is $8 trillion. That's the cost of the post-9/11 wars from FY 2001 to FY 2022. The Pentagon is a five-sided money pit, into which Congress regularly dumps even more billions than the president proposes. That bloated budget dwarfs the spending of other nations. In 2022, America was spending more on the military than the next nine nations combined, including Russia and China. But that staggering level of spending does not always ensure safety. A handful of zealots, armed only with boxcutters, were able to slaughter 3,000 Americans on 9/11, and all of the Pentagon's billions were unable to stop them. Writing in the *Nation*, William Hartung, the author of deeply researched, fiercely critical books on military spending, and a senior research fellow at the Quincy Institute, summed up the stubborn budget dominance of the military: "America has a national security problem. But it goes well beyond the challenges posed by Russia or China. The biggest threat is right here at home: the Pentagon's stranglehold on our national budget, alongside the woefully inadequate investments in addressing urgent, nonmilitary problems like climate change, pandemics, and racial and economic injustice."

One factor in that reality is a powerful force called political engineering. Take the F-35, a fighter jet designed to meet the needs of different branches of the armed forces. In a windfall for Lockheed Martin, the manufacturer, the Pentagon wants to spend $1.7 trillion to acquire 2,500 of these jets over the life of the program, despite a spotty performance record. Just one example: In the version designed for aircraft carrier landings, the plane's tail hook repeatedly failed to engage the arresting wire on the carrier deck. That required a redesign of the tail hook. In general, repairs to the aircraft took much longer than expected. But political engineering pretty much guarantees continued

Pentagon purchases of F-35s. Manufacturing of parts of the plane is spread through 350 congressional districts, which means jobs in those districts and reliable votes in Congress for funding the plane, no matter what its defects. It's a weapon so important to so many members of Congress that they formed the House F-35 Caucus to advocate for the ongoing flow of dollars to the manufacturer of the aircraft that I have dubbed The Little Plane That Can't.

To be fair, the F-35 is not the only military aircraft that too often can't. In November 2022, the Government Accountability Office (GAO) issued a report on the performance of 49 military aircraft, examining their mission-capable rate, defined as "the percentage of total time when the aircraft can fly and perform at least one mission." The GAO found that only four of these aircraft "met their annual mission capable goal in a majority of the years from fiscal years 2011 through 2021." In fact, 26 of these aircraft "did not meet their annual mission capable goal in any fiscal year." The Marine Corps version of the plane, the F-35B, met its mission-capable goal in zero out of nine years. Ironically, just a few weeks after that GAO report, an F-35B crashed during a vertical landing in Texas. The pilot ejected, and his parachute opened just before he hit the ground.

Even though other aircraft may underperform, for critics of weapons spending, the F-35 is the most frequent target—and for good reason. "The F-35 really is the biggest poster child for a program that's gone way over budget and has taken far longer than it was supposed to to be developed," Koshgarian said. The whole Transformer-like concept envisioned one basic fighter, built with varying configurations, to meet the needs of the different branches. "At least in hindsight, but probably at the time, it should have seemed like it was too good to be true," Koshgarian said. The manufacturer of the F-35, the subject of one of Hartung's books, *Prophets of War: Lockheed Martin and the Making of the Military-Industrial Complex*, is a powerful company. But it is not the only defense contractor to benefit from the congressional taste for ever-bigger military funding. Roughly half of the defense budget goes to corporations with chief executive officers who get paid millions of dollars a year—*not* to individual members of the armed forces, who too often end up needing food stamps to feed their families.

Of course, those huge corporations with impossibly wealthy executives also employ many thousands of people in jobs that pay reasonably well for middle-class families. That's another reason why cutting military spending is so difficult.

"It's the argument that 'I have to maintain the defense industry, because that's where the jobs are at,'" said Gregory Daddis, a West Point graduate, former tank platoon leader during Operation Desert Shield/Desert Storm in the Gulf War, and later, a history professor at West Point. At some point, if this nation ever does get around to making real cuts to defense spending, we'll need a conversation about "just transition." That's a concept that climate-change activists are grappling with: As the nation phases out fossil fuels for more renewable and less planet-heating energy sources, what happens to those who lose their jobs in the oil, gas, and coal industries? How can we help them transition to adequate new jobs? But the just-transition conversation for workers in the defense industry depends on a major change in public attitudes about military budgets. Right now, Daddis argues, Americans don't see this massive spending as really hurting anyone. So legislators don't yet feel sufficient constituent pressure to tackle significant cuts in the Pentagon's budget. "I think, until we get to that point, you're not going to have any discussions about making a just transition," Daddis said.

One argument that supporters of ever-higher military budgets make is that the nation needs to spend a given percentage of gross domestic product (GDP) on the military. Critics of the nation's bloated defense spending maintain that a percentage of the size of a nation's economy is a useless marker for deciding how much a nation needs to spend to defend itself. In any case, the United States is already near the top of that GDP pyramid. In the Stockholm International Peace Research Institute's 2022 list of defense spending by nations, the United States was spending 3.5 percent of its GDP on the war machine. Among the top 10, only Russia at 4.1 percent and Saudi Arabia at 6.6 percent were spending a higher percentage. On the Stockholm institute's list, the United States spent more than the next nine nations combined, including Russia and China.

Despite the ability of political engineering and pliant lawmakers to keep military spending high, some members of Congress have tried to lower it. Sen. Bernie Sanders (D-Vermont) is a prime example. So are Representatives Barbara Lee (D-California) and Mark Pocan (D-Wisconsin), who sponsored a bill called the People Over Pentagon Act of 2022, to cut defense spending by $100 billion in fiscal year 2023. In the annual wrangling over passage of the National Defense Authorization Act in the winter of 2022, however, efforts to trim the defense budget failed. It ended up at $857.9 billion, $45 billion more than what President Joseph R. Biden had originally requested. The $857.9 billion included $816.7 billion for the Department of Defense and $30.3 billion for national security programs in the Department of Energy. And Congress passed that huge authorization bill only a few weeks after the Pentagon admitted that it had failed for the fifth consecutive time to pass an audit of its spending.

In his blog, *Bracing Views*, William Astore offered a sweeping prescription for savings: "How about this as a start: that the production of F-35s—an overpriced 'Ferrari' of a fighter jet that's both too complex and remarkably successful as an underperformer—should be canceled (savings: as much as $1 trillion over time); that the much-touted new B-21 nuclear bomber isn't needed (savings: at least $200 billion) and neither is the new Sentinel Intercontinental Ballistic Missile (savings: another $200 billion and possibly the entire Earth from doomsday); that the KC-46 tanker is seriously flawed and should be canceled (savings: another $50 billion)," Astore wrote. "Now, tote it up. By canceling the F-35, the B-21, the Sentinel, and the KC-46, I singlehandedly saved the American taxpayer roughly $1.5 trillion without hurting America's national defense in the least."

Sadly, given the military-industrial complex that President Dwight D. Eisenhower warned us about as he left office, nothing even close to the cuts Astore suggested is likely to happen. Still, for those who monitor defense spending and argue for using a large part of that money for human needs, giving up the fight is not an option, and history provides some reason for optimism. "During the 1990s, there was a period of a few years of military budget cuts that were sort of the beginning of what people thought would be the peace dividend at the end of the Cold War," Lindsay Koshgarian said. "The military budget actually went down by about 25 percent over those few years. So it has happened before. And then, of course, you get into 9/11 and everything goes completely out of control, in terms of both the wars we start and what the budget looks like, which are directly connected." For her, the bottom line is this: "I definitely don't think it's hopeless."

AN EMPIRE OF BASES

Since World War II, the United States has created a vast array of permanent military bases in foreign countries. The public knows little about them, and you don't hear members of Congress or presidential candidates raising the issue. If people think about those bases at all, the fuzzily formed assumptions tend to run along these lines: America is the one indispensable nation, the great and noble protector of liberty, the global force for good. So why wouldn't any foreign country welcome the presence of well-trained American troops to defend that nation against possible aggression by big bullies such as China and Russia?

Though the issue has not risen to the level of broad public debate, academics and activists have urged a change in our policy on bases. One of those is David Vine, professor of political anthropology at American University in Washington, DC, and author of *Base Nation: How U.S. Military Bases Abroad Harm America and the World*. "Although few U.S. citizens realize it, we probably have more bases in other people's lands than any other people, nation, or empire in world history," Vine wrote. And he proposed a compelling thought exercise to put in perspective how unusual—even unique—this arrangement is. "For most in the United States, the idea of even the nicest, most benign foreign troops arriving with their tanks, planes, and high-powered weaponry and making themselves at home in our country—occupying and fencing off hundreds or thousands of acres of our land—is unthinkable.

Rafael Correa, the president of Ecuador, highlighted this rarely considered truth in 2009 when he refused to renew the lease for a US base in his country. Correa told reporters that he would approve the lease renewal on one condition: "They let us put a base in Miami—an Ecuadorian base. If there's no problem having foreign soldiers on a country's soil," Correa quipped, "surely they'll let us have an Ecuadorian base in the United States." Just try to imagine the cries of outrage, of betrayal, of surrender that the construction of this Ecuadorian base would elicit here, especially from those on the Right. How would Florida Gov. Ron DeSantis, for example, respond to the proposed Ecuadorian base?

The military justifies these bases as an essential element in its "forward strategy," a modern-day term of art that serves as an echo of Alexander Hamilton's dream of a standing army that would help the new nation to global dominance—in contrast to the fears of a standing army expressed by James Madison and others. This forward strategy does not come cheap. Vine estimates that it costs $10,000 to $20,000 more to station a member of the military in an overseas base than it does to maintain that same soldier in the United States. And what do all those bases cost? In his book, Vine offered an estimate of $71.8 billion a year, but added that the real number could be as high as $120 billion. That doesn't even take into account the loss to the United States economy. Dollars that members of the armed forces spend in bases in Germany or South Korea are dollars that they don't spend domestically in the American economy.

Those expensive bases didn't help much on September 11, 2001. In fact, one of the reasons that Osama bin Laden listed for the 9/11 attacks was the continuing presence of American troops after the 1991 Gulf War in Saudi Arabia, the location of two of Islam's holiest sites, Mecca and Medina. In 1998, bin Laden wrote that "for over seven years the United States has been occupying the lands of Islam in the holiest of places, the Arabian Peninsula, plundering its riches, dictating to its rulers, humiliating its people, terrorizing its neighbors, and turning its bases in the Peninsula into a spearhead through which to fight the neighboring Muslim peoples." Note his specific reference to "bases in the Peninsula."

In the immediate aftermath of the 9/11 attacks, it was stunning to hear the sudden repetition of the word "homeland," to describe the sudden realization by American military and civilian leaders that defense of the homeland should be a top priority. Secretary of State Colin Powell, a former chairman of the Joint Chiefs of Staff, told CNN, "It's going to require a greater emphasis on homeland defense, to defend ourselves against those who are still trying to get into our country to hurt us." And Paul Wolfowitz, deputy secretary of defense under President George W. Bush, talked about the administration's "initial plans for a sizable increase in the military that would be focused on defending the homeland." (Later, Wolfowitz became a major cheerleader for the Anglo-American invasion of Iraq, which turned out to be not at all focused on defending the homeland.) At the time when all this homeland talk was echoing throughout the nation, as we grieved for those killed on 9/11, my own reaction was essentially, "Well, duh!" Shouldn't defense of the homeland be the primary function of any military, rather than projection of force elsewhere in the world?

But that initial surge of emphasis on protecting the homeland has not exactly borne fruit. *19 Years Later*, a study by the Quincy Institute, said that the government had spent "roughly six times more" on waging counterinsurgency war than on homeland defense. With that continuing focus on what's happening outside the country, far more than on protecting the homeland, the nation still has hundreds of bases abroad. One factor in the persistence of those bases is the economic benefit to the host countries. The bases employ local citizens of the nation where they are located, and American troops spend a lot of money on the local economy. Catherine Lutz, cofounder of the Cost of War Project and editor of *The Bases of Empire: The Global Struggle against U.S. Military Posts*, cited one example of economic benefit when we spoke: "If it's in the interest of the Korean beef growers association to get a trade deal in exchange for these bases that lets them export their beef, well, there you go. That's what's going to happen."

As of mid-2022, the Republic of Korea was third among the nations with the largest number of American troops, behind Japan and Germany. In recent years, the alignment of bases in South Korea has slightly changed. My focus on South Korea as a prime example of US bases is understandable enough: In 1968 and early 1969, I was an intelligence officer in a nuclear-capable Honest John missile command at Camp Page, in Chuncheon. In 2005, Camp Page closed. That was one result of talks in Washington called the Future of the Alliance Policy Initiative, which produced the Land Partnership Plan for the return of American bases to South Korea. The closure of Camp Page, after some significant environmental cleanup, made that site part of a complex of theme parks, including one of the world's many Legoland resorts. But elsewhere in South Korea, bases have expanded.

"South Korea, of course, is a politically charged landscape," said Theodore Hughes of the Center for Korean Research at Columbia University. "So it is difficult to generalize about attitudes to the US bases. It is pretty clear, though, that generally Koreans have grown weary of the large bases that occupy space in urban areas. Thus the US pullout, for example, from Yongsan in Seoul. But accompanying base closures throughout South Korea has been the construction of new bases. Prominent among the new construction is the recently completed expansion of Camp Humphries, which I believe is now the largest overseas US base in the world. The Camp Humphries-Osan Air Base complex is a significant forward US presence. Recent construction on Jeju Island also will serve US military interests. In each case, locals who lost their land combined with progressive political and environmental groups to protest."

Dissatisfaction with the bases flows not only from lost land, but from incidents caused by members of the US military who live on those bases. Even as a mostly clueless young artillery officer in Korea, I understood this simple reality: Young Americans stationed far away from home can behave badly. In my training as a Cold War instructor, I learned of a violent incident in Turkey that became part of my please-behave-yourselves lecture to young troops before they left Camp Page for their first weekend pass in Chuncheon. It's not that young American soldiers are necessarily more obstreperous than soldiers of other nations. But soldiers of other nations don't have bases in America from which to go into town and cause trouble. In sharp contrast, more than 200,000 members of the American armed forces, stationed in that still-vast empire of bases, have ample opportunities to raise hell in the host nations. "Deadly accidents, violent crime, and local anger have been a constant almost everywhere there are bases," David Vine wrote in *Base Nation*. Bases abroad almost always generate protest against US forces.

One frequent accompaniment of American bases is prostitution. That includes sex-worker "camptowns" in South Korea near US installations. The feminist scholar Cynthia Enloe has written about the way this institutionalized sexuality helps create "militarized masculinity." That too often leads men to behave violently toward women, and it can create friction with outraged men of the host nation. In an interview with South Korean anthropologist Joowon Park, Vine learned that "frequent bar fights" arose in Seoul between American soldiers and local men, and that the root cause of the fighting was militarized masculinity, plus a racist sense of the superiority of Americans.

That toxic equation goes all the way back to the days after World War II, when America started building its empire of bases. In the aftermath of the war, as American forces occupied the defeated nation, Japan established something called the Recreation and Amusement Association. That innocent-sounding organization was actually a collection of houses of prostitution. The purpose was to protect Japanese women from rape by giving occupying soldiers a less violent way of expressing their militarized masculinity. Once the association was ended, the number of rapes soared. In the modern era, sexual misbehavior by American troops in the Japanese prefecture of Okinawa continues to be such a significant problem that it gave birth to organizations such as Okinawa Women Act Against Military Violence and the Rape Emergency Intervention Counseling Center Okinawa.

But sex is not the only cause of friction between American troops living in bases abroad and the people of the host nations. Vine cites a 1998 incident in Italy, when a Marine Corps jet, "flying too low and too fast," crashed into a gondola cable, killing twenty skiers. The pilot avoided prosecution in Italy and was found not guilty in a court-martial in North Carolina. In a 2002 accident in Korea, an American armored vehicle involved in a training exercise killed two teenage girls.

At the end of the Cold War, Vine said, the United States had 1,600 bases in 40 countries. By the 2020s, the number stood at about 750 bases in 80 countries and colonies. "Most of the closures came in the first few years after the end of the Cold War," Vine told me. "Most were in Germany, the UK, Italy, and other parts of Europe, and were related to the removal of forces there. Some closures have taken place in South Korea and Okinawa and other parts of Japan, with consolidation at other larger bases. I think protest played a much bigger role in the closures in Asia (including in the Republic of Korea after the killing of two schoolgirls and the protests that followed). Generally, my sense is that the military knows US bases are an irritant and spur protest most everywhere eventually."

The protests continued in South Korea in 2022, in the weeks before the midterm election in the United States. The target was something called the Terminal High Altitude Area Defense system, known as THAAD, a missile interceptor installed five years earlier in a small rural village southeast of Seoul. The installation stirred up fears among the residents that it would anger China. "Now, if there is war, our village will become the first target because of that machine up there," Do Geum-yun told the *New York Times*. She was part of a group of 20 protesters who made their objections clear near the THAAD base, despite a large police presence. The United States continued to beef up THAAD after a North Korean missile test rattled nerves, and protests continued, with signs proclaiming sentiments such as, "Stop THAAD Deployment. KOREAN people oppose THAAD."

The whole issue led Vine, Lutz, the late Chalmers Johnson, and others to study deeply and write cogently about bases. Military analysts, veterans, and scholars came together to form the Overseas Base Realignment and Closure Coalition. In May 2022, they sent a long letter to President Biden opposing new bases in Europe, despite Russia's war against Ukraine. The empire of bases continues, but so does the campaign to shrink it. As Lutz wrote in *Militarism: A Reader*, "The work to expel overseas U.S. military bases is considered by many, including an international body that met in Indonesia in 2003, to be one of the four pivotal goals of the global peace movement."

FUBAR AND SNAFU

The acronym SNAFU (Situation Normal, All Fucked Up) pops up regularly in civilian conversations. Its roots go back to the World War II military, as a comment on both the military's love of acronyms and the reality it describes: In the military, in both the fog of war and the relative calm of peacetime, things tend to go wrong. Anyone who has ever been in the armed forces is familiar with that phenomenon. Another acronym expresses the same reality: FUBAR (Fucked Up Beyond All Recognition). It's just an accepted fact of military life. Ask people about their experience of SNAFU, and they'll tell you stories. I asked Pamela Schmidlin, a former army intelligence analyst, whether she had encountered incompetence in the military. "Only on a daily basis," she said. "I mean, how could you not? It's the military, right?" Screwing up becomes a subject of laughter and a part of your identity. "People just do stupid stuff all the time," air force veteran Kat Maier said. "In the aviation community, how you earn your nickname is you do something stupid enough to earn a nickname." And that nickname sticks with you.

"It is the nature of military operations to go wrong, in whole or in part," retired Lt. Gen. Daniel Bolger wrote in *Why We Lost: A General's Inside Account of the Iraq and Afghanistan Wars*. "It amounts to Murphy's Law: What can go wrong will go wrong. A lot of stuff goes wrong in military operations. So it is with sports, politics, commerce, and the construction business. What makes armed conflict even more subject to Murphy's Law, and renders even simple acts so difficult, involves the danger of sudden death or serious injury."

Even in the brief, inglorious 1983 invasion of Grenada, cases of SNAFU cropped up. Ann Wright, peace activist and retired army colonel, told me about some of them. She had been teaching a class in the law of land warfare at the School of International Studies at Fort Bragg, N.C. Some members of the legal team for the XVIII Airborne Corps and the 82nd Airborne Division had attended some of her classes, and they were part of the invasion. "They called me up and said: 'We're already starting to have some problems that are going to bite us pretty quickly. We have soldiers that are looting people's houses. We've already bombed a mental hospital and killed 20 people in that.'" So, three days into the operation, Wright went to Grenada and stayed for six months.

Wright remembers the tragic case of some members of a Navy SEALs team who were dropped from a C-130 transport aircraft on a reconnaissance mission. "Their raft didn't open up," she said. "They drowned." In a less lethal but still painful Grenada SNAFU, Wright recalled what happened when the invading forces tried to drop 82nd Airborne Division paratroopers on an airfield. An antiaircraft weapon kept firing at the transport planes until the planes changed their procedure and approached the field at an altitude too low for the antiaircraft weapon to aim at them: 500 feet. Unfortunately, that was far too low for paratroopers to jump safely, but the soldiers were forced to jump anyway. "So the numbers of guys that broke their legs as they landed on the airfield, that was one of the things that really hasn't come out publicly," Wright said.

In addition to the dead and injured, the invasion led to continuing legal troubles for the souvenir-hungry paralooters and some scary threats toward Wright. "I got into a big brouhaha with them after Grenada, because one of my jobs as part of the international law team was to clamp down on all of the thievery and looting that our military was doing down in Grenada. And these guys were so brazen. They would just strip people's houses and bring all this stuff to the airport and put it on the planes going back to Fort Bragg." At Bragg, one young paratrooper managed to get his diary published in the Fayetteville newspaper. "It was a diary of looting," Wright said. "Talk about stupid. We were able to identify exactly which house he had gone into." As she worked to get the aftermath of the looting under control, Wright didn't get much help from the units at Bragg. So she went to the Judge Advocate General. She gave a long deposition about the looting, and the Criminal Investigation Division became involved. That didn't earn her any friendships among the paratroopers. "There were posters that were put up around the base, saying, 'If you see this woman, take her out.'" By "take her out," of course, they didn't mean inviting her on a date, but subjecting her to lethal violence.

In the current politically charged era, one SNAFU event was widely publicized, but not immediately understood as an example of incompetence. At a crowded Republican presidential debate in 2016, Texas Sen. Ted Cruz blustered: "Today, many of us picked up our newspapers, and we were horrified to see the sight of 10 American sailors on their knees, with their hands on their heads. In that State of the Union, President Obama didn't so much as mention the 10 sailors that had been captured by Iran."

Cruz made it sound as if the sailors were innocent victims in imminent danger. In fact, as then-Defense Secretary Ashton Carter admitted, the sailors on two riverine vessels had fouled up the basic naval task of navigation and entered Iranian territorial waters near Farsi Island. Naval elements of the Islamic Revolutionary Guard Corps seized them, held them briefly, then let them go, after negotiations between then-Secretary of State John Kerry and the Iranian foreign minister. That was not good enough for the chest-pounding Cruz, whose resume does not include a single day in the military. "I give you my word, if I am elected president, no service man or service woman will be forced to be on their knees," Cruz said, "and any nation that captures our fighting men will feel the full force and fury of the United States of America." In other words, he'd reject the delicate negotiation that led to a quick resolution. Instead, he'd bomb first and ask questions later. If he ever had the chance to use that overheated approach, it would almost certainly become another prime example of both SNAFU and FUBAR.

Once Donald Trump emerged from that 2016 Republican primary and was elected president, he couldn't stop talking about the Iranian incident, blaming Obama for mishandling it. But a team of reporters from the nonprofit investigative newsroom ProPublica—Robert Faturechi, T. Christian Miller, and Megan Rose—dug relentlessly into what they called "a spying mission" and found where the fault really lay: with military commanders. "The Farsi Island mission was a gross failure, involving issues that have plagued the Navy in recent years: inadequate training, poor leadership, and a disinclination to heed the warnings of its men and women about the true extent of its vulnerabilities," the ProPublica team wrote.

Those three reporters were able to pry out the facts on the Farsi Island farce during 2019, a year when they were spending a lot of time investigating three other naval incidents. In 2017, two navy ships, first the USS *Fitzgerald*, then the USS *John S. McCain*, crashed into commercial vessels. Then, in 2018, two Marine Corps aircraft crashed in midair. In all, the three events took the lives of 17 sailors and six marines. In a February 2020 story about a House Armed Services Committee hearing on the tragedies, Faturechi summed up: "In each of the accidents, ProPublica found that the crews were dangerously undertrained, undermanned and working with faulty or degraded equipment. Warnings about unsafe conditions were ignored up the chain of command." Three months after that story, ProPublica's collection of articles on the 7th Fleet's problems won the 2020 Pulitzer Prize for National Reporting.

The attitudes they found in interviewing senior officers included what Megan Rose told me was a "real push from on high to modernize and build more ships, more ships, without really thinking through what it takes to man those ships and whether you need them." Rose's background included time working for the military publication *Stars and Stripes*, Associated Press, and the *Las Vegas Sun*. She joined ProPublica in 2013. With all her experience covering the military, at ProPublica and before, she developed a sense of burn-out and needed a change of journalistic scene. So she switched to covering criminal justice. But when the disasters in the Pacific happened, she jumped back into covering the military again. When we spoke, I asked her how she and her colleagues managed to navigate their way through the Pentagon's wall of silence and learn the truth.

"The reason all those admirals spoke to us was because they had such a high level of frustration, of having stars on their shoulders and still not being able to get what they needed or be listened to," Rose said. "It just seemed that, in the 7th Fleet in particular, they were just tasked with doing so much that nobody wanted to push back on any level really, of saying, 'We can't do it.'" That inflated, misplaced can-do attitude, that don't-complain-just-get-it-done mantra, lay at the heart of the problems. "I think in the 7th Fleet, they wanted to own their territory. They didn't want to say, 'You're stretching us too thin,' because they didn't want to give anything up," Rose said. "Then, of course, there's the good aspects, too, of people just believing in the mission and what they're doing and wanting to make it happen. It's not like this is all malicious or idiocy. It's just a combination of all these things coming together."

Military incompetence is a widespread enough reality to have inspired a literature of its own. One book, published in 1971, was *From the Jaws of Victory: A History of the Character, Causes and Consequences of Military Stupidity, from Crassus to Johnson and Westmoreland*, by Charles Fair. Johnson, of course, was Lyndon B. Johnson, the president who presided over the escalation of the disastrous war in Vietnam. Westmoreland was Gen. William C. Westmoreland, the best-remembered officer from that war. In his introduction, Fair places responsibility for Vietnam where it belongs, with the government and the military, and he pokes fun at those who tried to shift the blame to war protesters: "The more obvious our failure in Vietnam became, the more we heard it was not due to military incompetence or the stupidity of the State Department. Far from it; we were being sabotaged by dissidents at home. Our generals were being 'held back,' presumably by those too cowardly to sanction the use of bacterial warfare or tactical nuclear weapons."

Another book along those lines, published in 1976, was *On the Psychology of Military Incompetence*, by Norman F. Dixon. On the failure of Vietnam, Dixon pulled no punches: "In this most ill-conceived and horrible of wars there was the Commander-in-Chief, Lyndon Johnson, aided by his advisers, dreaming up policies and even selecting targets at a nice safe distance of 12,000 miles. And there was the man on the spot, General Westmoreland, a by no means unintelligent military commander but bemused by the sheer weight of destructive energy and aggressive notions supplied by his President. Together, the Machiavellian mind of the one, coupled with the traditional military mind of the other, produced a pattern of martial lunacy...." Dixon also wrote about the ill-fated Bay of Pigs invasion of Cuba. President Dwight D. Eisenhower had set it in motion, but his successor, President John F. Kennedy, let it go forward—and regretted it. Dixon wrote, "Kennedy was stricken. 'How could I have been so stupid as to let them go ahead?' he asked."

Kennedy's experience with the military started in World War II. As a young naval lieutenant in the Pacific, he commanded a patrol torpedo boat, and a Japanese destroyer lived up to its name, plowing into the PT-109 and destroying it. Kennedy, who had been on the swim team at Harvard, led his men on a long swim to safety. That feat earned him a reputation as a hero, which he drily debunked. "It was involuntary," he said. "They sank my boat." Once he became president, Kennedy observed the failings of generals, admirals, and intelligence agencies, in the Bay of Pigs in 1961 and the nearly planet-ending Cuban missile crisis in 1962. He often expressed a sarcastic disdain for their seemingly bottomless capacity for giving bad advice. In a 2013 JFK issue of the *Atlantic*, published on the fiftieth anniversary of Kennedy's assassination, biographer Robert Dallek wrote a long article, "Kennedy vs. the Military," leaving no doubt about the president's contempt for the senior military officers in the fancily decorated uniforms and caps who had led him astray on the Bay of Pigs. In rising from a junior naval officer to commander in chief, he had developed a healthy skepticism about the military—especially its senior leaders. Dallek quotes Kennedy: "Those sons of bitches with all the fruit salad just sat there nodding, saying it would work."

During the Cuban missile crisis, Air Force Chief of Staff Gen. Curtis LeMay infamously urged the bombing of nuclear missile sites in Cuba. Kennedy's solution, the less dangerous naval blockade, averted nuclear war. His interactions with the generals led him to wonder whether their advice could lead to the mushroom cloud-shrouded end of planet Earth. Dallek wrote: " 'These brass hats have one great advantage,' Kennedy told his longtime aide Kenny O'Donnell. 'If we ... do what they want us to do, none of us will be alive later to tell them that they were wrong.'" That level of near-cynicism about military leaders, Dallek wrote, led Kennedy to tell White House guests, "The first thing I'm going to tell my successor is to watch the generals, and to avoid feeling that just because they were military men, their opinions on military matters were worth a damn." What Kennedy didn't know was that the assassination would make Johnson his successor, and Johnson failed to "watch the generals," as they kept asking him to send more and more troops to Vietnam, where 58,000 young Americans died.

In the years since Vietnam, in addition to the forever war in Iraq and the one that Biden finally ended in Afghanistan in 2021, the parade of SNAFU and FUBAR incidents continued.

In 2020, a Marine Corps amphibious vehicle sank off San Diego, killing eight marines and one sailor. The corps acknowledged that the accident resulted from failed maintenance and human errors.

A 2017 massacre at a Baptist church in Texas also turned out to have roots in military incompetence. The shooter was a former airman named Devin Patrick Kelley. During his time in the military, a court-martial had convicted him of assault. A Department of Defense investigation later found that Kelley had a history of violence stretching back a decade, but that the air force had failed to report his history to the FBI. In a lawsuit arising from the shooting, the plaintiffs argued that, if that assault conviction had been properly reported to the FBI's National Criminal Information Center database, Kelley might not have been able to buy the weapon that he used to kill 26 people. A judge found the air force 60 percent liable. In 2023, the Department of Justice announced a $144.5 million settlement with the plaintiffs.

In 2022, a Navy SEAL trainee died after the brutal Hell Week part of the training. "The course began with 210 men," the *New York Times* reported. "By the middle of Hell Week, 189 had quit or been brought down by injury." Though Seaman Kyle Mullen, a former captain of the Yale football team, had been coughing up blood that week, his instructors didn't make him quit. Soon after he completed Hell Week, he lay down, his heart stopped beating, and he died. For years, the SEAL course has been the object of criticism for its brutality and its lethality. "Since 1953, at least 11 men have died," the *Times* reported after Mullen's death.

Over the years, those deaths in SEALs training and the reports of brutality have done little to tarnish the SEALs image, as exemplified by the famous exclamation by Katie Couric of *The Today Show*, early in the invasion and occupation of Iraq, "I think Navy SEALs rock!" That earned her a "P.U.-litzer prize" in the "Military Groupie" category from the progressive media watchdog group Fairness & Accuracy in Reporting. But Couric's admiration for the SEALs is far more typical of the nation's attitude than FAIR's mock prize. Association with the SEALs has come to be as glorious a résumé item as time spent in the Marine Corps. Like "former marine," the term "former SEAL" has become a terse, unassailable assertion of a person's excellence and bravery.

That SEAL of approval, the Teflon-like immunity to lasting reputational damage that the SEALs enjoy, applies as well to the military at large. It remains the most trusted American institution, far higher in public esteem than the government that sent it to fight, the newspapers that supported the wars, or the churches that too often went along, even blessing the killing. No story or series of stories about its fallibility seem to erode its position of trust: Not the stories about the epidemic of sexual assault in the ranks. Not Martha Mendoza's reporting about recruiters sexually abusing recruits. Not her work—with Charles Hanley and Sang-Hun Choe—exposing the war crime by American troops in Korea at the bridge at No Gun Ri. Not navy vessels plowing into civilian ships. Not accounts of the corruption of Leonard Glenn "Fat Leonard" Francis, the defense contractor who admitted bribing dozens of navy officers in what the *New York Times* called "the worst corruption scandal in Navy history." Not the 2004 revelations, complete with photos, about American soldiers torturing inmates at the Abu Ghraib prison in Iraq. Not *Kill Anything That Moves: The Real American War in Vietnam,* the deeply researched Nick Turse book showing that My Lai was not the only American war crime in that wicked war. Not the *Washington Post* revelations of a practice that the American government tried for years to keep secret: retired American generals and admirals supplementing their pensions by serving as consultants to the oppressive, journalist-murdering Saudi regime—as well as Libya, Turkey, Kuwait, and others. Not the Pentagon Papers nor the Afghanistan Papers. Not the failure of the military to screen adequately for white supremacists entering the ranks. Not the charges filed against current and former members of the military who joined in the January 6 attack on the Capitol. Not the imprisonment of Daniel Hale, a former airman and intelligence analyst for the National Security Agency, who revealed the extent of civilian casualties from American drone strikes. Not stories about the American military being the world's largest institutional contributor to global warming, with a purportedly climate-friendlier plan that critics call "military-grade greenwash."

So far, all those stories about the problems of the military have not broken through the Teflon and created a widespread realization that it is a flawed organization that needs to be carefully watched, not abjectly worshiped. Yes, it's true that some right-wing TV and social media commentators—Tucker Carlson is a prime example—began in about 2022 to criticize the military for its perceived "feminization" and "wokeness." Another sign of declining admiration for the military was a poll by the Ronald Reagan Institute in late 2022, which found that 48 percent of the American public trusts and has confidence in the military, compared with 70 percent in 2018. But that bit of tarnish on the military's halo—which 62 percent of the poll's respondents attributed to excessive politicization of military leaders—did not bring about significant change in the reflexive adulation. Until Americans see its imperfections and get serious about correcting them, Congress and the president won't do the hard work of reexamining America's most trusted institution. Our leaders won't get around to deciding whether to shrink the numbers of active-duty soldiers, to take the pressure off the recruiters who are having such a hard time meeting their quotas. They won't seriously trim the defense budget and stop buying expensive weapons systems that are not making us safer. They won't address the knotty question of why the nation still needs an amphibious force like the Marine Corps, at a time when massive amphibious landings are essentially a thing of the past. They won't consider whether to apportion to the army and the navy the functions of the corps, which would be "resized to the small police force it was prior to World War I," as Norman R. Denny, a retired navy commander, suggested in a 2021 article. (Spoiler alert: Its mystique is so potent that the Marine Corps is unlikely to go away. "No politician's going to be the guy who ends the institutional history of the United States Marine Corps," Megan Rose said.)

In short, none of the much-needed rethinking of the shape and size of our military can really happen as long as our politicians—and our citizens—simply utter rote phrases like "finest fighting force in the history of the world" and don't scrutinize that force closely, intelligently, and skeptically.

Chapter 7
FEELING A DRAFT?

Beyond the question of how fine a fighting force today's American military is—or is not—lurks the matter of how America will populate its future armed forces in the event of another major war. Will the nation continue to rely exclusively on the all-volunteer force, or will a draft at some point become necessary? Is the current system of mandatory, males-only draft registration working, is it needed, and is it constitutional?

Inaction on major issues is a feature, not a bug, of the United States Congress. So its failure to act on two unpalatable choices about the future of draft registration is hardly surprising. A federal court ruled in 2019 that males-only draft registration is unconstitutional. So it appeared for a short time that Congress would have to decide: Either change the law to register women, as well as men, or eliminate the legal requirement to register for the draft and shut down the Selective Service System that administers it. But the Supreme Court declined to take sides in the appeal, leaving it up to Congress to choose between two alternatives—and both of them pose political problems.

Though the future of draft registration remains very much in doubt, the history of the draft offers some insights into the sources of the modern-era impasse. As far back as the Civil War, the draft has caused trouble. In 1863, Congress passed legislation to conscript men into that epic struggle over the enslavement of human beings. At that time, people with enough money could avoid the draft by hiring substitutes to replace them on the battlefield. This did not go over well with people who didn't have enough money, including many Irish immigrants. In the City of New York, a protest of the draft quickly escalated into a lethal race riot. "Irish immigrants, who would not have had anything against any one group upon arrival and were escaping famine and persecution of their own under the British, were pitted against black residents when they were drafted to fight a war over slavery from which they did not benefit and that they did not cause," Isabel Wilkerson wrote in her magisterial work, *Caste: The Origins of Our Discontents*. "They hung black men from lamp poles and burned to the ground anything associated with black people—homes, businesses, churches, a black orphanage—in the Draft Riots of 1863, considered the largest race riot in American history."

A draft was also in effect during World War I (2,810,296 men conscripted), World War II (10,110,104), and the "police action" in Korea (1,529,539). But by the 1960s, as the draft-age population grew and the military's needs diminished, the draft became less and less necessary. In fact, the system was more focused on granting draft deferments than on drafting new soldiers, wrote Bernard Rostker in *I Want You! The Evolution of the All-Volunteer Force*, his book about the draft. Then along came Vietnam, and the number of men drafted quickly soared. In 1965, the year when President Lyndon B. Johnson began the major troop buildup in Vietnam, the nation drafted 230,991 men into the military—including me. By the time that misbegotten war had ended, the Selective Service System's statistics show that it had drafted a total of 1,857,304 men for it. And that draft became the subject of intense protests, as men took to the streets, burning their draft cards in public. The most spectacular protest was a break-in at the office of the Selective Service System in Catonsville, Maryland, followed by the burning of draft files in the parking lot. That event in May 1968 made the nine protesters famous in poems, songs, documentary films, and a play and a movie called *The Trial of the Catonsville Nine*. The best known of the nine were two priests, Philip Berrigan and his brother Daniel.

In a radio speech four months after Catonsville, as the presidential election drew to a close in October, Republican candidate Richard M. Nixon took note of all the unrest and came out in favor of an all-volunteer force. "Today all across our country we face a crisis of confidence," Nixon said. "Nowhere is it more acute than among our young people. They recognize the draft as an infringement on their liberty, which it is. To them, it represents a government insensitive to their rights, a government callous to their status as free men. They ask for justice, and they deserve it."

During the presidential campaign, Nixon had said he had a "secret plan" to end the war in Vietnam. But by late 1969, months after his inauguration, Nixon had not yet begun to withdraw troops from Vietnam. On November 15, 1969, activists staged the largest anti-war protest in the nation's history. A little more than two weeks later, on December 1, the nation reinstated—for the first time since 1942—a lottery system for determining the draft order. In a large glass container, 366 blue plastic capsules each held a birth date. If your birth date was among the first picked, you'd be among the first to be drafted in 1970. If it was picked later, you had a good chance of not getting drafted.

In February 1970, the President's Commission on an All-Volunteer Force, which Nixon had appointed soon after he took office, rendered its final report. "Selection by lottery compels some to serve who have neither a talent nor a taste for military life," the commission said, in an understated-but-accurate assessment of the draft. "These men present morale and disciplinary problems which otherwise might not arise."

An all-volunteer force was not going to be cheap. It would require elevating pay levels for soldiers and increasing the number of recruiters. In fact, the commission expressed surprise that recruiting efforts hadn't ratcheted up as the American presence in Vietnam expanded. "In view of the increased need for enlistments since 1965, the stability of relative recruiting expenditures and the number of recruiters are surprising," the commission said. "They reflect the low priority assigned to recruiting so long as the draft is available to ensure an adequate supply of manpower for the lower ranks. Clearly, elimination of the draft will increase the need for effective recruiting and the budget required."

Still, costly or not, the commission opted to recommend the change. "We unanimously believe that the nation's interest will be better served by an all-volunteer force, supported by an effective standby draft, than by a mixed force of volunteers and conscripts…." On January 27, 1973, Secretary of Defense Melvin Laird announced the end of the draft. The last draftee was Dwight Elliot Stone, a plumber's apprentice from California, who reported for basic training at Fort Polk, Louisiana, on June 30, 1973.

The attitudes of many Vietnam War draftees—a growing sense that the war was wicked, and they wanted no part of it—led to draft law violations that resulted in thousands of indictments and convictions. In *Soldiers in Revolt: GI Resistance During the Vietnam War*, David Cortright wrote brilliantly about that anti-war feeling and showed that it wasn't confined to civilians: Active-duty soldiers also pushed back against the war, and Cortright was among them. Drafted in 1968, he began developing an antipathy to the army when he noticed in basic training the instinctive cruelty of drill sergeants. Then, at his first post—Fort Hamilton, in Brooklyn, New York—he encountered veterans returning from Vietnam. "These vets were the most embittered, burned-out people I had ever met," Cortright wrote. "I came to see the war as not just a mistake, but a crime." His work documenting the GI resistance informed Cortright's analysis of the attitudes that ultimately led the nation away from reliance on the draft. "The all-volunteer force was introduced and accepted, in my view, primarily because of the political and social pressures caused by resistance to the military," Cortright wrote.

Though Nixon felt no love for protesters, he had ultimately decided to end the draft that had caused so much turmoil and rely instead on an all-volunteer military. Within the government, however, the debate continued over the shape of the system for registering men for a draft that no longer existed. Some argued that completely abandoning registration would send a signal to potential enemies that the United States was simply not ready to mobilize in the event of a major war. In March 1975, the year after Nixon resigned to avoid impeachment, his successor took action. President Gerald R. Ford signed a proclamation titled "Terminating Registration Procedures Under the Military Selective Service Act, as Amended." But the document made clear that Ford's purpose was "to evaluate an annual registration system" and that the previous system would "be replaced by new procedures which will provide for periodic registration."

So the Selective Service System limped along, in "deep standby," with a sharply reduced budget, not registering men for a potential draft. And that fit well with the new doctrine of the army: The old mobilization plan was no longer needed anyway, because bases of American troops in Europe, helped if necessary by the National Guard and Army Reserve, would be quick enough to respond to any crisis in Europe. When Jimmy Carter defeated Ford in 1976 and became president in 1977, he established the Presidential Reorganization Project to look at ways of cutting expenses. One of the issues it faced was what to do about the vestigial Selective Service System. The project's staff did not see the necessity for active draft registration. The Joint Chiefs of Staff took the opposite position, pushing for peacetime registration. Meanwhile, recruiters for the all-volunteer military were having a tough time. "As the Carter administration started its third year, the manning of reserve forces and medical services, particularly physician manning, had not improved," Bernard Rostker wrote. "Now, recruiting for the active force was sliding. This trend had been noticed during the last days of the Ford administration, but it was obvious now across the board." Some members of Congress became concerned that the nation would not be able to mobilize quickly for a major war. But Stuart Eizenstat, Carter's domestic policy assistant, wrote to one congressman that the administration "opposes new legislation to reimpose peacetime registration for the draft. The President already has adequate authority to require registration if circumstances warrant." A few days later, Sen. Sam Nunn of Georgia, a leading skeptic about the all-volunteer force, wrote an op-ed in the *Washington Post* under the headline "The Case for Peacetime Registration."

In the middle of all that, Carter nominated Rostker, who had just finished working on civil service reform in the Department of the Navy, to be the new director of the Selective Service System. Rostker responded unenthusiastically to the person who was leading the search for a director: "Why should I be interested in moving from the Navy and the Department of Defense to a backwater agency in deep standby?" But saying no to a presidential nomination is seen as bad form. So Rostker said yes. His confirmation hearing, delayed for months, unfolded toward the end of 1979. He was confirmed and sworn in as director near the end of November, just a few weeks before the January 1980 congressional deadline for Carter to submit a report on alternative mobilization approaches—including the possibility of draft registration. In mid-January, Rostker produced a document that would presumably be the basis of the president's report to Congress. He did not recommend year-around peacetime draft registration, but rather a system that would start operating only once actual mobilization occurred in a crisis.

Despite Rostker's recommendation, a few hours before the State of the Union Address on January 23, 1980, Secretary of Defense Harold Brown passed the word down the chain of command that Carter had decided to support peacetime registration—and that decision had to be added to the text. Near the top of the speech, Carter sounded this ominous note: "At this time in Iran, 50 Americans are still held captive, innocent victims of terrorism and anarchy. Also at this moment, massive Soviet troops are attempting to subjugate the fiercely independent and deeply religious people of Afghanistan. These two acts—one of international terrorism and one of military aggression—present a serious challenge to the United States of America and indeed to all the nations of the world. Together, we will meet these threats to peace." Further down in the speech, he got to the point: "I believe that our volunteer forces are adequate for current defense needs, and I hope that it will not become necessary to impose a draft. However, we must be prepared for that possibility. For this reason, I have determined that the Selective Service System must now be revitalized. I will send legislation and budget proposals to the Congress next month so that we can begin registration and then meet future mobilization needs rapidly if they arise."

It was a staggering historic irony that Carter used the Soviet Union's invasion of Afghanistan as a key reason for reinstating a peacetime draft, in light of the later revelation that America had taken action that made that invasion more likely. The Russians argued that they moved into Afghanistan in order to fight against secret American involvement in that nation, but no one believed them. The official version was that the United States began to help the Mujahideen guerrilla forces in Afghanistan only *after* the Soviet invasion began on December 24, 1979. "But the reality, closely guarded until now, is completely otherwise: Indeed, it was July 3, 1979, that President Carter signed the first directive for secret aid to the opponents of the pro-Soviet regime in Kabul," admitted Carter's national security advisor, Zbigniew Brzezinski, in an interview years later. "We didn't push the Russians to intervene, but we knowingly increased the probability that they would." When the interviewer asked Brzezinski if he regretted any of that, Brzezinski answered: "Regret what? That secret operation was an excellent idea. It had the effect of drawing the Russians into the Afghan trap, and you want me to regret it? The day that the Soviets officially crossed the border, I wrote to President Carter, essentially: 'We now have the opportunity of giving to the USSR its Vietnam war.'"

Though Brzezinski delighted in helping to nudge the Soviet Union into a long, losing slog of a war, in a nation infamous as the graveyard of empires, the decision to aid the Mujahideen came back to haunt the United States. One of the leaders of those guerrilla forces was Osama bin Laden, who accepted American help but later declared war on the United States and engineered the 9/11 attacks. That led the United States into a long, losing slog of a war in Afghanistan, from 2001 to 2021. And the Soviet invasion provided a reason for Carter to revive the peacetime draft, at the start of a year when he'd be running for re-election. Given the Iranian hostage situation and the invasion of Afghanistan, Carter was certain to face Republican attacks for being soft on national security. Ronald Reagan had declared his candidacy for president a few days before Carter's State of the Union, and in the campaign ahead, Reagan was highly likely to attack Carter's national security policies as weak. Another irony of Carter's decision is that Reagan was not a fan of the peacetime draft. "Reagan had actually said during the campaign that he opposed the draft," said Edward Hasbrouck, who has an unusual array of expertise, as a travel writer and author of *The Practical Nomad*, and as a deeply committed, preeminent leader in the fight to eliminate the Selective Service System. "It wasn't a big campaign platform, but there were libertarians who believed that, and there were libertarians very close to him who were on the leading edge of some of his other radical programs who were anti-draft." In fact, Reagan wrote to Sen. Mark Hatfield (R-Oregon) in May 1980 that "this proposal is an ill-considered one, and should be rejected. Advanced registration will do little to enhance our military preparedness." Nonetheless, Carter's decision flowed from anticipating Republican attacks on his national security positions. "It was a campaign stunt," Hasbrouck said, "and we're still stuck with the consequences."

Those consequences have included significant constitutional challenges to a males-only draft registration requirement, the gradual realization that the lists of addresses of draft-registered young men were significantly inaccurate, and the imposition of civil penalties for those who have failed to register. The first challenge that draft registration faced, within months after it began, was a lawsuit declaring that registering men only was unconstitutional.

The issue of the constitutionality of a males-only draft had arisen years before Nixon ended the draft in 1973 and Carter revived draft registration in 1980. Indicted for failing to register and carry a draft card, a Fordham University student, James St. Clair, asked a Manhattan federal court in 1968 to dismiss the indictment. He argued that the law violated his constitutional right to due process because it unfairly discriminated against him based on sex: Only men, not women, were subject to the draft. During oral arguments, US District Court Judge Dudley Bonsal asked a flippant question that didn't seem to bode well for St. Clair's case, but pretty much summed up a prevailing attitude toward women in the military, "The theory was that women would stay home and have children so there'd be some soldiers for the next war, wasn't it?" And in his written opinion, Bonsal slammed the door shut: "In providing for involuntary service for men and voluntary service for women, Congress followed the teachings of history that if a nation is to survive, men must provide the first line of defense while women keep the home fires burning. Moreover, Congress recognized that in modern times there are certain duties in the Armed Forces which may be performed by women volunteers. For these reasons, the distinction between men and women with respect to service in the Armed Forces is not arbitrary, unreasonable or capricious."

Even after the St. Clair case, the sex-discrimination issue persisted. In the spring of 1971, a group of Philadelphia-area high school students brought a lawsuit claiming, among other things, that the Military Selective Service Act denied them equal protection under the Fourteenth Amendment because the draft affected only males. The United States Court of Appeals for the Third Circuit rejected all of the claims except for the one based on sex discrimination. That didn't please the plaintiffs. "The case had begun, after all, as an anti-war, antidraft enterprise; gender discrimination was thrown in almost inadvertently," wrote Linda Kerber in *No Constitutional Right to Be Ladies: Women and the Obligations of Citizenship*. "To argue primarily on the grounds of gender discrimination was to concede that if women were drafted, a draft would be acceptable. This was not at all what the four Philadelphians had signed on for." So the plaintiffs didn't want to go forward, but the attorneys found a new plaintiff who did. Robert Goldberg, a medical student, joined the case in 1975 and was willing to make the argument that the draft was unconstitutional because it didn't include women. The government managed to drag the case out for years, through the whole Carter presidency.

Though congressional committees rejected the Pentagon's request that they lift the ban on using women in combat, it was clear by 1981, the first year of the Reagan administration, that women who had voluntarily enlisted were valuable as members of the military. That year, nearly 74,000 women served in the army alone. Compared with men, women went AWOL far less often and behaved much less violently in their off-duty hours. They also tended to stay in the military longer. When Carter had submitted his formal proposal to revive the peacetime draft, he made clear the case for equality: "There is no distinction possible, on the basis of ability or performance, that would allow me to exclude women from an obligation to register." But he didn't exactly push hard for that equality. "Women in the military was a second-order issue for the President—who believed in equal obligation but was primarily concerned with responding to the Soviet Union," Kerber wrote.

The congressional debate on the issue did not produce a gender-neutral draft registration, but it did elevate the visibility of Goldberg's long-dragged-out lawsuit challenging the constitutionality of males-only registration. Ironically, by the time it reached the Supreme Court in 1981, the defendant/appellant in the case was Bernard Rostker, who had recommended against draft registration as one of his first acts as director of the deep-standby Selective Service System. In the case of *Rostker v. Goldberg*, Chief Justice William Rehnquist delivered the majority opinion on June 25, 1981. That opinion said that the primary purpose of registration was to replace combat troops. In 1981, women were not permitted to be combat troops. So, the opinion said, the "existence of the combat restrictions clearly indicates the basis for Congress' decision to exempt women from registration." The result was an opinion that preserved all-male registration: "Congress acted well within its constitutional authority when it authorized the registration of men, and not women, under the Military Selective Service Act."

Not long after that case had made it clear that women couldn't be registered for a future draft, the Selective Service System had to acknowledge that it was having significant trouble getting men to comply with the registration requirement. In November 1981 the system said that 1,336,000 men born in 1963 were supposed to register as of Sept. 1, but that only 1,029,000, or 77 percent, did. That shortfall of 300,000 men was the largest number of registration violators in one year. Then Congress began adding civil penalties to crack down on males who failed to register. Starting in 1982, Congress passed a series of what came to be known as Solomon Amendments to the federal education bill. No, they were not named for the biblical king whose baby-bisecting compromise in 1 Kings 3:16-28 gave birth to phrases such as "Solomonic wisdom" and "split the baby." This Solomon was Rep. Gerald B. H. Solomon, a Republican from upstate New York. Solomon had some military history as a marine—with a haircut to match, when I first saw him during his days as a member of the New York State Assembly—and his election to the House of Representatives in 1978 gave him a platform to act on behalf of the military. The first of the Solomon Amendments focused on denying federal financial aid for higher education to anyone who had failed to register for the draft. Over the years, Solomon Amendments built into the law another incentive for young men to register for the draft: If you haven't registered, you can't get a job in federal agencies. Different agencies enforce this prohibition with varying levels of zeal, but it's still an obstacle for many.

Not everyone who fails to register for the draft even knows about the requirement. Often, young men aren't aware of it as they turn 18, and they don't find out about it until after they turn 26. But that 26th birthday does not release you from the tentacles of draft registration. "Once you turn 26, it's too late to register," the Selective Service System says. If you're looking for a job with a federal agency, that agency can ask you to request a "Status Information Letter" from the Selective Service System, to give potential employers information on your registration or lack of it. "You will have to describe, in detail, the circumstances you believe prevented you from registering and provide copies of documents showing any periods when you were hospitalized, institutionalized, or incarcerated occurring between your 18th and 26th birthdays," the Selective Service System says. "If you are a non-citizen, you may be required to provide documents that show when you entered the United States." Even if you are an immigrant who has managed to get through the naturalization process and have become a citizen, you can be forced to jump through this Status Information Letter hoop. And the burden of proof is on you to show that your failure to register was not "knowing and willful."

It's no wonder, really, that people can go through their normal lives and be utterly unaware that they have to register for a draft that does not exist—and may never actually exist. You might see a poster in the post office—or you might not. In some states, when you apply for a driver's license, you might learn about the requirement, because the motor vehicle department will ask your consent to register you for the draft. Or you might get a mailing directly from the Selective Service System. "They send out a lot of junk mail," Hasbrouck said. "They go out and buy commercial mailing lists, which are neither complete nor accurate, especially when it comes to things like undocumented people.... If some other list shows you as having turned 18, but you don't show up on the Selective Service list, they send you a threatening letter, saying, 'Hey, it appears that you have turned 18 without having registered. You're supposed to have registered. Register or else.'"

But the "or else" is really not much of a threat. Though your failure to register can keep you from getting a job in a federal agency or a federal college loan, your chances of facing criminal charges are remote. "They turn over a couple hundred thousand names, between 100,000 and 200,000 a year, to the Department of Justice," Hasbrouck said. "The Department of Justice does nothing." With so many other crimes to pursue, since the late eighties DOJ has not regularly pursued criminal prosecutions for failure to register for the draft. But in the early eighties, DOJ did prosecute 20 men who had not registered, including Hasbrouck. The department obviously recognized the power of his voice on the issue. For simply declining to register for a draft that may never happen, Hasbrouck spent four months in a federal prison camp. That small number of prosecutions did not help encourage registration. Summing up that bit of draft history, the National Network Opposing the Militarization of Youth said, "These trials served only to call attention to the government's inability to prosecute more than a token number of nonregistrants, and reassured nonregistrants that they were not alone in their resistance and were in no danger of prosecution unless they called attention to themselves."

Between Carter's decision to revive draft registration in 1980 and the 9/11 attacks, America's most visible wars were the invasions of Grenada in 1983 and Panama in 1989. Neither of those incursions raised the specter of reviving the draft itself. The all-volunteer force was more than sufficient for overwhelming two tiny countries. In the 1990–91 Gulf War, the all-volunteer force was more than equal to the task of crushing the Iraqi army, which included both professional volunteer soldiers and draftees. But the 9/11 attacks led to a new focus on the draft. For one thing, Rep. Charles Rangel (D-New York), a Bronze Star and Purple Heart veteran of the Korean conflict and the first Black chairman of the House Ways and Means Committee, thought a fair draft was needed. So, starting in January 2003, as it was becoming increasingly clear that the United States was preparing to invade Iraq, Rangel introduced the Universal National Service Act, which proposed to "provide for the common defense by requiring that all young persons in the United States, including women, perform a period of military service or a period of civilian service in furtherance of the national defense and homeland security." That was the first of many times that Rangel proposed essentially the same legislation.

Rangel's core ideas were that everyone should make a commitment to national service and that America gets into wars too easily with an all-volunteer force, because not enough people know someone who is in harm's way in the military. When I asked what gave him the idea to propose the legislation, he said: "It was the number of funerals I was attending as a congressperson. I had to explain to people, some of whom were not even citizens, why their sons, brothers, and fathers were in that coffin." It deeply annoyed Rangel that so many nonveterans in the House advocated for "sending our young people into harm for some cause that had nothing, absolutely nothing, to do with our national security." Those members, Rangel argued, had no skin in the game. "Since almost all of them did not know anybody that knew anybody that was in the volunteer army, the whole idea of people getting wounded or missing in action or being killed is a non-existing thought in the House of Representatives and certainly the Senate."

A few months after Rangel introduced that bill, Americans were talking nervously about the draft, but not because of him. In November 2003, the Pentagon caused a stir by asking on its antiterrorism website for volunteers to work on draft boards and appeals boards that would decide whether men can get deferments or exemptions from the draft. The Selective Service System denied that a draft was coming, but a lot of people volunteered for those boards. Given my own experience with the draft almost four decades earlier, I wrote a column about this for *Newsday* and interviewed J. E. McNeil, executive director of the Center on Conscience and War, which opposes conscription.

The center had received a large number of emails and calls about the draft, and McNeil told me that she had heard from Republican legislators that there might be a draft after the presidential election of 2004. But McNeil saw no reason to believe the skin-in-the-game argument that a draft would prevent the nation from jumping into war. "The reality is that the draft has never kept us out of war," McNeil said. She also rejected the notion that a draft would get the attention of legislators because their children would be affected. "During Vietnam, not one single member of Congress had a child who was drafted," McNeil said. "The reality is that the middle class and the upper middle class always have more options than the lower class in the face of the draft."

Despite the draft scare of late 2003, the government did not call for a draft for the wars in Iraq and Afghanistan. The military continued to be an all-volunteer force. But something significant did change. In January 2013, Defense Secretary Leon Panetta rescinded a 1994 rule that had excluded women from being assigned to units whose primary mission was direct combat. In the years that followed, as the forever wars continued, the number of women involved in combat increased. So the changing role of women rendered essentially moot a core finding in the 1981 majority opinion in *Rostker v. Goldberg* that "existence of the combat restrictions clearly indicates the basis for Congress' decision to exempt women from registration." Congress no longer had a rational basis for allowing this unequal treatment of men and women.

In that new reality, another lawsuit challenged again the constitutionality of the males-only registration system. That suit started in California in 2013, the same year that Panetta did away with the rule excluding women from combat units. *National Coalition for Men v. Selective Service System* ran into some procedural problems over the standing of plaintiffs to sue, and it ended up transferred from California to Texas, where one of the plaintiffs lived. The Selective Service System argued that the case was not ripe for a decision because Congress was studying the issue and had established the National Commission on Military, National, and Public Service to examine the whole question of registration and make recommendations on altering or abolishing the draft registration requirement set up by the Military Selective Service Act. But in his February 2019 decision, Senior United States District Judge Gray H. Miller did not buy that argument. "There is no guarantee that the

Commission will recommend amending or abolishing the MSSA—and, even if it does, Congress is not required to act on those recommendations," Miller wrote. "Congress has been debating the male-only registration requirement since at least 1980 and has recently considered and rejected a proposal to include women in the draft." So Miller ruled unequivocally: "The male-only registration requirement of the Military Selective Service Act ... violates the Due Process Clause of the Fifth Amendment to the United States Constitution...."

That ruling in Texas looked for a moment like the nationwide death knell for males-only registration. It appeared that Congress would have to take one of two actions: expand registration to include women or eliminate the Selective Service System's draft registration entirely. Unsurprisingly, however, the Selective Service System appealed. Meanwhile, in March 2020, the commission appointed by Congress to study the issue issued its final report, finding draft registration necessary, but recommending that it should include women. In August 2020, a three-judge panel of the United States Court of Appeals for the Fifth Circuit in New Orleans reversed Miller's ruling that the males-only draft was unconstitutional. The National Coalition for Men asked the Supreme Court to review the Fifth Circuit's reversal of the Miller ruling. In June 2021, the Supreme Court declined to hear the case. Agreeing with the court's decision, Justice Sonia Sotomayor wrote: "It remains to be seen, of course, whether Congress will end gender-based registration under the Military Selective Service Act. But at least for now, the Court's longstanding deference to Congress on matters of national defense and military affairs cautions against granting review while Congress actively weighs the issue."

Reacting to the Supreme Court's decision in his blog, Edward Hasbrouck wrote, "Today's decision is bad news—the worst news in years, perhaps decades—for opponents of the draft and draft registration." Now that the Supreme Court had made clear that it is unwilling to pressure Congress on this issue, that frees Congress to do what Congress does so well: postpone a decision. Both solutions—eliminating draft registration entirely or expanding it to include women—have supporters in Congress. But two of those key lawmakers chose not to run for re-election in 2022: Rep. Jackie Speier, a California Democrat who favors expanding draft registration to include women, and Rep. Peter DeFazio, an Oregon Democrat who favors ending draft registration. The issue will continue to be part of the conversation in the annual process of the National Defense Authorization Act.

In late 2022, language expanding registration to women appeared in one version of the NDAA, but for the third time in six years it was deleted from the NDAA's final draft. So, in the early 2020s at least, the draft registration system would continue to operate—poorly. During the hearings by the National Commission on Military, National, and Public Service, a key piece of testimony came from Bernard Rostker, who had opposed peacetime registration until Jimmy Carter decided to revive it in 1980. Then Rostker, as director of the Selective Service Commission, had to administer the registration system that he considered unnecessary. In his statement to the commission, Rostker made clear that the current system of registration is not accurate. "It systematically lacks large segments of the eligible male population and for those that are included, the currency of information contained is questionable," Rostker said. Currency of information is a fancy way of saying what is obvious: Young people move around a lot, and they don't always tell the Selective Service System their new address, as the law requires. In his testimony before the commission, Hasbrouck cited the Government Accountability Office about the accuracy of the addresses on the Selective Service System's list of potential draftees. "There's been no independent audit of the addresses in the Selective Service System database since 1982, but even then, only two years after the start of the current registration process, the GAO estimated that 20–40 percent of the addresses were already out of date, and that up to 75 percent would be obsolete by the time registrants reached age 26," Hasbrouck told the commission.

On the question of drafting women or ending the Selective Service System, its former director Rostker didn't mince words in his statement to the commission. "I cannot think of a more divisive issue than the conscription of women, an issue that clearly does not need to be addressed at this time, given that a return to a draft is so unlikely," Rostker testified. "This is a 'fight' we really don't need to have." If that meant that the Military Selective Service Act (MSSA) would have to be repealed, Rostker said, "So be it."

Remember, early in his tenure as director of the Selective Service System, Rostker had recommended against reviving peacetime draft registration, but Carter decided to show strength to the Soviet Union by reinstating registration.

In the years since, Rostker did not change his mind about his original view. "Today the Army does not need and cannot absorb the mass of untrained and unskilled men, and potentially women, the draft would provide," Rostker told the commission in April 2019. "If history tells us anything, it is that when we have needed to build a mass Army, as we did for World War I and World War II, there was sufficient time to develop a new Selective Service System from scratch…. So, my bottom line is there is no need to continue to register people for a draft that will not come, no need to fight the battle over registering women, and no military need to retain the MSSA."

What do women think about the two options? A 2021 Ipsos poll showed that support for drafting women had declined since 2016, and women weren't enthusiastic about the possibility of being conscripted. "In 2016, 63% of Americans supported drafting women, as well as men, if the military draft were reinstated," Ipsos said. "In this most recent poll, only 45% of Americans are in favor. In 2021, over half of all men (55%) support drafting women, compared to about a third (36%) of women." When we spoke in March 2022, Hasbrouck continued to have doubts about the binary way polls have framed the question, for or against expanding draft registration to women, without asking about multiple options: retaining the male-only status quo, expanding registration to women, or eliminating registration entirely. "I am confident that most women of potential draft age don't want to be subject to a draft, and would prefer that draft registration and contingency planning for a draft be ended rather than expanded to women," Hasbrouck said. "Despite the distorted framing of the question, it is clear from polls that most people in the US don't support actually drafting women, even if there were to be a draft of men, and that this opposition to drafting women is much stronger among women than among men."

While the outcome of the register-women question remains to be seen, it is clear that the current males-only draft registration system maintains a list of draft-age young men that is so outdated and inaccurate that it is likely to be useless if America ever decides to use that list to draft people. Even the former director of the Selective Service System believes that the registration is unnecessary, because the government has shown itself capable in past major wars of raising a conscripted army on short notice. Meanwhile, even though the Department of Justice has shown no real interest in criminal prosecutions of those who have failed to register, the Solomon Amendments have erected a series of obstacles to young men who have failed to register but want federal student aid or federal jobs. Given all that, what is the real purpose of this faulty draft registration system? Hasbrouck, who follows draft issues as closely as anyone, offered an answer.

"The existence of Selective Service registration serves a function independent of whether it would actually work, if called upon," Hasbrouck told me. That function is this: It allows Pentagon war planners greater freedom in launching future wars without having to bother achieving broad enough public approval to attract the necessary number of volunteers. They have the possibility of a draft as a fallback. "So, it's not actual workability," Hasbrouck said. "It's just the perceived availability. It's not that it even enables war-making, but that it enables war planning. So, does it serve that function? Yes, and I think there are war planners and there are hawks who really don't like the idea, who know the Selective Service is a failure at actually enabling a draft. Part of the reason they don't want to admit failure is just loss of face. It's really embarrassing for the government to admit this whole thing is a fiasco, and they've kept it going for decades, even though it's a complete failure and has been a failure from day one." Yet registration continues, and its critics continue to sound off. "The goal of the draft resistance movement is not to prevent the draft," Hasbrouck said, "but to force constraints onto war planning."

In Vietnam, Afghanistan, and Iraq, we have seen vivid examples of war planning that vastly overestimated the prospects of success and disastrously underestimated the indicators of impending failure. So, if draft registration is enabling Pentagon war planners and their civilian leaders to forge ahead with future wars, without having to calculate whether the nation will have enough troops to fight those wars, we ought to be thinking seriously about scrapping a system that is unlikely to actually work anyway.

"The bottom line is, I think that Selective Service needs to be disbanded and defunded," said Rick Jahnkow, a leading counter-recruitment activist. "Whether or not Congress is willing to do that is an open question." With the Supreme Court declining to intervene and put pressure on lawmakers, there is little reason to believe that Congress will resolve that question anytime soon.

Chapter 8
HOME TO THE WORLD

The military loves acronyms. So let me offer a new one, EGOS: Empty Gestures of Support. Those gestures don't even come close to meeting veterans' needs for healing from the mental and physical wounds of war. Veterans Day parades don't pay the mortgage. The rote recitation of the ubiquitous thank-you-for-your-service mantra doesn't get them past the eligibility obstacles that prevent many veterans from access to health care and other benefits from the Department of Veterans Affairs. Other EGOS include the Support Our Troops bumper stickers, the yellow ribbons, the veteran-of-the-game ceremonies at baseball games, the widespread use of military-style camouflage in clothing. But no amount of adulation can ease the desperation that leads so many veterans to homelessness and even suicide. For veterans, adulation and desperation too often live side by side.

"The disconnect between patriotic celebration of veterans and how returning soldiers are actually treated has a long history in the United States," wrote Suzanne Gordon, Steve Early, and Jasper Craven in *Our Veterans: Winners, Losers, Friends, and Enemies on the New Terrain of Veterans Affairs*. This comprehensively researched, heavily footnoted book examines the hurdles confronting the nation's 20 million veterans and the forces at play in their lives: the VA itself, the Big Six veterans service organizations, the smaller VSOs that have grown up in recent years, even as the larger legacy organizations struggle with declining memberships, and the forty thousand nonprofits providing services to veterans—many of them admirable, but some of them improperly using donations for the benefit of their leaders.

Veterans seeking education have also had to navigate for-profit schools that are focused too much on their own earnings and not enough on learning.

In that complex post-military world, one of the realities that veterans encounter is the two powerful, contradictory images of who they are. The prevailing perception of veterans is glorious and heroic. Politicians and corporations take advantage of that patriotic glow by virtually wearing veterans as a magic cloak to provide cover for their own interests. The authors of *Our Veterans* call that phenomenon "rent-a-vet," citing as a prime example a Vietnam veteran turned lobbyist named Pete Conaty: "After Conaty opened his Sacramento lobbying shop in 1996, he signed up, as clients, VSOs directly representing over 800,000 veterans in the state, who belonged to more than 1,000 local posts of the Legion, VFW, and other groups. Conaty's well-advertised connection to this grassroots network enabled him to devise a 'rent-a-vet' strategy that's been a big moneymaker for his firm and a winner for corporate clients in several high-profile California referendum campaigns." In one of those referenda, he used his rent-a-vet clout to help Big Pharma kill a California ballot proposition that would have mandated that state health plans not pay more for drugs than the deeply discounted prices that the VA pays. One billboard attacking that proposal featured an older man, wearing a veterans cap, warning that this proposition would hurt veterans. The proposition lost by a substantial margin. There's another name for this phenomenon, offered by Jon Soltz of VoteVet, who cited as one example a call he received. " 'We need a veteran who's under 25, who's African American, who lost a leg below the knee,'" the caller told him. "The term we've given that is called pet-a-vet, where people generally who haven't been in the military want to use veterans for some other agenda." This pet-a-vet notion, he said, is grounded in "the idea that people who served in war should be worshiped."

The other image is a nasty stereotype that facilely files combat veterans in the category of "too deeply damaged" to be useful citizens. Sadly, many veterans really do have to live with serious damage as a result of their time in the military: the fear, sleeplessness, flashbacks and other symptoms of post-traumatic stress, drug addiction, homelessness, loss of limbs blown off by improvised explosive devices, a variety of illnesses arising from toxic exposure to the Agent Orange herbicide used in Vietnam, the fumes emanating from burn pits in Iraq and Afghanistan, or the contaminated drinking water at the

Marine Corps base in Camp Lejeune, North Carolina. Too many veterans live with the soul-searing pain of moral injury, the deep sense that, in the process of performing the murderous duty of combat, they have violated their own inescapable moral beliefs. And they face serious mental health issues arising from the horror of war.

The cabinet-level agency tasked with helping veterans with those health challenges can provide excellent care, but many veterans can't get access to it because of the other-than-honorable discharges that followed them from the military into civilian life. That "bad paper" forces them to jump through an exhausting set of hoops to upgrade their discharge status and gain the right to get the health care they need from the Veterans Health Administration. Without medical help and other benefits from the VA, veterans can slide into a spiral of homelessness and despair.

Bad paper is generic shorthand for any discharge that is not an honorable discharge. The most damaging kinds of discharges, reserved for those convicted at a court-martial, are in the punitive category: bad conduct or dishonorable. The administrative category, decided by commanders without a court-martial, includes honorable, general, and other than honorable discharges. It takes a major effort to upgrade other types of discharge to honorable, but it doesn't take much to acquire that life-altering bad paper in the first place. "It could be, in the navy, from having a bad urine test one time," said Craig Bruno, an attorney who has experienced scores of these cases at the Veterans and Servicemembers Rights Clinic at the Jacob D. Fuchsberg Law Center of Touro University on Long Island. "It could be smoking pot in any of the branches. It could be stealing one time. It could be disobeying orders. It could be a lot of things."

One case that remains vivid in Bruno's memory involved a woman who had experienced something far worse than her bad paper, but wasn't telling him about it. "She was in the service for a long time, over 10 years," Bruno said. "Her service record was outstanding, and at some point just dropped off a cliff. I said, 'What happened?' Nothing was forthcoming." So Bruno dug into her 750-page record. "Halfway through, I see a piece of paper with a copy of a Post-it, and it says, 'Raped, 1978.'" Beyond that Post-it, he found nothing else in her file about the rape. Then he called the veteran and apologetically asked her if she had been raped in 1978. She said she had. He asked why the file contained nothing about that event, and she told him, "Because I reported it, and they told me to suck it up, stop wearing my emotions on my sleeve."

Unfortunately, that connection between sexual abuse and bad paper is not rare. Kenneth Rosenblum, a former Judge Advocate General's Corps officer and Vietnam veteran who served as director of the veterans clinic at Touro, put it this way: "In reading and talking to other vets' advocates, I found a common experience, that it presents as 'disagreement with my first sergeant.' Then, when you develop a high level of trust, the rape will come out." Conflict with a sergeant doesn't even have to involve sexual abuse to lead to bad paper. In the case of Pamela Schmidlin, all it took was a rocky relationship with a noncommissioned officer, an E-5 sergeant, one step above her rank as an E-4 specialist. "It took him nine or ten years to get his E-5," Schmidlin said. "It took me nine or ten seconds—no wait a minute, it didn't even take me that—to get my E-4. He hated me for that. I don't know if he ever said that part out loud. He hated the fact that I was a female in the military." The sergeant's warped view was that she had joined the military to find a husband. "He gave me a hard time, from I want to say day zero, not day one." When she left the army in 1998, she had an other-than-honorable discharge. "It was between him and me," Schmidlin said. "I couldn't really face it for the longest time." When we spoke, in 2020, she was still going through the upgrade process.

The scope of the problem becomes clear in a deeply researched 2016 report, *Underserved: How the VA Wrongfully Excludes Veterans with Bad Paper.* It was a cooperative effort, written by the Veterans Legal Clinic at the Legal Services Center of Harvard Law School, working with a California-based veterans group, Swords to Plowshares, and the National Veterans Legal Services Program, based in Arlington, Virginia. As the report describes it, the bad paper problem is getting much worse. "Today, the VA is excluding these veterans at a higher rate than at any point in our history," the report said. The exclusion rate was 1.7 percent for World War II-era veterans and 2.8 percent for Vietnam-era veterans. For veterans of the forever-war era, from 2001 to the time of the report, the exclusion rate was 6.5 percent. That high rate is "due almost entirely to the VA's own discretionary policies, not any statute."

The key statute governing veterans was the Servicemen's Readjustment Act of 1944, commonly known as the G.I. Bill. As the report analyzes it, the problem is that the VA has chosen not to be as forgiving of bad paper as Congress prescribed in 1944. "Indeed, Congress intended for the VA to provide services to almost all veterans with bad paper discharges," *Underserved* said. "Congress explicitly chose to grant eligibility for basic VA services even to veterans discharged for some misconduct, provided that the misconduct was not so severe that it should have led to a trial by court-martial and Dishonorable discharge." The current rate of rejection of veterans with bad paper varies, depending on the location of the VA regional facility. In Indianapolis in 2013, the VA denied eligibility to 100 percent of the veterans with bad paper. In Boston, it was 69 percent.

The veteran's branch of service also makes a big difference. "Marine Corps veterans are nearly 10 times more likely to be ineligible for VA services than Air Force veterans," *Underserved* said. Ineligibility is not just some meaningless status. It's a matter of life and death. "Veterans with bad paper discharges are at greater risk of homelessness and suicide, yet it is nearly impossible for such veterans to navigate the bureaucracies to get VA healthcare or homelessness prevention services," the report argued.

The short-term remedy for an individual veteran is a time-consuming "character of discharge" review process while the VA looks through a veteran's entire record. The report said that the average time for this process was more than three years. The more sweeping recommended remedy of the system was clear, but not easily achievable. The report called on the vast agency to "revise its regulations to more accurately reflect congressional intent to exclude only those whose misconduct should have led to a trial by court-martial and Dishonorable discharge. It should do this by requiring consideration of positive and mitigating factors and by not disqualifying veterans for minor misconduct."

Too often, the bad paper results from some commander's determination that a subordinate has an underlying "personality disorder," when the real problem is post-traumatic stress or traumatic brain injury, or some other condition caused by exposure to combat. Too often, 84 percent of the time, the VA denies applications for upgrading the discharge because it finds the veteran guilty of "willful and persistent misconduct." That category can include some pretty minor conduct, like the twice-deployed marine who had a toothpick in his mouth while speaking with his sergeant and got discharged after failing one drug test.

After reading *Underserved*, I spoke with its lead writer, Dana Montalto of the Veterans Legal Clinic at the Legal Services Center of Harvard Law School, and she explained its origins. "Because we prioritize certain populations, like veterans who have mental health conditions, traumatic brain injury, who have experienced military sexual trauma, that also means we serve a lot of veterans who have less-than-honorable discharges, because they are over-represented in those populations," Montalto said. In serving those veterans, the clinic learned a lot about their difficulty in upgrading the status of their discharges and in gaining access to the VA services that they needed. "So we connected to a number of other organizations that were doing similar work and seeing similar problems—among them, Swords to Plowshares and the National Veterans Legal Services Program. This was back in 2014–2015." One of those she worked with was Brad Adams, then a staff attorney at Swords to Plowshares, who was trying to get the VA to amend the regulations that were making it so difficult for veterans to upgrade their discharges and get the services that they needed. "He found some surprising receptivity at VA to looking at these rules, because they were excluding people who really needed help," Montalto recalled. "VA was saying at the time, and they still say now, that they're very serious about addressing veteran suicide, addressing veteran homelessness. You can't 'fix' either of those problems if you are not thinking about how to support veterans who have received less-than-honorable discharges." In petitioning the VA for the rule-making process to change its regulations, Adams got help from the National Veterans Legal Services Program, Montalto's clinic at Harvard Law School, and a law firm willing to donate pro bono time, Latham & Watkins.

The rule-making petition, asking the VA to revisit its rules for dealing with bad paper, was a complex document. "It was a mix of presenting data, presenting individual stories, presenting both legal arguments about why we think the regulations are unlawful, but also some policy arguments about why they're harmful, why they're bad, regardless of the lawfulness of the regulations," Montalto said. "After submitting that to VA, we thought that it would be valuable to create something that was better for public consumption and better for people to read and really grasp." That decision led to the creation of the *Underserved* document. The authors used Freedom of Information Act requests, and they were also able to get existing information online, such as the website of the Board of Veterans' Appeals, where they harvested all of the board's decisions from 1992 to 2015. Though Montalto was the lead writer, if she got stuck, she checked with Brad Adams at Swords to Plowshares to get his advice on the best way to explain their findings to the public. They started the writing in late 2015 and issued the report in March 2016.

"By the end of May, the VA had actually granted the petition for rulemaking," Montalto said. "But granting it doesn't mean they changed the regulations. It just means they agreed, 'Yes, we should revisit those.'" As to the exact form of the new rules, that was still up in the air years later, in the summer of 2023. The VA did hold two rounds of public comment, in July 2020 and September 2021, and some public listening sessions in October of 2021. Some senators and members of the House of Representatives did submit comments. But lawmakers might have been more helpful in past years if they had given the VA the funding it needed for staffing. It seemed at least possible to me that the agency's narrow view of which veterans were entitled to services might have been a result of that inadequate funding. With more funding from a Congress that loves to be seen as veteran-friendly, the VA could have hired more staff to run the character-of-discharge process and could have paid for the health care and other benefits to larger numbers of veterans.

"I do get the sense that cost is something that is very much on VA's mind," Montalto said. "They had to do some cost estimates, and that was a factor that was considered in deciding, 'OK, if we're going to change the regulations, how do we change them? How far do we go?'"

For those who do manage to get their discharges upgraded and gain access to treatment at Veterans Health Administration facilities, like all VHA patients, they will have to endure a wait that can be frustratingly long as the staff-starved agency struggles to respond to claims that the veteran's illness is connected to time in the military. Beyond that, another problem looms on the horizon: an effort by conservative forces to shift veterans' health care from the VHA to the private sector, where their care would be in the hands of doctors without deep knowledge of veteran-specific ailments. Suzanne Gordon is among the leaders of an effort to keep that privatization from happening. Before joining Craven and Early to write *Our Veterans*, she had written two books on healthcare for veterans: *The Battle for Veterans' Healthcare: Dispatches from the Frontlines of Policy Making and Patient Care* (2017) and *Wounds of War: How the VA Delivers Health, Healing, and Hope to the Nation's Veterans* (2018). Like Early, she protested the war in Vietnam when she was young. Like Craven, she serves on the Veterans Healthcare Policy Institute. She is an excellent example of the way someone can both criticize the war and work to help the warrior in life-enhancing ways. In early 2022, Gordon moderated a virtual conference of an organization that arose within Veterans for Peace, called SOVA, the Save Our VA National Campaign. Its purpose was to push back against the forces of privatization. At that conference, Gordon spoke powerfully about the Veterans Health Administration (VHA).

"The VA is probably the most successful healthcare system in the United States, and what you're defending is the only actual national health system in the country. It's the only publicly funded national health system in the country. It's the only integrated and coordinated health system in the country. And that's why its outcomes are so stellar," Gordon said. "For the past 10 years, the media, thanks to the Koch brothers' multimillion-dollar effort to tarnish the reputation of the VA, which was wonderful previous to their effort, the people really think now that the VA is a bad system." A 2015 Pew survey showed that the agency's favorability had plunged precipitously in two years, from 68 percent to 39 percent.

The Koch brothers whom Gordon mentioned are Charles and the late David. The source of their wealth is Koch Industries, the mammoth energy company founded by their father, Fred. In the first two decades of this century, the two brothers used that wealth to construct a network of like-minded, libertarian thinkers and donors who favor shrinking the size of the federal government and suppressing government regulation. The Koch network is a major funder of the conservative-leaning Concerned Veterans for America, which supports privatization of healthcare for veterans. On its website, Concerned Veterans for America praises the work of a major Koch entity, the Americans for Prosperity Foundation, which has been using the Freedom of Information Act to get data from the VHA on wait times for appointments. Wait times exploded as an issue in 2014, with a scandal surrounding the VHA facility in Phoenix, Arizona, where some veterans had to wait for an average of 115 days to see a primary healthcare provider. In the middle of the scandal, CNN reported: "At least 40 U.S. veterans died waiting for appointments at the Phoenix Veterans Affairs Health Care system, many of whom were placed on a secret waiting list. The secret list was part of an elaborate scheme designed by Veterans Affairs managers in Phoenix who were trying to hide that 1,400 to 1,600 sick veterans were forced to wait months to see a doctor, according to a recently retired top VA doctor and several high-level sources."

In examining the scandal, the online news site *Vox* listed two key factors. One was the fast-increasing demand for VHA's health care. "The VA had way more patients than it could handle," *Vox* reported. "The VA has seen a net gain of 700,000 unique patients in the past few years, including veterans from theaters in Iraq and Afghanistan. At the same time, the agency had struggled to fill 400 vacancies in its team of primary care doctors, which in 2013 totaled 5,100."

Of course, the duality of congressional attitudes toward veterans lies at the core of the VA's inability to hire enough doctors. Members of Congress love to fund the Department of Defense (DOD) lavishly, and they love to praise veterans, but when it comes time to fund the agency that serves them, lawmakers simply don't provide enough resources. "Unfortunately, in Congress, the harm-inflicting DOD has a bigger fan club than the caregiving VHA," *Our Veterans* reported. The VA gets criticized routinely as scandal-ridden, but the Pentagon doesn't encounter nearly as much flak, despite its record of failing to pass five consecutive audits—and failing to win a major war since 1945.

"We have hundreds of studies that document that VA delivers superior care to the private sector, at less cost—and this is, by the way, doing it with one hand tied behind their back, because they have never been adequately funded and adequately staffed," said Suzanne Gordon. "Wouldn't it be great if, every time they increase the Pentagon budget by 20 percent, they increase the budget of the VA by the same thing? Actually, that should be a demand." Jeff Roy, coordinator of the steering committee of SOVA, the Save Our VA National Campaign, points to his own experience as a clue that the below-market pay rates at VHA, caused by chronic underfunding, are a real problem. "I have a private-sector physician, primary care, who I'm moving slowly, slowly further away from, as I put all my health care into the VA," Roy told me. "He's excellent, but I remember him saying, 'You know, I wanted to work for the VA.' He may have actually even begun to. And he says, 'But the pay just wasn't high enough.' So, then you have to ask, 'OK, is the pay alone having an impact on driving people who may have great skills into the private sector and away from the VA?'"

The second factor that the *Vox* examination of the Phoenix scandal identified was the system of financial bonuses designed to reward VHA facilities that manage to provide timely appointments for patients and avoid long delays. "The combination—staffing shortages and financial incentives to see patients quickly—encouraged workers at the Phoenix VA hospital to act inappropriately, falsifying records about how quickly they were seeing patients in order to come closer to federal expectations," *Vox* reported. In a 2014 report, NBC News cited internal memos demonstrating that VA employees for at least six years had been using dozens of different scheduling tricks "to hide substantial delays in health care for America's veterans. And whenever the VA tries to stop its staffers from 'gaming the system,' the staffers come up with new techniques."

Within months after the story of the Phoenix scandal broke, Congress acted with uncharacteristic alacrity in passing the Veterans Access, Choice, and Accountability Act of 2014, commonly known as the Choice Act. Its stated purpose was to allow veterans receiving VHA health care to get treated instead in the private sector if they are told they'd have to wait for more than 30 days for an appointment or if they live more than 40 miles from the closest VHA facility. Even if they live within 40 miles of the VHA facility, veterans could use the private sector if they faced "an unusual or excessive geographical burden" in getting there. The bill included the creation of a commission "to examine veterans' access to VA health care and to strategically examine how best to organize the VHA, locate health care resources, and deliver health care to veterans over the next 20 years." The Commission on Care's final report, issued on June 30, 2016, was a mixed blessing for the VHA. The good news was that the report found VHA health care to be "in many ways comparable or better in clinical quality to that generally available in the private sector," and it recommended more generous funding for the VHA, so it could offer more competitive salaries and do a better job of recruiting. The bad news in the report was the caveat that VHA health care "is inconsistent from facility to facility, and can be substantially compromised by problems with access, service, and poorly functioning operational systems and processes." So the commission recommended the creation of something called the "VHA Care System," which would blend private-sector health-care providers into a network supervised by the VHA for the roughly nine million veterans eligible for VHA care. "The commission estimated that over the next few decades, about 40 to 60 percent of veterans will receive some, if not all, of their healthcare from private-sector providers," Suzanne Gordon wrote in *The Battle for Veterans' Healthcare.* One member of the commission, Vietnam veteran Michael Blecker, executive director of Swords to Plowshares, dissented in part from the report. He accepted the possibility of a limited expansion of private-sector care for veterans, but he worried that sending more veterans to the private sector would weaken the base of patients that the VHA needed to keep operating efficiently.

In September 2016, VA Secretary Robert McDonald forwarded to Congress President Barack Obama's response to the Commission on Care report. McDonald said that the president and the VA found 15 of the report's 18 recommendations "feasible and advisable," and he said that the VA had either accomplished or was working on 12 of the 18 items. Then McDonald rolled out a statistical analysis, boasting of 5.3 million completed appointments inside the VHA system in March 2016, which was 730,000 more than in March 2014. On the choice side of the ledger, McDonald reported that veterans had received more than three million authorizations to get care in the private sector from October 2015 to July 2016—up 42 percent. The year of the commission's report was also the year of a presidential election, and the issue of private-sector care for veterans found its way into the campaign, through a nonveteran named Donald J. Trump. His proposal was to give all veterans vouchers to buy health care in the private sector, which would have essentially killed the VHA. Veterans groups pushed back against that idea. But Trump won that election and was soon in a position to do something about health care for veterans. In his administration, the privatization trend continued.

The Choice Act of 2014 was to have been a three-year pilot. But in 2018, Trump signed into law a more permanent piece of legislation, the VA Maintaining Internal Systems and Strengthening Integrated Outside

Networks Act of 2018. That torturous title produced yet another congressional acronym for legislation: the MISSION Act. It continues the march toward privatization. The late Sen. John McCain and Trump had their share of fights at the end of McCain's life, but they were clearly on the same page on the MISSION Act. McCain was a primary mover and shaker for this legislation, and a lot of Democrats went along with it. It wasn't quite the voucher plan that Trump had proposed in 2016, but it was a definite step forward for the forces of privatization. "This was a Trump initiative that, tragically, the veterans service organizations lobbied very hard for," Gordon said during the 2022 SOVA conference. "This law allowed more outsourcing of care to the private sector than the Choice Act that had preceded it, which was supposed to be temporary and last three years and sunset."

The man Trump appointed in early 2017 as secretary of the Department of Veterans Affairs, David Shulkin, had supported the MISSION Act and presided over increased privatization. "When I became under secretary, roughly 19 percent of veterans received care in the community," Shulkin wrote in *It Shouldn't Be This Hard to Serve Your Country*. "When I left the VA as secretary at the end of March 2018, the figure was nearly 36 percent." Ultimately, after Shulkin had held the top VA job for a bit more than a year, Trump fired him—in a tweet, of course. "To me, it was clear: I was pushed out of the VA because of a partisan desire to get rid of me and any other obstacles standing in the way of privatizing the VA," Shulkin wrote.

Trump lost the 2020 election, which put President Joseph R. Biden in charge of overseeing implementation of the MISSION Act. Dan Caldwell, senior advisor at the Koch-funded Concerned Veterans for America, thought the Biden White House wasn't sufficiently enthusiastic or comfortable with the idea of pushing forward the goals of the MISSION Act. "So our concern is that veterans aren't being able to access the care that they've earned, and most importantly, haven't been able to effectively choose the option to get care outside the VA," Caldwell said. "I think that the Biden administration recognizes that VA choice is here to stay, that the VA is going to be integrated with the private health care system in a way that it hasn't been before." To Caldwell, the fight against privatization seems to be about more than just the health care of veterans. He said public employee unions are aligned against further privatization, "mainly the American Federation of Government

Employees," whose opposition is rooted in the fear that more privatization means fewer VA employees and fewer members for the union.

If Trump's successor was less than energetic in pursuing the privatization goals of the MISSION Act, *Our Veterans* reported that there were legitimate reasons: "Faced with a private healthcare system in bad shape—and reshaped for the worse, due to COVID-19—the Biden administration had good reason to rethink the diversion of billions of tax dollars from the VA to costly, less-qualified, and not-even-more-accessible outside providers." The MISSION Act also created the Asset and Infrastructure Review (AIR) Commission, which could lead to the closing of VA facilities and could block the proposed creation of new facilities.

The VA privatization struggle is also part of the larger fight over the future of health care for all Americans. "On the progressive Left, there's a lot of discomfort with too much health care choice within the VA," Caldwell said. "If the VA becomes primarily a payer, as opposed to a provider, it undermines their narrative about the VA being a model government-run health care system that the rest of the country could benefit from." In fact, one of the members of the Commission on Care, Phillip Longman, wrote a book in 2012, before the Phoenix scandal, called *Best Care Anywhere: Why VA Health Care Would Work Better for Everyone.* And in her 2017 book, *The Battle for Veterans' Healthcare*, Gordon quotes Longman briefly on his work-better-for-everyone assertion. "I believe the VA can become the mechanism by which universal, government-provided healthcare comes to the United States," Longman told Gordon. "The VA model of care, with its emphasis on integration, prevention, and evidence-based, cost-effective care, is also in the forefront of where the rest of the U.S. healthcare needs to go. If we lose the VA, the cause of real healthcare delivery system reform will be set back by at least another generation, with incalculably dire consequences to the health and finances of the American population."

Whatever the broader political implications of the future implementation of the MISSION Act and the growth of privatization, it's clear that offering high-quality health care to veterans is a real challenge for non-VHA doctors. "The private sector doesn't have their eyes on the ball when it comes to veteran health care," said SOVA's Jeff Roy. "So, when a veteran comes to them, they don't even ask if you are a veteran. If someone comes to them, Vietnam era, and they have either Agent Orange exposure or something else that may be causing the symptoms that the veteran is presenting and concerned about, if the doctor doesn't ask, the doctor is going to be going through all sorts of tests and so forth that may be unnecessary."

Doctors in the private sector are simply not accustomed to seeing the types and range of problems that confront veterans—not just from combat, but from exposure to toxins on military bases run by the Pentagon, a world-class polluter. "The veteran population may be declining in broad numbers, but the number of people who need health care because of reckless practices by the military and being in wars and so forth is actually increasing, and the number of problems is increasing," Gordon said. "In World War II, you might have had somebody with four problems. In Iraq, they have 16. This is true. The average Medicare beneficiary at 65 has three to five presenting problems. The average Vietnam vet has nine to 12. So you have a very complex patient population. And this is important to note, because private-sector providers, where they're outsourcing patients to, don't know about the problems that you have. They don't know how to recognize the difference between regular asthma and burn-pit-related respiratory problems."

During the forever wars in Iraq and Afghanistan, the military burned immense amounts of trash in open-air burn pits. But it wasn't until 2022 that Congress passed and Biden signed the Promise to Address Comprehensive Toxics Act—better known as the PACT Act. The legislation set aside $300 billion over 10 years for veterans coping with the health effects of the burn pits, from Agent Orange sprayed in Vietnam, and from other exposures to toxics. The legislation also contained the Camp Lejeune Justice Act, opening the door to lawsuits arising from contaminated water at the Marine Corps base, and spawning numerous television commercials by law firms looking to represent what could amount to a million plaintiffs. The PACT Act was the latest development in the long struggle by veterans to get the VA to acknowledge that their current illness is related to something that happened to them in the military. Slowly over the years, the VA has expanded the list of ailments that are presumptively tied to a veteran's days in uniform. The PACT Act codifies the updated way the VA evaluates these illness claims, a new process that has added significantly to the list of illnesses presumed to have arisen during a veteran's military career. The legislation lays out additional illnesses that should be added to the presumptive list, but they will be phased in gradually. Meanwhile, the law sets aside funding to hire additional claims processors and reduce the backlog of disability claims that are overdue for final decisions. So, as the movement toward privatization of VA health care continues at the national level, veterans at the local level continue to work through issues such as upgrading their discharges so that they are eligible for VA health care, getting their disability claims adjudicated, and dealing with a variety of problems that confront them in their post-military life.

"We deal with a lot of veterans that are alone in the world. They might have some mental or physical problems that deprive them of working, making a good income," said Craig Bruno of the Touro veterans clinic. "So, all it takes is a few tickets on their car, and then they're behind the eight ball—or a hospitalization, so they're not working." Many of those nagging, day-to-day problems can lead veterans into homelessness. So can bad paper.

The *Underserved* report on discharge upgrades said that veterans with bad paper discharges "are estimated to be at seven times the risk of homelessness as other veterans." Another factor leading to homelessness is "intimate partner violence." Monica Diaz, executive director of the VHA Homeless Programs Office, referred to that violence in an October 2022 message, reporting that research suggests that veterans are twice as likely to experience this intimate partner violence as people in the general population. "We know that too often, individuals stay in relationships with abusive partners simply because they have nowhere else to live," Diaz wrote. "Furthermore, fleeing domestic violence is often cited as the origin of an individual's experience with homelessness." The Department of Housing and Urban Development's Annual Homeless Assessment Report gives point-in-time estimates of the numbers of homeless persons, based on a single night in the third week of January each year. The 2022 report estimated that 33,129 veterans were homeless. That was a 55 percent decrease from the estimate of 77,367 in 2009, the first year when this information went public. In recent years, the VA has made important strides in reducing homelessness, with something called Project CHALENG—not a misspelling, but an acronym for Community Homelessness Assessment, Local Education and Networking Groups. This was the result of congressional legislation in 1992, followed by additional bipartisan public laws signed in 1994 and 1997.

The purpose of that legislation was to require the VA "to really start engaging with the community, in response to the emerging issue in the late eighties and the early nineties of veterans who were experiencing homelessness," said Jessica Blue-Howells, the lead and subject matter expert for Project CHALENG and the deputy national director for veterans justice programs. She said the legislation required two things: "a survey that both VA homeless providers and community homeless providers took, kind of ranking needs among veterans who were homeless, and then it required meetings, community meetings with community homeless providers and VA homeless program staff."

In 2021, 4,149 people responded to the CHALENG survey, including 1,773 homeless veterans and 2,376 providers. That survey produced a ranking of unmet needs. "Consistent with 2020 data and with the previous 20 years of CHALENG data, in 2021 unmet needs are primarily services that VA cannot provide directly," the CHALENG fact sheet reported in April 2022. "This underscores the importance of collaboration" to meet the needs of homeless vets. The top 10 unmet needs reported by veterans included legal help on such problems as expunging criminal records, debt collection, court fees and fines, discharge upgrades, divorce and child custody, child support, eviction and foreclosure, and restoration of driver's licenses.

The VA does give $700 million in grants annually to more than four hundred nonprofit agencies that help homeless veterans. But until recently, Blue-Howells said, the VA didn't have "the explicit authority to deliver legal services." Then Congress passed the Veterans Health Care and Benefits Improvement Act, signed into law on January 5, 2021—one of Trump's last substantive actions before the January 6 attack on the Capitol. The bill contained a variety of provisions, including better health care for women veterans, and the ability of the VA to start something called the Legal Services for Homeless Veterans and Veterans At-Risk for Homelessness Grant program, which will let VA offer grants to agencies that help with legal services on problems that could lead to homelessness. "The legislation used a lot of the language that has come out of the CHALENG surveys, to be sure that our grants would be able to address these issues that keep coming up," Blue-Howells said. "Of course, law schools and other pro bono legal clinics can and will continue to operate. They also, though, would qualify to apply for funding."

The unmet needs identified in the CHALENG survey also include the broad area of tax issues and, in the number four spot, registered sex offender housing. All across the nation, municipalities have passed legislation saying that registered sex offenders are forbidden to live within a specified area of schools and other places where they might find victims. It's not clear whether the powerful urges that drive sex offenders would be deterred by a government-mandated longer walk from home to a potential victim, but it is clear that this kind of legislation does narrow housing options. The presence of sex offender housing on the list of the unmet needs of veterans does beg the question: How often do veterans show up as sex offenders, compared with the general population?

"The data on that is not known," Blue-Howells said. What is known is the data on veterans in prison. "Veterans are more likely to be incarcerated for a sex offense than nonveterans, and that is persistent," Blue-Howells said. "The 'why' is kind of not known, but in studies that take a look at it, potential reasons are childhood events that happened before people joined the military, kind of those adverse childhood events and those risk factors. Trauma from the military could potentially be involved, especially military sexual trauma." That sexual trauma seems like a good bet to be part of the explanation for this sex offender problem among incarcerated vets, given the continued problem of sexual abuse in the military, outlined in Chapter 5: The Pentagon's own annual estimate for fiscal year 2021 estimated that 36,000 members of the military had experienced sexual abuse.

Sex offenses are far from the only crimes that ensnare veterans in the unloving arms of the criminal justice system. In a recognition that the roots of some of their crimes can be found in problems that arose from their time in the military, such as drug addiction or mental illness, court systems around the nation have established hundreds of veterans treatment courts. The goal is to find alternatives to incarceration where possible, based on the same operating principles that guide drug treatment courts and mental health treatment courts. "Really, the intention is to offer folks an opportunity to have their sentence supervised in the community," said Blue-Howells, who, in addition to her Project CHALENG work, is the deputy national director for veterans justice programs. "So you have the diversion from what would have otherwise been a jail sentence, with the oversight of probation."

At the turn of the century, the idea of specialized treatment courts for a variety of populations was growing throughout the country. "We weren't as concerned in these kind of courts with counting cases, or counting filings in and out, dispositions," said Jonathan Lippman, a former chief judge of the New York State Court of Appeals. "Rather, what's the outcome for people who come into our courts that need justice?"

As veterans began to be seen as a population that needed outcomes-oriented treatment courts of their own, New York became a pioneer. In upstate Buffalo, City Court Judge Robert T. Russell launched the first one in the state, in 2008. Later, to spread the idea further, Lippman turned to one of his predecessors as chief judge: Sol Wachtler, a veteran of the Korean War and an ardent advocate of veterans treatment courts. "Sol was the main proponent of this," Lippman said. "He was in my ear all the time." Lippman wanted to advocate for veterans treatment courts downstate, and he asked Wachtler to craft a speech for him. "I said, 'Sol, you know so much more about this than I do. See if you can sketch something out,' which he did. That speech, and so many other ways to get our message across, were instrumental in getting the public support that we needed to do these courts. There's nothing like the head of the system coming in and giving it a high profile. That's what Sol, in every way, helped me to do. Sol was the driving force of this, without any question."

Wachtler offered a sadly succinct account of the journey that too many veterans take from the military to trouble with the law. "What happens is, these guys get shot up or suffer from PTSD, and they would be hospitalized, and while they're hospitalized, they're treated with addictive drugs. Then they're discharged, and they're addicts, and they go out on the street," Wachtler said. "A dealer comes up to them and says, 'Look, here's five pills. Sell two, and you can keep three.' That's trafficking. That's drug dealing. Then what happens is, they arrest the kingpin, they get the kingpin, and they say, 'OK, who are your mules?'" Too often, the mules get rounded up, and the kingpin does not. The mules, the veterans, find themselves in serious, long-lasting trouble. "They're sent to prison, and for long terms, because they had a kilo with them when they were arrested. So now they're out of prison," Wachtler said. "They have no job. They have no benefits because they have bad paper. So they end up homeless, suicide, or back in prison for another offense."

Wachtler spoke highly of the judge who had created a veterans treatment court in Suffolk County, on the eastern end of Long Island, not long after the start of the court in Buffalo. That was County Court Judge Jack Toomey, an infantry combat veteran of Vietnam. When he became a judge, his military background attuned him to noticing some distressing trends among veterans, the same military-to-prison pipeline that Wachtler had described.

"A lot of guys were coming back from overseas, and they were having problems: emotional problems, criminal problems, drug, alcohol problems," Toomey said. "And a lot of times those problems would intersect with the criminal justice system. People started realizing that there's a correlation between being in combat and coming home and acting out and getting in trouble, and that they had to look at it in a different way."

The origin of the Suffolk treatment court was a request from the administrative judge for Suffolk County, Patrick Leis. At the time, as far as Toomey knew, he was the only judge in Suffolk who was also a combat veteran, and Leis presented him with the idea. "He just kind of gave it to me and said, 'Do whatever you want, whatever you think you want to do with it,'" Toomey said. "So we started it."

Without the benefit of any printed judicial playbook, Toomey just began. In the treatment court setting, he didn't wear his judicial robes or ask security guards to accompany him as he walked through the courtroom, meeting the veteran defendants and the family members who accompanied them. "I'd talk to them, see what their problems were, what their charges were, what they had to do," Toomey said. "I would just explain that we're here to help you, that you shouldn't have done it, but there are extenuating circumstances, and the people owe you this, and we're going to do everything we can to get you through it. I never acted like a judge. I always knew them by their first name."

The crimes that brought them to Toomey's courtroom varied. Any quick online search about veterans treatment courts during the infancy of the idea would have produced a statement saying they were only for misdemeanor offenses. But that's not the way Toomey experienced it. "We had armed robberies, we had homicides, we had drug deals, serious assaults, shootings," Toomey said. "One guy was on his motorcycle with his girlfriend on the back. They're both high and hit a guardrail. He got injured. She was killed. And he came into the veterans court, successfully completed it." In that case, and in many others, Toomey and the treatment court developed a rapport with the veterans, while keeping close watch on their progress. "We knew what they were doing. I would say 95 percent of them really did well."

That even applied to a major violent felony, a case Toomey remembers vividly. "He's a combat marine, had been wounded in action, came back completely bonkers, and got involved in an armed robbery," Toomey recalled. That drug-related robbery resulted in an arrest and indictment. But when prosecutors in the Suffolk County district attorney's office found that the defendant had been a marine, they asked Toomey if he would take the case in the treatment court.

One of the mentors who volunteered with the court was Ralph Zanchelli, a Vietnam veteran who had worked in law enforcement in Suffolk for 31 years, starting as a patrolman, rising to detective, and ending up working undercover out of the district attorney's office on organized crime cases. Zanchelli and an assistant district attorney worked with the former marine. "The whole idea is, he served his country, and naturally the judge wanted to give him an opportunity to come into veterans court," Zanchelli recalled. At first, though, the defendant was reluctant. So Sullivan told Zanchelli to be more emphatic in his persuasion. "We turned around and said to him: 'You're in a position right now that you could be going to jail for a long time. Now you've got an opportunity, because you served your country, to get into veterans court,'" Zanchelli said. Ultimately, that argument carried the day, and the defendant saw the value of veterans treatment court.

Once the former marine was in veterans treatment court, he cooperated. "He goes through the program, does everything he's supposed to do," Toomey said. "He gets his life in order." Ultimately, Toomey received a phone call from Suffolk County District Attorney Thomas Spota, with a suggested disposition for the case. " 'Are you OK if we dismiss the charges on this? He's done so well,'" Spota asked. "I said, 'Tom, I think he deserves it. That's really great. We'll do that.'" Toomey appreciated Spota's position in the marine's case. What followed was a sad irony of criminal justice that Toomey recounted wistfully: A day after Toomey dismissed the charges, Spota found himself under indictment, standing before a federal judge, accused of helping to cover up the misdeeds of a senior police official whom Spota had mentored for years. The felonious marine had his charges dismissed, but Spota ended up sentenced to five years in prison—more time than the rogue cop he had helped.

The VA itself has nothing to do with the establishment of the treatment courts, but it does contribute something valuable to the enterprise: the services of veterans-justice outreach coordinators, who work for the local VA facility and coordinate with the treatment courts. They also work on other initiatives to help keep veterans out of the criminal justice system and to guide them if they fall into it. A major national effort to help veterans is the Justice Involved Veterans network. It's led by the National Institute of Corrections within the Department of Justice, in partnership with the VA and the Substance Abuse and Mental Health Services Administration. This network includes people along the whole route of the criminal justice journey, including sheriffs, county jail administrators, and prison officials. The network's name sounds like murky jargon, but the basic idea is clear: to intervene as early as possible in a veteran's problems. "If local police can find someone who's in distress and address the issue if it's safe to do so while that person's in distress and never even need to arrest them, you've prevented all of those downstream consequences of having a charge or having an arrest or having a conviction, spending time in jail, spending time in prison," Jessica Blue-Howells said.

In Toomey's case, the veterans justice outreach coordinator was Eric Bruno, the son of Craig Bruno of the Touro veterans clinic. "He's not a veteran, but he's just great—a great, great guy with the veterans," Toomey said. If veterans came before Toomey and admitted to violating one of the conditions the treatment court had set, such as refraining from drugs or alcohol, Toomey would commend them for their honesty, and he and Eric Bruno would help them chart the next steps. If they needed more frequent treatment, that's what Toomey and Bruno would arrange. "They always seem to respond well to it. We talk to them like they were regular people, not like they were criminals."

The underlying philosophy of Toomey's treatment court was simple: "No veteran left behind," Toomey said. "We would do everything we could to get a veteran—especially combat veterans, especially guys who were really suffering from PTSD or traumatic brain injury—and get them through the program, do everything we could, without leaving them behind. It was my job to get them through. They did the work, but it was really up us to make sure, through the mentors and through Eric and everybody that was affiliated with it, we wanted them to make it. We weren't there to trap them or find ways that you could punish them more severely."

As we spoke, I asked whether Toomey had taken any incoming fire, or even gentle pushback, from people who weren't veterans and got a less customized treatment in his court, or people who had been the victims of a crime committed by a veteran. "I can't remember anybody coming in and screaming, saying, 'No he shouldn't be in here,' or anything like that," Toomey said. Even in the case where a young woman had died when her boyfriend, high on a recreational drug, ran his motorcycle into a guardrail, her parents seemed to understand. "They were on board with it," Toomey said. "They used to come to veterans court, and I talked to them before I put the defendant, the boyfriend, in."

Now, in retirement from County Court, Toomey serves as the judge in a village court, where traffic tickets are the predominant violation he adjudicates. He looks back at his time dealing with veterans as a jewel in his decades-long legal and judicial career. "It was the most rewarding experience I ever had in my professional life, at the veterans court, because you could see, however long it lasted, you were definitely changing their lives and making a difference."

Despite efforts like the treatment courts and the work thousands of nonprofits focused on helping veterans, many continue to live with the debilitating effects of traumatic brain injury, which can include anxiety and depression, and with the flashbacks and nightmares of post-traumatic stress disorder. The acronym is now nearly universal, but the full understanding of PTSD is a fairly recent development, outlined by David Morris in *The Evil Hours: A Biography of Post-Traumatic Stress Disorder*. Morris did not contract post-traumatic stress while he was in the Marine Corps, deployed in the Gulf War. It happened later, when he was a journalist covering the war in Iraq, and a roadside bomb almost killed him in 2007. "Later, I interviewed a prominent psychoanalyst, who told me that trauma destroys the fabric of time. In normal time, you move from one moment to the next, sunrise to sunset, birth to death," Morris wrote. "After trauma, you may move in circles, find yourself being sucked backwards into an eddy, or bouncing about like a rubber ball from now to then and back again." His memory of what happened to him in a seemingly quiet neighborhood of Baghdad is inescapably vivid, including the question that a soldier asked him just before the bomb went off: "Have you ever been blown up before, sir?" That one explosion continues to reverberate through his life. "I have been blown up so many times in my mind that it is impossible to imagine a version of myself that has not been blown up."

As the biographer of this condition, Morris dove deeply into the history of war-induced trauma, back to ancient times and forward to the "nostalgia," insanity, and other nervous disorders reported among soldiers in the Civil War, to "shell shock" in World War I, to the official acknowledgment of PTSD in the post-Vietnam War era. "A condition that went unacknowledged for millennia, and began its public life with a handful of disgruntled Vietnam veterans 'rapping' in the offices of an anti-war group in midtown Manhattan in December 1970, has spread to every nation on the globe," Morris wrote. In 1980, it was included for the first time as a three-page, 1,500-word section of the *Diagnostic and Statistical Manual of Mental Disorders*, a thick reference work published by the American Psychiatric Association. "A species of pain that went unnamed for most of human history, PTSD is now the fourth most common psychiatric disorder in the United States. According to the latest estimates, nearly 8 percent of all Americans—twenty-eight million people—will suffer from post-traumatic stress at some point in their lives. According to the Veterans Administration, which spends more annually on PTSD research and treatment than any organization in the world, PTSD is the number one health concern of American military veterans, regardless of when they served."

Beyond post-traumatic stress is another war wound that goes even deeper: moral injury. "Moral injury results when soldiers violate their core moral beliefs, and in evaluating their behavior negatively, they feel they no longer live in a reliable, meaningful world and can no longer be regarded as decent human beings," wrote Rita Nakashima Brock and Gabriella Lettini in *Soul Repair: Recovering from Moral Injury after War*. "They may feel this even if what they did was warranted and unavoidable."

One survivor of the post-9/11 wars, Matthew Hoh, has written piercingly of his own experience with moral injury, after returning from his second tour in Iraq with the Marine Corps. "I wanted to step away from the war entirely," Hoh wrote in an essay in *Paths of Dissent*. "There was an enormous dissonance between what I had taken part in during my time in Iraq and who I thought I was as a person. The dissonance was causing chaos, dismay, and desolation within my mind and spirit. This was moral injury: the harrowing feeling of having transgressed—whether through thought or deed, action or inaction—against your moral code. It is a betrayal of who you thought you were…. I was in a bad way. I cannot emphasize enough the destructive effects—mental, emotional, and spiritual—of moral injury. It is believed by many to be the primary driver of combat veteran suicides."

The numbers of suicides among veterans and active-duty members of the military in the current forever-war era are staggering. "This paper estimates 30,177 active duty personnel and veterans of the post 9/11 wars have died by suicide, significantly more than the 7,057 service members killed in post-9/11 war operations," wrote Thomas Howard Suitt III in a 2021 study written for the Costs of War Project at Brown University. "High suicide rates mark the failure of the U.S. government and U.S. society to manage the mental health costs of our current conflicts." The estimate was even higher in 2019 testimony before the House Committee on Oversight and Reform by Terri Tanielian, a senior behavioral scientist at the RAND Corporation. "We all know the of-ten-cited statistic: 20 veterans die by suicide each day," she testified. "Since this figure became a rallying cry 2,256 days ago, we have lost 270,720 Americans to suicide, 45,120 of whom have been veterans or service members."

Both the Department of Defense and the VA have worked to address the suicide problem. The VA's Office of Mental Health and Suicide Prevention, for example, publishes annually a long, highly detailed, statistically robust study of suicide among veterans. The report issued in September 2022 offered some "Anchors of Hope," including this: "There were 343 fewer Veterans who died from suicide in 2020 than in 2019, and 2020 had the lowest number of Veteran suicides since 2006. From 2001 through 2018, the number of Veteran suicides increased on average by 47 deaths per year. From 2019 to 2020, there were consecutive reductions, of 307 and 343 suicides, respective-ly, an unprecedented decrease since 2001…. The overall downward trends in Veteran suicide in 2019 and 2020 are encouraging. They followed VA's launch of the 2018 *National Strategy for Preventing Veteran Suicide*." But in her 2019 House testimony, Tanielian, who later moved from RAND to the White House as a special assistant for veterans affairs, made this clear: "We can and must do more to address this problem."

What is the "more" that needs to be done, to keep veterans from becoming homeless, from falling into drug addiction, from committing suicide? For starters, Congress needs to follow the advice of Suzanne Gordon and increase the funding of the VA whenever it throws more money at the Pentagon. Until the VA is fully funded and staffed, veterans will continue to encounter problems in getting their claims for service-related illnesses processed. The VA also has to live up to the congressional intent dating back to 1944 and stop denying health care based on bad paper for offenses that do not warrant a court-martial. "Nearly five hundred thousand Vietnam-era veterans have received less-than-honorable separations, often resulting in a lifelong barrier to GI benefits and decent employment," David Cortright wrote in *Soldiers in Revolt: GI Resistance During the Vietnam War*. But he didn't just gripe about that situation. He offered a sweeping plan: "The only just solution is to establish 'one discharge for all': the current system of five separate discharge classifications should be completely abolished and replaced with a single, ungraded certificate denoting completion of service."

The VA could also do more to ease the transition from combat to civilian life. In World War II, battle-scarred veterans on the ships returning them to America at least had some time to begin thinking about civilian life. In today's world, a soldier can be in combat one day and back in the world a day or two later. That is a jarring transition. On top of all the other adjustments they have to make, they need to figure out whether they are eligible for VA health care. "As far as I know, there is no smooth transition from your discharge to the VA," said Craig Bruno of the Touro veterans clinic. So Bruno has proposed that the VA "streamline that process so that, when you're discharged, your DD-214, your discharge paper, be provided directly to the VA and that you automatically, despite whatever income you might have, you automatically get filed with the VA. And in this way, the VA can track their veterans wherever they go."

In short, veterans have a lot of real needs, which Congress and the VA must address. They also need us all to adopt an attitude toward them that acknowledges the problems they face, without spreading a false stigma about all veterans being so needy that they can't function in society. Jessica Blue-Howells outlined the "anti-stigma work" that the veterans justice program at VA does, helping veterans without stigmatizing them. "We talk a lot about exactly that issue: kind of over-labeling people as at risk for homelessness or at risk of criminal justice interventions or those types of things," she said. "I think what's important is remembering that, in most cases, veterans are successful. People have a successful experience in the military, they leave the military successfully, and they move on with their lives successfully in most cases. Issues of being in homelessness are critical, and it's important for us to address. Issues of veterans being involved in criminal justice are important for us to address. But they are not the norm."

What veterans definitely do *not* need is EGOS, the Empty Gestures of Support that so many Americans so unthinkingly throw at them, gestures that fix nothing, that do nothing to make the lives of veterans better, that fail to ease the crushing burdens of war. Let me allow two combat veterans, one from the Vietnam era and one from the post-9/11 era, to have the last word on Empty Gestures of Support and real needs.

In his book *Un-American: A Soldier's Reckoning of Our Longest War*, West Point graduate and Afghanistan veteran Erik Edstrom put it this way: "Soldiers and veterans don't need priority boarding, 10% discounts at gimmicky chain restaurants, or a few crinkled bills stuffed into a charity's coffee can. What they need is a nation that can find the courage and conviction to stop misusing their service." Andrew Bacevich, another West Point graduate and Vietnam veteran, and the father of a son killed by an improvised explosive device in Iraq, wrote this in *Paths of Dissent*: "On a recent Veterans Day, merchants in my corner of New England offered vets an abundance of good deals: free coffee, free doughnuts, free pizza, free car washes, and as much as 30 percent off assorted retail purchases. Here was 'thank you for your service' as something more than an empty sentiment. I got my car washed and took a pass on the rest. What we Americans owe vets is not free pizza but the decency to hear them out and ponder what they have learned. There is value in their testimony. To listen attentively is the least the rest of us can do."

Chapter 9
ONE DOES WHAT ONE CAN

Worshiping warriors is far from a uniquely American mindset. It's been going on for centuries, around the globe. Ancient Greek and Latin epic poetry sings the praises of war and the warriors who wage it. My own introduction to this universal lionization happened in high school, where we studied an epic poem by Publius Vergilius Maro, the *Aeneid*, and I wrote my own translation of its opening verses for the school's literary magazine. The *Aeneid* begins with these simple, scene-setting Latin words: "*Arma virumque cano,*" meaning, "Of arms and a man I sing." Another translation for "*arma*" is "war."

Virgil portrays Aeneas in heroic colors, as a warrior fighting valiantly in the Trojan War, to save Troy from the Greeks. When Troy fell, Aeneas headed for Italy, navigating his way through the mythological displeasure and quirks of multiple gods and goddesses. Ultimately, when Aeneas reached Italy, Virgil described him as a founder of the Roman state. Centuries before Virgil, in the epic poem the *Iliad*, the Greek poet Homer had also praised Aeneas in heroic terms, using such phrases as "great-hearted."

In the two millennia after Virgil, the world offered many opportunities for those seeking the glory of war. To name just a few of those long-lasting struggles, the Romans battled the Persians, the Crusaders fought the Muslims for control of the Holy Land, and the English fought the French for more than seven hundred years—a remarkable level of lethal enmity spanning many, many generations. Then the English and the French were on the same side, this time against the Germans. In the United Kingdom during World War I—also known as the Great War and, ridiculously and inaccurately, the War to End All Wars—young men eagerly, almost giddily, enlisted in a war to defeat "the Hun." They saw it as a glorious struggle that they felt sure would be over by Christmas. Of course, it wasn't. In the trench warfare and epic battles of Europe, the modern, ever-more-lethal weapons of war, such as machine guns and fighter planes, dramatically elevated the body count. For so many young men, what had started as a hunt for glory became the ugly, gory reality of mechanized battle. The British poet Wilfred Owen, who lost his life in combat in France, one week before the war ended, put it this way:

> If you could hear, at every jolt, the blood
> Come gargling from the froth-corrupted lungs,
> Obscene as cancer, bitter as the cud
> Of vile, incurable sores on innocent tongues,—
> My friend, you would not tell with such high zest
> To children ardent for some desperate glory,
> The old Lie: *Dulce et decorum est*
> *Pro patria mori*

That stubbornly long-lasting lie, "It is sweet and fitting to die for one's country," dates back to the Roman poet Quintus Horatius Flaccus, who died not long before the birth of Jesus. For many young Americans enlisting in today's wars, even those who have never heard Horace's Latin words about the sweet and fitting death in combat, the idea of fighting for one's country, either out of pure patriotism or out of a hunger for combat glory, is still a powerful force—along with such dollars-and-cents recruitment incentives as help with college tuition. For anyone contemplating enlistment, influenced even unknowingly by Horace's glory-tinged view of dying for one's country, one powerful antidote is a book by veteran war correspondent Chris Hedges, *What Every Person Should Know About War.* Based on his deep research and broad reading, including a series of army field manuals, Hedges asks questions about living and dying in war, and he answers them in dry, almost matter-of-fact language. The book's second question is "Has the world ever been at peace?" Hedges reports, "Of the past 3,400 years, humans have been entirely at peace for 268 of them, or just 8 percent of recorded history."

In the chapter on dying in battle, Hedges writes about last words: "Those who die in combat often call for their mothers." That was true not only of American troops in Vietnam but of the Viet Cong (VC). Hedges quotes one account of an American who had a good enough grasp of the Vietnamese language to understand what dying Vietnamese were saying: "When someone gets wounded, they call out for their mothers, their wives, their girlfriends. There I was listening to the VC cry for the same things." And when they die, the gory overshadows the glory. Hedges writes about "death agonies" and "random spasms of muscles" and reports: "Your body will have the flaccid feel of a slab of meat."

For young Americans, in the years before they are old enough to enlist, the dominant image of warfare is not that of soldiers dying painfully and ingloriously, crying piteously for their mothers. It is the high-tech imagery of video war games such as Call of Duty, which allows them to score points by killing realistic images of a computer-generated "enemy." In an earlier time, before the rise of those games, boys emulated military glory by playing war in the streets and in backyards, making do with whatever was at hand to simulate weapons of war: branches, sticks, rocks. In their make-believe foxholes, they felt vaguely heroic as they voiced aloud the sounds of battle they had seen printed in their war comic books: Kapow! Bam! Those imaginary childhood battles planted the seeds of war glory in young minds.

In our own country, the founding generation found some glory in the need to revolt against what they considered the oppressive monarchy of England. But some of them also had strong doubts about the military, arising largely from their experience with British troops based in the American colonies. Like many members of the founding generation, James Madison deeply distrusted the idea of a standing army for the nation that they were working to create. "A standing military force, with an overgrown Executive, will not long be safe companions to liberty," Madison argued. "The means of defense against foreign danger, have been always the instruments of tyranny at home." Later, he called the nation's establishment of a standing army a "calamity."

In contrast, Alexander Hamilton favored a standing army and wrote a defense of it in the *Federalist Papers*. George Washington, who had led the Continental Army during the Revolutionary War, had the same view. "He felt that militia were unreliable," said Gordon Wood, author of *The Radicalism of the American Revolution*, on *Constitutional*, a 2017 *Washington Post* podcast. "Whenever they confronted real regular British soldiers, redcoats, they often ran and dispersed. They didn't stand up to the enemy, and he had a strong objection to the militia, and he wanted regular soldiers. He and Hamilton were strongly in favor of what we would call a standing army, a professional military force. Both of them, especially Hamilton, wanted to build up the United States as a military state capable of taking on the European powers on their own terms. And that meant a large army, a large navy." In the *Journal of the American Revolution*, Griffin Bovée wrote, "Hamilton and his likeminded peers thought that an irrational fear of standing armies stood in the way of the creation of a great nation state."

But Madison's fear of that kind of powerful army had a long history, dating back to England in the 1600s, when Parliament and King Charles I disagreed sharply. An army created by supporters of Parliament staged what amounted to a military coup, lopped off the king's head, installed Oliver Cromwell as the nation's leader, then began making demands on Parliament.

Actually, the framers didn't have to think all the way back to Cromwell. In the 1750s, during the French and Indian War between the French colonies in North America and the English colonies, England sent soldiers here. The war in the colonies ended in 1763, but the British soldiers stayed. In 1765, Parliament passed the Quartering Act, requiring the American colonies to house British soldiers in such places as barns and inns. This did not go over well, and it became part of the grievances leading to the Revolutionary War. The presence of those troops became particularly unbearable in Boston. That influx of troops—4,000 of them in a town of 15,000—led to friction with the citizens. "Throughout 1769, reports of assaults, robbery, harassment, and rape by soldiers were commonplace," wrote David Vine, in *The United States of War: A Global History of America's Endless Conflicts, from Columbus to the Islamic State*. On March 5, 1770, British soldiers fired on a crowd in front of Boston's Customs House. "Five locals were killed in what became known as the Boston Massacre," Vine wrote. "The killings were another spark leading toward revolution."

In 1776, the presence of British troops became part of the long list of complaints against the British monarch, King George III, laid out in the

Declaration of Independence. "He has kept among us, in times of peace, Standing Armies without the Consent of our legislatures," the declaration griped. More than that, the declaration accused the king of sending "swarms of Officers to harrass our people, and eat out their substance," of "quartering large bodies of armed troops among us," and of "protecting them, by a mock Trial from punishment for any Murders which they should commit on the Inhabitants of these States."

Years before the sweaty, contentious process in Philadelphia in 1787 that gave birth to the Constitution of the fledgling nation, the constitutions of Massachusetts and Virginia had used the exact same phrase to describe standing armies: "dangerous to liberty." So, it should come as no surprise that Madison, in sponsoring the Bill of Rights, included an amendment focused totally on the quartering of troops. It is exactly one sentence long, a sentence almost universally ignored today: "No Soldier shall, in time of peace be quartered in any house, without the consent of the Owner, nor in time of war, but in a manner to be prescribed by law."

It isn't the Third Amendment that draws endless attention these days, but another one-sentence addition to the Constitution, the Second Amendment: "A well regulated Militia, being necessary to the security of a free State, the right of the people to keep and bear Arms, shall not be infringed."

Both amendments, with eight others, won ratification at the end of 1791. The Third Amendment has never evoked much controversy or Supreme Court attention, but the issue of a standing army remained a touchy one in the early years of the republic. In fact, Treasury Secretary Hamilton became the target of a Connecticut editor who accused him not only of trying to create a standing army, but also of adultery. Hamilton was guilty on both counts, but the Alien and Sedition Acts, which President John Adams had signed into law the year before the Connecticut editor aimed his barbs at Hamilton, outlawed any "false, scandalous and malicious writing" against the government. The editor ended up paying a $200 fine and spending three months in jail.

Today, hardly a day goes by without a high-decibel, high-intensity debate about the Second Amendment. But only a vanishingly small percentage of Americans would discern any connection between the two one-sentence amendments. In fact, however, many historians argue that, when the framers wrote that much-parsed, much-misunderstood sentence about militias and arms, they were thinking mostly about state militias as a defense against any future oppression by a federally controlled standing army.

Yet we have one. The battle over a standing army ended long ago, and no reasonable person can expect that the United States will ever be without one. America has an active-duty military of well over a million people, plus almost as many reserves. Are those troops, as Madison dreaded, "the instruments of tyranny at home"? Certainly not in the sense that the troops are quartered in "any house," as the Third Amendment prohibited, but they are quartered in hundreds of military bases around the world. Domestically, the troops have become an instrument of rigid conformity, if not tyranny. That's not a result of what the troops themselves are doing. It's the work of the political class, which uses them as an almost magical incantation, in support of war or other causes, like suppression of dissent.

In the struggle among the founding generation over the question of a standing army, all Madison got out of it was the Third Amendment, permanently buried in obscurity. What Hamilton got was a standing army. But America is not unique. There are tiny exceptions, like army-less Costa Rica. But Russia and China, the major nations seen as rivals to the United States, have substantial armies. In fact, any argument for a reduced American military is bound to run into a counterargument that both Russia and China are rising threats. Latin American and African nations also have standing armies, and they come to our attention periodically when the army stages a military coup. We now live in an era of standing armies. None of them will be going away.

But surely we can ask some useful questions about our army—including all the branches of the nation's armed forces. Question number one should be this: Is it realistic to plan for a clash of American ground forces in a classic land battle with Russia or China, in an era when the major powers have so many other ways of waging war, from cyberattacks to nuclear weapons, that do not involve infantry and artillery clashes on the ground in Europe or Asia? If that plan for land warfare exists, isn't it just another example of generals planning to fight the last war?

Beyond that core question, we need to ask: How big does the military need to be? Where does it need to be? As we explored in Chapter 6, we should be asking: How many overseas bases should a nation maintain? Do those bases really provide a swifter response to potential enemies than the airlift of troops from bases in the continental United States? Why can't Congress do a top-to-bottom review of these bases, from the huge Camp Humphreys in South Korea to the minuscule army garrison in Garmisch-Partenkirchen, a ski resort in Bavaria? If our military failed to protect the nation on 9/11—and it did fail, spectacularly—what does it need to do differently? Many in the Pentagon and in Congress would argue for more troops, more aircraft carriers, more fighter jets, more stealth bombers. More spending is always the answer we hear, despite what President Dwight D. Eisenhower famously said in his farewell address, warning about the dangers of the military-industrial complex. "In the councils of government, we must guard against the acquisition of unwarranted influence, whether sought or unsought, by the military-industrial complex," said Eisenhower, a five-star general who commanded American troops in Europe during World War II. "The potential for the disastrous rise of misplaced power exists and will persist."

Unfortunately, Eisenhower's warning has not succeeded in curbing the growth of America's vast share of the world's military budget. The Stockholm International Peace Research Institute estimated that total military spending around the globe in 2022 was $2.24 trillion. The biggest spender was the United States. On Tax Day 2023, the National Priorities Project estimated that the average taxpayer paid $1,087 for Pentagon contractors in 2022, compared with $270 for K–12 education and $43 for the Centers for Disease Control and Prevention (CDC).

The Pentagon is not the only customer for defense contractors: The United States leads all other nations in arms exports. "Today we have become what Eisenhower's worst nightmare predicted in his farewell address," said retired army Col. Lawrence Wilkerson. "We are the merchants of death for seven billion people." Wilkerson was chief of staff to Secretary of State Colin Powell when Powell told the United Nations in 2003 that Iraq had weapons of mass destruction. That speech helped lay the groundwork for the invasion of Iraq, and Wilkerson has expressed real regret about his own role in it. He is now one of the experts on the Eisenhower Media Network, made up of former national security officials, military and civilian. "Our experts offer alternative analyses untainted by Pentagon or defense industry ties," the network's website proclaims. "They oppose systemic corruption, nepotism, and the undue influence that the military-industrial-congressional complex—through its money and army of 'revolving door' lobbyists—has on the policymaking process."

The Eisenhower Media Network and the National Priorities Project are not the only entities seeking a more rational, less reflexively bellicose approach to national security. The Quincy Institute for Responsible Statecraft is one example. "The practical and moral failures of U.S. efforts to unilaterally shape the destiny of other nations by force requires a fundamental rethinking of U.S. foreign policy assumptions," the institute says, describing its work. "We connect and mobilize a network of policy experts and academics who are dedicated to a vision of American foreign policy based on military restraint rather than domination." The chairman of the Quincy Institute board is Andrew Bacevich, the West Point graduate and Vietnam veteran quoted often in this book. Bacevich is just one of many soldiers who have learned from their time in the military and written books critical of the way America conducts itself around the world. The title of one of his books makes the point admirably: *The New American Militarism: How Americans Are Seduced by War.*

That seduction, the overwhelming temptation to cheer for war and for warriors, is powerful, not only among impressionable, military-age youth, but among men and women with enough experience of the world to know better. Historian Adam Hochschild describes one historic moment of war-whooping in his *American Midnight: The Great War, a Violent Peace, and Democracy's Forgotten Crisis.* The scene was President Woodrow Wilson's address to Congress in April 1917, announcing that he had come down on the side of joining in the fight against Germany. Pressure had been building on the United States to join "the Great War" since it began in 1914, but the slogan of Wilson's victorious 1916 re-election campaign had been, "He kept us out of war." Wilson's reluctance to send Americans into the bloodbath in Europe did not please people like Theodore Roosevelt, the combat-loving former president. Hochschild describes Roosevelt's frustration. In a letter to his friend Henry Cabot Lodge, a Republican senator from Massachusetts, Roosevelt wrote, "If he does not go to war with Germany I shall skin him alive."

In his speech to Congress, Wilson made clear that America was now ready for war. This line elicited a huge roar of approval: "There is one choice we cannot make, we are incapable of making: we will not choose the path of submission," Wilson said. At that moment, the chief justice of the United States, Edward Douglass White, reacted with overwhelming happiness and gratitude, and the legislators and others in that chamber also roared their approval. "If there was a single moment that epitomized the frenzy unleashed in these years, it was when the chief justice of the United States leapt to his feet and wept tears of joy at the certainty of war," Hochschild wrote. "That frenzy would only grow as time passed."

As the war frenzy grew, so did an era of repression in the United States, much of it aimed at those who dared criticize the war or refused to take part in it. Hochschild's *American Midnight* describes in painful detail what happened in the years right after Wilson's speech: the vigilantism, the citizens' arrests, the closing of magazines and newspapers, the physical abuse of conscientious objectors. In that period, other persistent societal ills—not directly related to war but exacerbated by the general frenzy of the time—gripped the nation: continued lynchings of Black Americans for the slightest of reasons, nativist fears of immigrants, and repression of an aggressive union, the Industrial Workers of the World, known as the Wobblies. "For anti-labor politicians and businessmen, the Wobblies were a convenient bogeyman, and the war a welcome chance to crush them," Hochschild wrote.

In our own era, the 9/11 attacks brought another large cohort of young people rushing into war. They were outraged by the deaths of three thousand Americans on one gloriously sunny day at the World Trade Center, the Pentagon, and in a field in Pennsylvania, and they felt the need to do something about it. So they enlisted. The administration of President George W. Bush dubbed it a war on terror, and Bush made the case for including Iraq in the "axis of evil," by arguing that it was producing weapons of mass destruction. Even though that assertion soon proved to be false, America invaded Iraq, costing hundreds of thousands of Iraqi lives. In the war on terror, the "Thank you for your service" and "Support the troops" mantras flourished.

To push back against that love of war and worship of warriors, I have quoted in this book other veterans, such as William Astore, Mac Bica, Philip Caputo, David Cortright, Erik Edstrom, Rory Fanning, Danny Sjursen, Kayla Williams, and Ann Wright. They have written about the seduction of war, describing in gritty language what combat is like and shining a powerful light on the underlying realities—the lies, miscalculations, and faulty intelligence that put them in harm's way on the other side of the world. I have cited the writing of Cortright and Jonathan Hutto on anti-war soldiers. I have quoted the wisdom of scholars and journalists such as Christian Appy, Andrew Bacevich, William Hartung, Chris Hedges, Jerry Lembcke, Catherine Lutz, Rosa Brooks, David Vine, and Nick Turse. But all of those books and articles have not yet sufficiently altered the near-idolatrous perception of America's armed forces. Nor do I imagine that this book will significantly change that perception. But I felt the need to try, to add my own contribution to the growing list of work that looks critically at our warriors and the wars that our politicians send them to fight. My own military experience did not include combat, but it did plant in me the seeds of an increasingly skeptical attitude about the universal adulation of our armed forces. The writing of these veterans, scholars, and journalists helped me to feel comfortable in adding my own journalistic perspective, focusing on the need to dial down the adulation.

That near-idolatry is one element in our nation's historic comfort with war. It is not, admittedly, the most powerful element. That title belongs to the military-industrial-congressional complex, which keeps the billions of dollars flowing, to build weapons and to contribute to the campaigns of lawmakers who support that weapons spending. Any substantial reduction of that spending seems like an impossible task. It reminds me of an often repeated story about optimism in the face of overwhelming odds: A horseman came upon a tiny sparrow lying on its back in the middle of the road, with its legs pointing to the sky. The horseman asked the bird to explain its posture. "I heard the sky is going to fall today," the bird chirped. Unimpressed, the horseman laughed and said, "And I suppose your spindly legs can hold up the sky?" Undaunted, the sparrow answered, "Well, sir, one does what one can."

In that spirit, each of us should ask, What can I do to curb the worship of war and warriors, to chip away at what Catherine Lutz calls "the military normal"?

First, resolutely set your own attitude a few notches below idolatry. When you encounter someone who has spent time in the military, don't reflexively mouth the "Thank you for your service" mantra. Instead, ask how life has been going after the military and express concern.

Demonstrate your concern by finding a nonprofit that works with veterans experiencing homelessness or suffering from war wounds, and volunteer to help. Be careful, though: Not every charity that purports to help veterans is equally deserving of your support. Check them out on Charity Navigator.

Do some volunteer counter-recruitment work. Chapter 2 outlined some of what counter-recruitment organizations are doing, especially focusing on giving high school students a more realistic view of the military recruitment efforts in their schools. Ask your school district's superintendent and school board about their policy on allowing military recruiters in the school.

Using online resources such as opensecrets.org, keep track of the flow of campaign contributions from the military-industrial complex to your own member of Congress. If your member is benefiting from the war machine, don't hesitate to gripe about it in a message to that member's office, a letter to the editor of a local newspaper, or a small campaign contribution of your own to the opposing candidate, if that candidate has pledged not to take large contributions from corporations.

Read some of the books listed in the bibliography, to elevate your own understanding of what war is like today and how it hurts the warriors and their families.

If a president attempts to build support for military action by calling on all of us to "support the troops," or asks you to remember the mythical spit-tsunami during the Vietnam War, push back with the truth, among your friends, in the local newspaper, or wherever you can express your doubts about the latest war. If you fall for "support the troops" or the spit myth, you're endangering the troops by clearing a path to where that will leave too many of them dead or badly injured, or suffering PTSD or moral injury, or both.

If you hear anyone, from the president to your local politician, blithely claiming that the troops are "fighting for our freedoms," don't be afraid to ask, "Really?" Too often, America's wars have not been about preserving the freedoms of Americans, but about imposing our will on other nations or preserving the flow of oil. In actual combat, the reality is this: Soldiers are usually not thinking about freedoms, but about staying alive and protecting the soldiers next to them.

The millennia-old love of war glory, dating back even before Homer, Virgil, and Cicero, and the modern-day influence of the military-industrial complex, are powerful forces, not easily overcome. But, like the scrawny sparrow trying to hold up the falling sky, one does what one can.

BIBLIOGRAPHY

Alexander, Michelle. *The New Jim Crow: Mass Incarceration in the Age of Colorblindness*. New York: The New Press, 2010.

Alford, Matthew. *Reel Power: Hollywood Cinema and American Supremacy*. London: Pluto Press, 2010.

Alford, Matthew, and Secker, Tom. *National Security Cinema: The Shocking New Evidence of Government Control in Hollywood*. Scotts Valley, California: CreateSpace Independent Publishing Platform, 2017.

Appy, Christian G. *American Reckoning: The Vietnam War and Our National Identity*. New York: Penguin, 2016.

Bacevich, Andrew J. *The New American Militarism: How Americans Are Seduced by War*. New York: Oxford University Press, 2005.

Bacevich, Andrew J. *Breach of Trust: How Americans Failed Their Soldiers and Their Country*. New York: Picador, 2013.

Bacevich, Andrew J. *The Limits of Power: The End of American Exceptionalism*. New York: Metropolitan Books, Henry Holt, 2008.

Bacevich, Andrew, and Sjursen, Daniel A., editors. *Paths of Dissent: Soldiers Speak Out Against America's Misguided Wars*. New York: Metropolitan Books, 2022.

Bakken, Tim. *The Cost of Loyalty: Dishonesty, Hubris, and Failure in the U.S. Military*. New York: Bloomsbury, 2020.

Belkin, Aaron. *Bring Me Men: Military Masculinity and the Benign Façade of American Empire 1898–2001*. New York: Columbia University Press, 2012.

Benedict, Helen. *The Lonely Soldier: The Private War of Women Serving in Iraq*. Boston: Beacon Press, 2009.

Bennis, Phyllis, and Wildman, David. *Ending the US War in Afghanistan: A Primer*. Northampton: Olive Branch Press, 2010.

Bica, Camillo (Mac). *Worthy of Gratitude? Why Veterans May Not Want to Be Thanked for Their "Service" in War*. Smithtown, New York: Gnosis Press, 2015.

Bolger, Daniel. *Why We Lost: A General's Inside Account of the Iraq and Afghanistan Wars*. New York: An Eamon Dolan Book, Mariner Books, Houghton Mifflin Harcourt, 2015.

Brock, Rita Nakashima, and Lettini, Gabriella. *Soul Repair: Recovering from Moral Injury after War*. Boston: Beacon Press, 2012.

Brooks, Rosa. *How Everything Became War and the Military Became Everything: Tales from the Pentagon*. New York: Simon & Schuster, 2016.

Burke, Carol. *Camp All-American, Hanoi Jane, and the High-and-Tight: Gender, Folklore, and Changing Military Culture*. Boston: Beacon, 2004.

Butler, Smedley. *War Is a Racket*. Rapid City: Vantage Point Press, 2010.

Caputo, Philip. *A Rumor of War*. New York: Henry Holt, 1977.

Carroll, James. *The Truth at the Heart of the Lie: How the Catholic Church Lost Its Soul*. New York: Random House, 2021.

Cohn, Marjorie, and Gilberd, Kathleen. *Rules of Disengagement: The Politics and Honor of Military Dissent*. Sausalito: PoliPoint Press, 2009.

Cortright, David. *Soldiers in Revolt: GI Resistance During the Vietnam War*. New York, Haymarket Books, 2005.

Cortright, David, Carver, Ron, and Doherty, Barbara, editors. *Waging Peace in Vietnam: U.S. Soldiers and Veterans Who Opposed the War*. New York: New Village Press, 2019.

Dixon, Norman F. *On the Psychology of Military Incompetence*. New York: Basic Books, 2016.

Drucker, David M. *In Trump's Shadow: The Battle for 2024 and the Future of the GOP*. New York: Hachette Book Group, 2021.

Edstrom, Erik. *Un-American: A Soldier's Reckoning of Our Longest War*. New York: Bloomsbury Publishing, 2020.

Elder, Pat. *Military Recruiting in the United States*. St. Mary's City, Maryland: Self-published, 2016.

Fair, Charles. *From the Jaws of Victory: A History of the Character, Causes and Consequences of Military Stupidity, from Crassus to Johnson and Westmoreland.* New York: Simon & Schuster, 1971.

Fanning, Rory. *Worth Fighting For: An Army Ranger's Journey Out of the Military and Across America.* Chicago: Haymarket Books, 2014.

Filkins, Dexter. *The Forever War.* New York: Knopf, 2008.

Gonzales, Laurence. *Deep Survival: Who Lives, Who Dies, and Why.* New York: W. W. Norton, 2003.

Gonzales, Laurence. *Surviving Survival: The Art and Science of Resilience.* New York: W. W. Norton, 2012.

Gonzalez, Roberto; Gusterson, Hugh; Houtman, Gustaaf, editors. *Militarization: A Reader.* Durham and London: Duke University Press, 2019.

Gordon, Rebecca. *American Nuremberg: The US Officials Who Should Stand Trial for Post-9/11 War Crimes.* New York: Skyhorse, 2016.

Gordon, Suzanne. *The Battle for Veterans' Healthcare: Dispatches from the Frontline of Policy Making and Patient Care.* Ithaca: Cornell Publishing, 2017.

Gordon, Suzanne. *Wounds of War: How the VA Delivers Health, Healing, and Hope to the Nation's Veterans.* Ithaca: ILR Press, 2018.

Gordon, Suzanne, Early, Steve, Craven, Jasper. *Our Veterans: Winners, Losers, Friends, and Enemies on the New Terrain of Veterans Affairs.* Durham: Duke University Press, 2022.

Greider, William. *Fortress America: The American Military and the Consequences of Peace.* New York: PublicAffairs, 1998.

Grossman, Lt. Col. Dave. *On Killing: The Psychological Cost of Learning to Kill in War and Society.* Boston: Back Bay, 1995.

Gutmann, Matthew C. and Lutz, Catherine, ed. *Breaking Ranks: Iraq Veterans Speak Out Against the War.* Berkeley and Los Angeles: University of California Press, 2010.

Hallock, Daniel. *Hell Healing and Resistance: Veterans Speak.* Farmington, PA: Plough Publishing, 1998.

Hanley, Charles J., Choe, Sang-Hun, and Mendoza, Martha. *The Bridge at No Gun Ri: A Hidden Nightmare from the Korean War.* New York: Henry Holt, 2001.

Hartung, William. *And Weapons for All: How America's Multibillion-Dollar Arms Trade Warps Our Foreign Policy and Subverts Democracy at Home*. New York: Harper Perennial, 1995.

Hartung, William. *Prophets of War: Lockheed Martin and the Making of the Military-Industrial Complex*. New York: Nation Books, 2011.

Hedges, Chris. *What Every Person Should Know About War*. New York: Free Press, Simon & Schuster, 2003

Herman, Edward S., and Chomsky, Noam. *Manufacturing Consent: The Political Economy of the Mass Media*. New York: Pantheon, 1988.

Hochschild, Adam. *American Midnight: The Great War, a Violent Peace, and Democracy's Forgotten Crisis*. Boston: Mariner Books, 2022.

Holmes, Burnham. *The American Heritage History of the Bill of Rights: The Third Amendment*. Englewood Cliffs, N.J.: Silver Burdett Press, 1991.

Hutto, Jonathan W. Sr. *Antiwar Soldier: How to Dissent Within the Ranks of the Military*. New York: Nation Books, 2008.

Jenkins, Tricia. *The CIA in Hollywood*. Austin: University of Texas Press, 2012.

Johnson, Chalmers. *The Sorrows of Empire: Militarism, Secrecy, and the End of the Republic*. New York: Metropolitan Books, Henry Holt, 2004.

Kerber, Linda. *No Constitutional Right to Be Ladies: Women and the Obligations of Citizenship*. New York: Hill and Wang, 1998.

Kershner, Seth, and Harding, Scott. *Counter-Recruitment and the Campaign to Demilitarize Public Schools*. New York: Palgrave Macmillan, 2015.

Kobes Du Mez, Kristin. *Jesus and John Wayne: How White Evangelicals Corrupted a Faith and Fractured a Nation*. New York: Liveright, 2021.

Lembcke, Jerry. *The Spitting Image: Myth, Memory, and the Legacy of Vietnam*. New York: New York University Press, 1998.

Longman, Phillip. *Best Care Anywhere: Why VA Healthcare Would Work Better for Everyone*. Oakland: Berrett-Koehler Publishers, 2012.

Lutz, Catherine. *Homefront: A Military City and the American 20th Century*. Boston: Beacon Press, 2001.

Lutz, Catherine, editor. *The Bases of Empire: The Global Struggle against U.S. Military Posts*. New York: NYU Press, 2009.

Merton, Thomas. *Faith and Violence: Christian Teaching and Christian Practice*. Notre Dame, Indiana: University of Notre Dame Press, 1968.

Morris, David J. *The Evil Hours: A Biography of Post-Traumatic Stress Disorder.* New York: Mariner Books, 2015.

Nelson, Deborah. *The War Behind Me: Vietnam Veterans Confront the Truth About U.S. War Crimes.* New York: Basic Books, 2008.

Network of Concerned Anthropologists. *The Counter-Counterinsurgency Manual.* Chicago: Prickly Paradigm Press, 2009.

Nicosia, Gerald. *Home to War: A History of the Vietnam Veterans' Movement.* New York: Crown, 2001.

Reed, George E. *Tarnished: Toxic Leadership in the U.S. Military.* Lincoln: University of Nebraska Press, 2015.

Robb, David. *Operation Hollywood: How the Pentagon Shapes and Censors the Movies.* Amherst, New York: 2004.

Robinson, Roxana. *Sparta.* New York: Sarah Crichton Books, 2013.

Rostker, Bernard. *I Want You!: The Evolution of the All-Volunteer Force.* Santa Monica, RAND Corporation, 2006.

Sewall, Sarah; Nagl, John; Petraeus, David. *The U.S. Army/Marine Corps Counterinsurgency Field Manual.* Chicago: University of Chicago Press, 2007.

Sheehan, Cindy. *Peace Mom: A Mother's Journey Through Heartache to Activism.* New York: Atria, 2006.

Shirer, William. *The Rise and Fall of the Third Reich: A History of Nazi Germany.* New York: Simon & Schuster, 1959.

Shulkin, David. *It Shouldn't Be This Hard to Serve Your Country.* New York, PublicAffairs, 2019.

Simon, Steven. *19 Years Later: How to Wind Down the War on Terror.* Washington: Quincy Institute for Responsible Statecraft, 2020.

Sjursen, Daniel A. *Ghost Riders of Baghdad: Soldiers, Civilians, and the Myth of the Surge.* Boston: ForeEdge, 2015.

Stahl, Roger. *Militainment, Inc.: War, Media, and Popular Culture.* Oxfordshire: Routledge, 2009.

Turse, Nick. *The Complex: How the Military Invades Our Everyday Lives.* New York: Metropolitan Books, Henry Holt and Company, LLC, 2008.

Turse, Nick. *Kill Anything That Moves: The Real American War in Vietnam.* New York: Picador, 2013.

Veterans Legal Clinic at the Legal Services Center of Harvard Law School; Swords to Plowshares, and the National Veterans Legal Services Program. *Underserved: How the VA Wrongfully Excludes Veterans with Bad Paper.* Cambridge, 2016.

Vine, David. *Base Nation: How U.S. Military Bases Abroad Harm America and the World.* New York: Metropolitan Books, 2015.

Vine, David. *The United States of War: A Global History of America's Endless Conflicts, from Columbus to the Islamic State.* Oakland: University of California Press, 2020.

Webb, Jim. *Born Fighting: How the Scots-Irish Shaped America.* New York, Broadway Books: 2004.

Wilkerson, Isabel. *Caste: The Origins of Our Discontents.* New York: Random House, 2020.

Williams, Kayla. *Love My Rifle More Than You: Young and Female in the U.S. Army.* New York: W. W. Norton, 2006.

Williams, Kayla. *Plenty of Time When We Get Home: Love and Recovery in the Aftermath of War.* New York: W. W. Norton, 2014.

Willson, S. Brian. *Blood on the Tracks: The Life and Times of S. Brian Willson.* Oakland: PM Press, 2011.

Willson, S. Brian. *Don't Thank Me for My Service: My Vietnam Awakening to the Long History of US Lies.* Atlanta: Clarity Press, 2018.

Wood, Gordon S. *The Radicalism of the American Revolution.* New York: Random House, 2011.

ACKNOWLEDGMENTS

This book could not have happened without the patience of my wife, Judy. She had to put up with long periods when I sat at my desk, manufacturing paragraphs, while she was doing what needed to be done around the house and in the garden. She was also an intelligent and generous reader of the chapters as they emerged. My daughter, Rachel Keeler, a former freelance book copyeditor, also contributed valuable insights.

Michel Moushabeck, the founder, publisher, and editor of Interlink Publishing, deserves my gratitude for saying yes to this book and for making smart, useful suggestions for revisions to the manuscript. David Klein was the epitome of professionalism and gentleness in the copyediting process.

For the book's title, I am grateful to my friend Mary Ragan, who pointed out to me that my original title, *Camo Nation*, would require too much explanation. As with so many aspects of my life, baseball had influenced me in choosing it: The camouflage-themed caps that the Mets wore on Military Monday put *Camo Nation* in my head. But Mary was right. So I looked around for another main title. William Rivers Pitt, the lead columnist of *Truthout*, an online nonprofit news organization, and the author of three books on the evils of war, had used the phrase "Sacred Soldier syndrome." I referred to it when I gave talks about war and peace issues. So I asked his permission to use "Sacred Soldier" as the main title of the book, and he graciously consented. Sadly, Will died young, at age 50, in September 2022.

In telling the story of sexual abuse in the military, I couldn't be content with a mere recital of the stunning statistics. I needed a more personal account of this pervasive scandal within our armed forces. So I am deeply grateful to

Rebekah Havrilla for sharing so honestly her own searing story of abuse. Her bravery and intelligence became a core focus of that chapter.

My former *Newsday* colleague, Larry Striegel, not only read the entire manuscript but spent a significant amount of time using his copyediting skills to make multiple detailed suggestions for clarification and improvement. I am grateful to the friends, family members, and sources who allowed me to send them part or all of the manuscript and, in many cases, offered helpful suggestions: Daniel Akst, Matt Alford, Linda Armyn, Kathy Barker, Robert Bilbro, Patty Briotta, Lisa Broughton, Fred Bruning, Patricia Buchenberger, Jane Coakley, Kate Connell, Beverly Coyle, Gregory Daddis, William Deresiewicz, Lara Edwards, Judith Ehrlich, Veronica Fellerath-Lowell, John Foote, Devon Giordano, Edward Hasbrouck, Ellen Hauskens, Roger Herman, Shoshana Hershkowitz, George Hochbrueckner, Jonathan Hutto, Steve Israel, Alexis Jetter, Renée Kaplan, Marguerite Kearns, Jerry Lembcke, Martha Mendoza, Anne Michaud, Sal Milano, Bill Millett, Dana Montalto, Sister Mary Beth Moore, Paul Moses, Arda Nazerian, John T. O'Connell, Annelise Orleck, Susan Perretti, George Reed, Karen Ann Roach, Marge Rogatz, Ken Rosenblum, Johanna Rotta, Jeff Roy, Peter Ruffner, Cathie Ryan, Darren Sandow, Sister Dorothy Sconzo, Tom Secker, Allison Singh, Daniel Sjursen, Jon Soltz, Roger Stahl, Marianne Szegedy-Maszák, Kai Teoh, Jack Toomey, Sol Wachtler, and Johnny Zokovitch.

Finally, let me thank my friends at Pax Christi Long Island, the local presence of the international Catholic peace movement, for helping me to start the long process of climbing out of ignorance and learning painfully the ways in which our nation has been far less than peaceful.

ABOUT THE AUTHOR

Robert F. Keeler is a Pulitzer Prize-winning journalist and military veteran who spent more than 45 years in journalism. At *Newsday* on Long Island, he wrote about town, county, and state politics and spent a decade covering religion. He served as Albany bureau chief, editor of the paper's Sunday magazine, and member of the editorial board. His previous books are *Newsday: A Candid History of the Respectable Tabloid*; *Parish! The Pulitzer Prize-Winning Story of a Vibrant Catholic Community*; and, with co-author Paul Moses, *Days of Intense Emotion: Praying with Pope John Paul II in the Holy Land*.